THE FIRST
ATLANTIC LINER

THE FIRST ATLANTIC LINER

BRUNEL'S *GREAT WESTERN* STEAMSHIP

HELEN DOE

AMBERLEY

Professor John Armstrong
(1944–2017)

distinguished maritime historian,
mentor and friend

First published 2017

Amberley Publishing
The Hill, Stroud
Gloucestershire, GL5 4EP

www.amberley-books.com

Typesetting and Origination by Amberley Publishing.
Printed in the UK.

Contents

Foreword   7

Acknowledgements   9

1 A Bold Idea   13

2 Building the *Great Western*   30

3 The First Record-Breaking Voyage   58

4 Masters and Crew   79

5 Looking after the Passengers   102

6 A Variety of Passengers   119

7 The Great Western Steam Ship Company   136

8 Changing Hands   165

9 Influence and Legacy   181

Appendix 1: Timeline   199

Appendix 2: Atlantic Voyages of the *Great Western*   201

Appendix 3: Transatlantic Steamer Comparisons   206

Appendix 4: Lydia Sigourney's Poem   207

Appendix 5: Claxton Letter to *The Times* (1843)   210

Appendix 6: Claxton Sea Chest Recommendations   213

Appendix 7: Hosken Letter to Lord Goulburn (1846)   215

Appendix 8: An English Businessman in New York   218

Appendix 9: *Great Western* Menu Comparison   223

Appendix 10: Mock Turtle Soup   228

Appendix 11: Roches Point and the Speed of
             Communications   230

Appendix 12: Passengers to New York in 1838   234

Notes   247

Sources and Bibliography   267

List of Illustrations   279

Index   281

Foreword

The *Great Western* was the first of Isambard Kingdom Brunel's three great ships. It is the least well known but arguably the most successful, certainly financially for Brunel and his co-investors, and was the only one that spent most of its service doing the job it was actually designed to do.

Conceived at a time when 'sail was king' and marine propulsion was in its infancy, the *Great Western* was intended to provide passengers with a scheduled, reliable service from London to New York, essentially as an extension of the Great Western Railway, a task it performed with considerable success.

Like each of Brunel's ships its design was a huge advance compared with contemporary vessels and represented a leap of faith that lesser men would have baulked at undertaking.

It can be argued that among Brunel's many engineering endeavours, his three ships stand out as individual encapsulations of his willingness to really push the technological boundaries at the time of their conception to create something far in advance of their contemporaries. As evidenced by the atmospheric railway and, to some extent, the *Great Eastern*, this sometimes did not work as well as IKB and his co-investors had expected. Indeed, even his most successful ship, the ss *Great Britain*, did not make money for the original investor, albeit more as a result of navigation error rather than any technical shortcoming. The ships also show how Brunel was as much concerned with how things look and feel as how they work, and his diaries and company records show that

IKB was equally focused on ensuring the best possible experience for users of his products.

The pace of innovation in the middle of the nineteenth century was so fast that, all too soon, the *Great Western* was superseded by more advanced vessels, not least Brunel's ss *Great Britain*, and the ship was sold to the Royal Mail Steam Packet Company to operate the Caribbean and South American routes.

Interestingly, towards the end of its life, the *Great Western* served alongside the ss *Great Britain* as a troop ship during the Crimean war, and she clearly occupied a special place in Brunel's heart.

Helen Doe's thoroughly researched book is a great read. It concentrates on the men and women behind the vessel – the designers, the operators, the crew and the passengers – and tells the human story behind this great ship.

Colin H. Green CBE
Chairman, ss Great Britain Trust
Bristol, March 2017

Acknowledgements

Despite so many years of record-breaking service across the Atlantic, and great fame in her heyday, Brunel's first ship has a very low, almost negligible profile. Yet she was a trailblazer, paving the way for her more famous successors and establishing the first reliable scheduled steam service across the Atlantic. In the biographies of Brunel she merits a few pages, while in the popular view she is overshadowed by the *Great Britain* and the *Great Eastern*, and there are few, even in some specialist circles, who can name Brunel's first ship. This book sets out to restore her reputation and to explore her influence and impact.

As with all research journeys, there were many unknowns and several assumptions in the course of my investigation. It has turned out to be quite a revelation, and there are still questions to be answered and more aspects worth exploring. The only previous full book treatment of the *Great Western* is by Denis Griffiths, who published *Brunel's Great Western* in 1985. He subsequently contributed to a book with Andrew Lambert and Fred Walker, *Brunel's Ships*, in 1999. Denis researched the ship and the company in great detail and, as an engineer, he brought an expertise and eye for detail in writing about the building of the ship and its engines. His work is the foundation on which I have based this book.

Not being an engineer, my interests are more social and economic; I wanted to pursue the people who travelled on the ship, either as crew or passengers, and the influence of the ship itself. This has led me into the realms of United States history and a little early

Canadian history. New York is a vibrant city and was experiencing fantastic growth in the pre-Civil War period. Getting a better understanding of the cities linked by the *Great Western* and the people within them has been really enjoyable. The *Great Western* linked Dickens's London with antebellum New York, and to get some idea of home life at the time I visited two small museums. The Merchant House, Fourth Street, New York was purchased new in 1835 by a china merchant, Seabury Tredwell, and the Dickens House, 48 Doughty Street, London was owned and occupied by Charles Dickens from 1837 to 1839.

I also had the great pleasure of crossing the Atlantic on more than one occasion on board Cunard's *Queen Mary 2*. Here I shared some early research material with the passengers, so I must thank my audiences on that beautiful ship and other audiences on *Queen Elizabeth* and *Queen Victoria* for letting me tell them a few stories about their predecessors on early steamships. The audience for my lecture at Hull University on the influence of the *Great Western* revealed the survival of the figurehead of the *Sirius*, which is held by the Maritime Museum in Hull. I thank my students on my University of Exeter course, 'Steaming Ahead', who have been great to work with and with whom I have shared a few research snippets.

Research on this period has been transformed by the wealth of rich and stimulating digital archives. Extensive reading around the many varied topics such as fashion, literature, finance and theatre was provided by the University of Exeter library, so much of which is online. My favoured websites for second-hand books were well used and, yes, I now need more bookshelves. The online newspaper archives are an endless source of fascination and one can spend many a happy hour browsing them with wonderful results. Websites such as Ancestry were well used, not just for the traditional material such as the census but also passenger lists. The New York passenger lists show everyone who landed of whatever nationality and their age, which helps to pin down some passengers with exactitude, but the lists for Bristol and Southampton, the alien lists as they are known, only show those who were non-British, while similar lists for Liverpool in this period have yet to be traced.

Passenger diaries have been illuminating and add enormously to the picture of life on board, and a very big thank you goes to

Caroline Welling Van Deusen for letting me use her ancestor's diary. Caroline kindly sent me not just her latest transcript, but also the images of James and Elizabeth Dixon, which were a real bonus. Almost all the diaries traced so far are American, with one rare exception by George Moore.

Online research can never replace visits to archives, where riches await and serendipity plays its part. In New York, my thanks go to the New-York Historical Society. In London, I spent many happy hours in the National Archives at Kew where the staff, as ever, were great to work with. A very big and special thank you goes to the Brunel Institute Archives at the ss Great Britain Trust. Under the watchful eye of Rhian Tritton and her team, they hold a world-class collection of archival material relating to Brunel, including the University of Bristol collection. The curator of the Brunel Institute, Eleni Papavasileiou, was an enthusiastic supporter and her successor as curator, Nick Booth, has similarly been tremendous in keeping an eye open for matters relating to the *Great Western* and helping to source images. My thanks too to Philippa Turner, assistant curator. Joanna Thomas, maritime curator, gave me some useful references to crew agreements and we had some beneficial debates on her early doctoral research on crews. The chairman of the ss Great Britain Trust, Colin Green, supported the book by writing the foreword and Matthew Tanner, the chief executive, has been a constant source of encouragement as have many others at the Trust.

Images are always a time-consuming task and I thank Sierra Dixon of the Connecticut Historical Society and the curators at the New-York Historical Society, Library of Congress and the New York Public Library. Thank you also to Julia Carver at Bristol Museum and Art Gallery and to Michael Hosken, who let me use the image of the portrait of his ancestor Captain James Hosken.

Any errors in this book are purely mine and are no reflection on the many kind souls who have helped me. Academic colleagues have let me pester them with questions and they include Dr Alston Kennerley. Dr Peter Malpass of the University of the West of England allowed me to see and cite from a draft of his book on Bristol. Professor Sarah Palmer and Dr Roger Owen each took the trouble to seek out and copy some hard-to-get articles for me.

Professor Andrew Lambert read an early rough version and encouraged me onwards and Dr David Williams answered a query on steamships and railway companies. One great sadness is that Professor John Armstrong, a friend of many years and one who has been consistent in his help and support for innumerable maritime historians, will not see the book. John died just a few weeks before the book was finished. His work, with David Williams, on the early years of steam navigation provides the context for this book.

Denis Griffiths has been more than supportive and I cannot express just how grateful I am for his help. His enthusiasm for this ship is undimmed and he has been more than generous in letting me use so many of his drawings. I have indeed been fortunate to work from his research. My greatest and most important thank you goes to my husband Mike. Only those who live with an author can truly understand the absorbing nature of the task and Mike continues to encourage and support my work in ways large and small.

Helen Doe
Mixtow
March 2017

1

A Bold Idea

Isambard Kingdom Brunel was the engineering inspiration behind three ships that connected the world in the nineteenth century. The *Great Western* connected Britain and the Americas, the *Great Britain* connected Britain and Australia and the *Great Eastern* laid the first telegraph cable across the Atlantic. Each one was the wonder of its time, pushing engineering boundaries and breaking records. A lesser-known project was his fourth ship, HMS *Rattler*, the world's first screw-propelled warship. Brunel's genius was in connecting places through ships, railways, bridges and canals, but he never lost sight of the people who would be transported via these projects and this he showed in his first truly successful ship, the *Great Western*.

It was a challenging question that led to the building of the *Great Western*. At a meeting of the directors of the Great Western Railway that was attended by their engineer, Brunel, it was pointed out that their proposed line between London and Bristol would be longer than any other railway line then contemplated. 'Why not make it longer,' came the question, perhaps posed half in jest, 'and have a steamboat go from Bristol to New York?'

It was a bold idea and an adventurous and risky project in 1835. The question is usually attributed to Isambard Kingdom Brunel and first appears in the biography written by his son.[1] After the board meeting, Brunel and Thomas Guppy, one of the railway directors and an enthusiastic supporter of the idea, talked long into the night debating the possibilities.[2] Steam propulsion for shipping was still in its infancy, and at this time no vessel had successfully completed a full passage across the Atlantic under steam alone.

While Brunel and the railway promoters were working to speed up internal connections in Britain as the Industrial Revolution continued, the other area of growth was Britain's shipping industry. Pace and progress in steamship development was a product of the industrial process which began in the late eighteenth century when James Watt patented the first true steam engine. By 1800, Britain had factories and mechanised power in place.[3] However, most of the population still lived in rural areas, and a fifth of the total labour force was in agriculture.[4] Since the end of the Napoleonic Wars, world trade had increased. Raw materials and people were needed to feed the growing manufacturing sector, and goods were flowing to and from the colonies. Investments were made in the infrastructure of canals, railways and ports to facilitate the movement of goods and people, and ships were built in increasing numbers to handle the growth of trade, both international and coastal.

That steam technology came at a time of enormous expansion in trade is reflected in the statistics. British coal production went from 7.6 million tons in 1790 to 16 million by 1816 and 54.7 million by 1854. Iron production in 1796 was 125,000 tons and rose to 2.5 million tons by 1854, with a concomitant fall in prices.[5] It was also a period of political change, much of which was of direct benefit to the business sector, particularly the shipping industry. The year 1833 saw the end of the East India Company's monopoly on Far East trade, and one year later Jardine Matheson sent home the first monopoly-free cargo from China, opening a rush of trade to the East. 'Free Trade' was the buzz phrase and the pressure was on the government to repeal the restrictive Navigation Acts. These acts limited all colonial trade to British-owned and British-manned ships. Such restrictions on foreign competition were largely supported by shipowners and shipbuilders but disliked by merchants, who sought greater freedoms.

Steam-powered vessels were highly experimental – and often dangerous – craft in the first two decades of the nineteenth century. In New York in 1807 the *Clermont* was the first successful commercial steamboat; built in New York with engines provided by the British engineers Bolton and Watt. In Britain the *Charlotte Dundas* had already proved the value of marine steam in an experiment drawing barges on the Forth–Clyde canal in 1803. The *Charlotte Dundas* was not much more than a platform with a steam engine on its deck to drive a primitive paddle wheel at the rear. However, naval architects and engineers warmed to the concept and the design race began. Henry Bell's *Comet* was launched on the Clyde in 1812 and ushered in a dramatically new type of shipping, one that was to have profound implications. It ran a service between Glasgow and Helensburgh and was the first British fully commercial use of steam on the water.[6] The *Comet* was a new design, both in the build of the hull and the engine, with the engine driving paddle wheels situated either side of the central deck. It showed the way, and soon other entrepreneurs were testing the possibilities of steam boats.

The use of steam spread quickly. In 1814 there were eleven registered steam vessels in Britain totalling 542 tons, and by 1829 this had grown to 342 vessels totalling over 31,000 tons. These steamships were wooden-hulled and powered by a side-lever steam engine driving paddle wheels. They came in many sizes, from as little as 10 tons to over 500 tons. Their function was the carriage of passengers, mails and high-value, low-bulk freight and the provision of towing services to sailing vessels. The improvements in efficiency in so many functions was a major factor in the rapid acceptance of the steamship and its spread across so many parts of Britain and Ireland.[7]

People were fascinated by these early steamboats even if their unreliability and propensity for boilers to blow up made some rather more interested in viewing them from a safe distance. Excursions were an early use, with passengers crowding on board to see the scenery from these new steamboats. The advantage of steam meant that the passenger could travel on a regular itinerary as timings could be exact and schedules kept; a major advantage to those for whom free time was a strange concept. The *Thames* steamboat that plied its way between the city and Margate advertised the benefits of no delays caused by weather or adverse tides. 'The public have the pleasing certainty of never being detained on the water after dark, much less over two nights, which has frequently occurred with the old vessels.'[8]

An indicator of the novelty of steam engines on water was the range of terms used; steamboats, steam packet, steamer, steam yacht or steam navigation were widely used. While previously it was thought that steamboats made relatively slow progress in the first decades of the nineteenth century, research has shown just how rapid and how widespread the new technology became. This rapid growth was due to the recognition of the unique abilities of steam navigation, which gave exciting prospects in both new and existing markets. They were wholly independent of wind and tide, timed voyages on regular itineraries enabled scheduled services and customers were offered speed and reliability. The possibilities were unprecedented and, after centuries of sail technology, steam provided versatility and potential. If the very early steam boats could carry little freight they could carry people and mail and were no threat to the sail-powered freight vessels in the bulk trades.[9] Towing sailing vessels in and out of port when there was little wind or along narrow rivers was an early application that was of benefit to both technologies.

Even if they could not yet compete fully in many trades, and though much experimentation and investment was required, the demand for steam vessels seemed unlimited. Contemporary commentators saw the rise of steamships as rapid. Steamboats were not just confined to the big cities; London, Liverpool, Glasgow and Hull had a significant number, but steam vessels were spread around Britain in seventy different locations in thirty-seven ports. All of this was accomplished within seventeen years of the *Comet*'s first appearance. Bristol was quick to see the benefits, and in 1814 the 43-ton 6-horsepower *Hope* was built in the port, making Bristol the fourth port to have a steam vessel after Glasgow, Port Glasgow and Yarmouth. By 1829 Bristol had eight vessels registering a total of 740 tons. Situated several miles from the sea up the long, winding River Avon, the steamboat provided invaluable assistance to the navigation of sailing vessels along the river. Sunderland, another city with plenty of river and a requirement for towing facilities, had ten vessels, but these were rather smaller than those in Bristol and totalled just 258 tons. Towing sailing ships was a very early use and between 1815 and 1818 the Clyde, Thames and Tyne had steam services. These numbers do not reflect all the steam boats built at this time as the early years saw a high number of losses and, more positively, many steam boats were sold abroad spreading the use of marine steam to other countries.[10]

This relatively fast and geographically widespread adoption of such a new technology was assisted by the extensive number of yards around the coast with wooden shipbuilding skills. Almost every coastal community had a shipyard and many of them were more than capable of venturing into the new era. Traditional wooden hull builders could respond to the new technology by buying in – and requiring the contractor to supply and fit – engines and wheels. Prominent specialist engine-building firms included Boulton and Watt of Birmingham, David and Robert Napier of Glasgow and Henry Maudslay of Lambeth, but there were other suppliers and steam-engine makers to be found in most industrial areas, particularly in mining districts.[11]

The early marine engines were inefficient users of coal. Their machinery took up a large amount of space and so the boats could only travel short distances, limited by the amount of coal they could carry on board and the availability of coaling stations on the way and at their destination. Initially they were confined to canals and rivers, and by 1815 there were twenty-three steamboats in operation. Then the *Thames* showed that steam need not be limited just to rivers and inland waterways by steaming from Glasgow to London, albeit with frequent stops along the coast to refuel. Soon steam was providing regular packet services, travelling further afield. A list of scheduled services supplied by Joshua Field to a parliamentary enquiry in 1822 shows that, even within the first decade, steamboats were operating scheduled crossings of the distinctly rough Irish Sea and lengthy routes such as the east coast Edinburgh to London, inaugurated in 1821. International links were in place between France and the Low Countries, and in 1821 the *Aaron Manby* was the first iron-hulled steam vessel. This travelled from London to Paris, confounding the doubters who could not believe an iron boat would float.[12]

By 1835 regular steam boat services were established around the coast and going further. Sailings were proved to be possible throughout the year even on the most exposed passages due to continuing improvement in marine engines and ship design.[13] London,

Liverpool, Glasgow, Hull and Bristol had regular steam connections with ports around the coast and across the Bristol Channel and Irish sea. Every year the steam services from Bristol increased in reach, linking ports around the Bristol Channel: to Cork, Dublin, Newport and Chepstow in 1822 and to Ilfracombe, Tenby and Swansea in 1823. By 1835 there were services between Waterford, Gloucester, Milford Haven, Hayle, Carmarthen, Cardiff and Bideford. While east coast and south coast ports developed services to the near continent, the Admiralty in 1830 saw the great benefit of the use of steam for their sailing packets and led the way for longer ocean passages. These packets carried government mail, valuables and some passengers and were a vital communication link. From Falmouth, the first navy steam packets travelled to Cadiz, Gibraltar, Malta and Corfu.[14] It was indeed a transformation in travel at sea.

The Atlantic, however, was a very different proposition, as Brunel and Guppy were aware. Severe gales, enormous waves, and icebergs and fog off Newfoundland all added to the dangers. But the prize was big. Textiles, iron engineering and coal were the cornerstones of Britain's emerging industrial economy.[15] The cotton mills needed the raw materials, and New York was an important hub for American cotton exports to Britain. New York was the great emporium of the Western world; American raw materials came out and British textiles and manufactured goods went in. Studies of transatlantic business partnerships show how well connected the two nations were, despite a recent war. Firms such as Bolton, Ogden and Company had built up networks and family connections to export West Indian, North American and South American sugar, coffee, cotton and rice and to import many European goods into the United States,[16] but all this growing trade across the Atlantic relied upon sailing ships. Steamships may have been in use in North America, but they were restricted to lakes, rivers, canals and the coast.

Vessels with steam engines had crossed the Atlantic but they had always done so under sail power, assisted occasionally by steam and on the eastbound crossing, which had favourable wind conditions. Captain Moses Rogers, with the backing of funding from the cotton port of Savannah, had a fully rigged 380-ton sailing ship built in New York in 1818. A boiler and engine made in New Jersey and detachable iron paddle wheels were then added. The *Savannah* crossed the Atlantic in 1819 on an experimental voyage, steaming for eighty-five hours on a twenty-seven-day passage. It was not repeated, and on her return her engines were removed. The next steam passage across the Atlantic was almost accidental. The *Royal William*'s voyage was 'conceived in financial desperation'. Built with Scottish expertise and financed in Canada in 1831, she initially steamed between Quebec and Halifax and was laid up in the winter months. Her manager and agent at Halifax was Samuel Cunard, a Canadian businessman. The *Royal William* was a commercial disaster for her owners and it was decided to send her to England for sale in 1833. The ship just about survived the eastbound crossing and much use was made of the sails as the engines frequently broke down and were highly inefficient. No buyers in England were interested and she was eventually sold to the Portuguese government.[17]

After the Great Western Railway board meeting in 1835, Brunel and Thomas Guppy were now convinced that sufficient engine improvements had been achieved; the time was right to take the Atlantic challenge. But if they found it an exciting proposition as an engineering concept, they still needed to convince potential investors about the financial benefits. The great project on which they were currently both engaged, the Great Western Railway, required vast sums of money and large numbers of investors since a railway requires a substantial infrastructure before it can run any trains. Bridges, tracks, tunnels and stations were all occupying Brunel's time. But a ship was a different prospect and the two men were confident that such investors could be found. Rewards would be quicker as once built or acquired a steamboat could be put to use immediately and use existing quays in most instances. Docks could prove to be a limiting factor, but ships could moor off and passengers be embarked into smaller vessels. Later problems were with the size of docks. Steamships, it would seem, were easy to assemble, and shipbuilders and engineers were eager to embrace the new technology – and, unlike the early steam experiments, there were no major constraints of patents.[18]

The cost of building a steamship was higher than for traditional vessels as everything was in addition to sails. Even if they were intended as back-up rather than a key item, sails were still required. Thus the cost involved a fully rigged ship plus sails, with the addition of boilers and engine and paddle wheels. Such ships also required stronger hulls to cope with the weight of engines, and the ship that was proposed would also need to handle the considerable strain of an Atlantic crossing.[19]

The expense and risk was high but so too were the rewards. Fast travel across the Atlantic was the dream of many. But it was not freight that had the attraction, it was passengers. Passengers had become the market for steamboats and both the business traveller and the tourist saw the benefits of scheduled travel. Those on excursions enjoyed the novelty and convenience of being able to walk around the deck during a journey. Added to this, another popular aspect was comfort: paddle steamers did not tend to heel over so much, or change angle drastically (unless the wind was directly behind), and so produced a smoother ride. On board a busy sailing vessel, with miles of rope and sail to manage, passengers were not actively encouraged on deck. A steamer had an unrivalled ability to provide scheduled service speed, reliability and greater comfort.[20]

For the shipowner the passenger trade was equally attractive. The business was on a cash basis, there were no lengthy contracts involved and they were assured of regular cash flow. Freight involved extra handling costs and delays in port while passengers came with the very considerable benefit that they loaded and unloaded themselves. Operating a steamboat did not require significantly new facilities to take on or discharge passengers or cargo. 'Steamships were mobile capital goods that could be easily relocated unlike railways which were fixed and required major initial capital investment and infrastructure.'[21] There was also the higher cost of internal fittings and decoration. The early steamboats recognised that passengers wanted not just a voyage or excursion but needed to be entertained and well fed. Longer passages required sleeping accommodation and competition drove higher standards on the quality of accommodation. As one witness before a parliamentary enquiry put it 'the steam packet owner looks only to the splendour of the saloon and the velocity of the vessel; it is upon these alone that he depends for success'.[22]

Ships make money when they are at sea and preferably with a full consignment of passengers, cargo or both. The transatlantic route offered great potential for a steam service which would surely prove to be immensely popular. Under sail the transatlantic passage could take fifty days, especially the westbound passage against prevailing winds, and was dependent on weather conditions. There was no shortage of shipping across the ocean and demand was high as trade and opportunities for work increased as the North American economy grew. Sailing ships would advertise to sail 'on the first available wind'.[23] This often meant a delay for the freight owner as only when the ship was full and the wind, and tide, was right did the ship sail. This changed in 1818 when the American Black Ball line instituted a hitherto unheard-of system in commercial terms, but it was only possible thanks to the potential use of steam boats to get the ships out of harbour when needed. In 1817 a letter was sent to two firms of Liverpool shipping agents, Cropper, Benson & Co. and Rathbone Hodgson & Co.

Previously to the receipt of this you may probably have been individually informed that it has been in contemplation of the owners of the Amity, Pacific and Courier to establish a line of Packets between this place and Liverpool, to sail from each port on a certain day in every month. – This information is correct. ....
It is our intention that these Ships shall leave New York, full or not full on the 5th, and Liverpool on the 1st, of every Month throughout the year: – and if it be necessary to employ a Steam Boat to tow them out of the River we wish it to be done.[24]

No doubt many shook their heads at this foolhardy commitment and prophesied ruin, with half-empty unprofitable ships crossing the ocean. But the system proved popular, and by 1836 regular scheduled sailings were provided by the Black Ball, Red Star, Black X, Swallow-Tail and Dramatic lines. New York, Boston and Philadelphia all had such services provided by fast packets with incentives offered for the masters to sail with a full load where possible. Losses were inevitable in such circumstances, but business boomed for these fast-sailing packets.[25] These packet lines developed a reputation for speed – with fair winds they could average thirty-six days out and twenty-four days home between Liverpool and New York – but if their start date was fixed, their arrival was not.[26] They did reduce the time gap, but steam had the potential to reduce it further while also providing fixed departure and reasonably fixed arrival dates, making a true liner service.

Bristol did not have regular connections with New York. Its main focus had been on the West Indies, where many Bristol merchants still had interests. Increasingly their attentions had turned to New York, and when a large fire swept through the island of Manhattan the Bristol community was supportive. Bankers, Members of Parliament, merchants and others urged the Bristol mayor to convene a public meeting for the purpose of 'expressing to the American nation their deep sympathy in the late conflagration at New York'. The same newspaper in which this was announced also added, with an eye to local commercial interests, that the merchants of New York 'have already sent large orders to Europe to make up for the loss of those destroyed by fire'.[27]

The market was there, but the great question-mark over steam was safety. Would sufficient passengers put their trust in a steam vessel for the sake of a speedier passage? The loss rate among early steamships was considerable. Certainly any voyage across the sea had its risks due to adverse wind or weather, but there were dangers peculiar to steam vessels such as boiler explosions, machinery breakdown and, in congested areas, collisions.[28] Among the many reasons for the accidents, a key factor was the lack of engineers and experience. Each new steamboat required a marine engineer, and these were in short supply due to demand. Exacerbating this, passengers were not always helpful. In the 'Report on Steam Vessel Accidents to the Committee of Privy Council for Trade' in 1839 the following unattributed anecdote was given as an example. It had come from an 'experienced commander of steam vessels' who saved his vessel and all on board from an untimely end.

A steamer on her passage from Ireland to Scotland was perceived by her commander during the night, and in a smooth sea, to be going with much greater than her ordinary velocity through the water. The engineer was not at his post; the captain enquired of the fireman how it was that the engines were going so fast: the man said 'he could not tell, for he had very little steam, and had been firing hard nevertheless'. The captain began to look about him, and approaching the chimney where the (exposed) safety-valves were fixed, he perceived a passenger fast asleep, with greater part of his body resting on the flat, cheese-shaped, weights of the valve. The man had contrived, with some luggage to make his bed there for warmth. On arousing and turning him off, the valve rose and the steam escaped with a roar which denoted its having attained very elevated pressure.[29]

Such incidents, although regularly reported in the press, seemed to have limited impact on the steady development of the steam vessel, but it was still a major concern as the new technology was expanded and tested. It was against this background that Brunel and Guppy entered into discussion. Brunel had been interested in steamships since 1829 and was a young witness to an early experiment. His father, Marc, was an advocate of steam engines, using them in his blockmills at Portsmouth and then in his shoemaking factory at Battersea.[30] Marc was convinced that steamboats would be of great value to the Navy and tried to persuade them to support some experiments, and these were witnessed by ten-year-old Isambard. Marc hired the *Regent*, a small steam boat registered on the Thames. She was built at Rotherhithe by Courthope and Sons, and launched on 27 March 1815. Described on registration as an 111-ton square-sterned steam packet, she was 79 feet in length and 17½ feet wide, with one deck and two masts. She had a double-acting steam engine manufactured by Maudslay and was fitted with cabins as her trade was to be in carrying passengers to Margate. The sole owner was Thomas Hall, of Brixton Place in Surrey, a Quaker merchant with connections in Whitby. The steamer was registered as a foreign-going vessel and not, as might be expected of a steamer heading along the Thames to Margate, a coastal vessel, which indicates that Hall had ambitious plans for her. Hall died in 1816 and his executors took over the ship.[31]

In a letter to the Admiralty in May 1817 following the experiment, Marc Brunel expanded on the benefits of steam for towing warships. His idea was that they would not only tow ships but also 'carry cables and anchors to the assistance of ships in distress'.

He also alluded to the difficulty he had in hiring the vessel, 'as the proprietors were most averse to allow her to be engaged on that service in any account'. The owners, Hall's executors, were right to be concerned: towing a large, heavy armed naval vessel was rather different to towing a lighter merchant vessel, the first application of small steamboats, and was, in any case, far from her intended purpose in steaming up and down the river with passengers.[32]

According to Marc's biographer, the towing trial was a great success and was witnessed by young Isambard Brunel and his siblings from London Bridge. The letter to the Admiralty shows that Marc was in some dispute with them over expenses related to the trial, and the Admiralty was clearly not interested in taking the trials any further. The Admiralty, short-handed and lacking funds, was adept at using private engineers' time and money. Marc continued his interest in steam navigation and filed several patents in 1822 for marine steam engines. He was later asked to act as consulting engineer for a scheme for a steamship between England and the West Indies. He turned it down as in his opinion 'steam cannot do for distant navigation'. Based on the state of the technology at that time, he was right. It was also claimed that the '*Regent* continued in service between London and Margate for many years without incident'. Not quite; it did provide a regular service between London and Whitstable carrying excursion passengers, but only for a short time, and it was one of several steamers on that route. It came to a sad and rather incompetent end in 1817.[33]

> The cause of the fire which destroyed the *Regent* steam packet on Wednesday last is stated to be as follows: the gale of wind being strong, blew the chimney flue away, and the wood-work, that is nearly breast high from the deck, at the bottom of the flue, for the purpose of keeping the people near the chimney from burning themselves, caught fire; the men in throwing the buckets over for water to put it out, lost them, consequently the fire was not checked by their exertions.[34]

Marc's son also had an interest in ships, which is hardly surprising given his father's Navy connections and that as a schoolboy he went to a school based on the Sussex coast. Isambard was at Dr Morell's school on the seafront in Hove up to 1820. Sailing ships and warships were a regular sight along the Channel and like many young boys Brunel turned his hands to making models. He wrote, 'I have been making half a dozen boats lately, till I've worn my hands to pieces.'[35] Hove was next to the port of Shoreham, which was a base for several noted shipbuilders including James Britton Balley, who was also an engineer. Many noted vessels of over 500 tons were launched from the shipyards there, and, to quote a local historian, 'they did much to raise the reputation of the port to its eminence for superior coasting vessels as well as those built for foreign service and foreign owners'.[36]

Brunel's father then sent him to France to train as an engineer, and on his return he worked with his father on the great scheme to build a tunnel under the Thames. During an enforced stay at home due to illness Brunel noted his dreams in his secret journal, among which was an ambition to build a fleet of ships and 'storm Algiers'.[37] Events had taken him away from the sea, but now, in 1835, aged twenty-nine, he had an opportunity to realise some early thoughts and to be at the forefront of steam navigation. He was still at a relatively early stage of his career, and through his many connections and his work in Bristol he knew the port well.[38]

The man with whom he was having such keen discussions over the possible steamship was Thomas Guppy. Born in 1798, Guppy came from an entrepreneurial family. His father was in the metal trade, a brass and iron founder and manufacturer of agricultural machinery with interests in a nail manufactory in New England. His mother, Sarah, was an unconventional woman, an inventor with many patents who was actively involved in a variety of schemes and held shares in the Great Western Railway. She was also in partnership with William Sommerton, the editor of the *Bristol Mercury*.[39]

Although Thomas Guppy later made his reputation as an engineer, he did not have a formal apprenticeship. He had applied to Henry Maudslay for an apprenticeship, but his timing was unlucky: in 1815 Maudslay was not taking on apprentices given the severe downturn at the end of the war. Instead he headed over to Philadelphia where he spent a year, including an unsuccessful attempt to persuade New York to use gas lighting. He then returned to Europe and studied architectural drawing in Germany in 1823 and finished his architectural education in Paris. Like many people of his time he was multi-talented and on his return to England submitted a patent for rigging ships. In 1826 with his brother Samuel they ran a successful sugar refinery at Bristol, but his first love was still engineering and in 1830 he was one of the first members of the company to establish the Great Western Railway and invested £14,300 in the scheme.[40] Guppy was a trustee of Clifton Suspension Bridge, a project for which his mother Sarah was an ardent supporter and fundraiser. He also had many shares in ships, both sail and steam. Politically he was on the Bristol town council from 1835 to 1837, and it is clear from the press reports that he had his fingers in many municipal pies.[41] Thomas Guppy is described as a natural ally for Brunel. This is reflected in the correspondence between the two between 1838 and 1840. 'They are written in a chatty and breezy style such as Isambard Kingdom Brunel reserved for his closest friends.' Later, in June 1838, Guppy would even suggest that the two of them should establish a partnership, a concept about which Brunel was slightly evasive.[42]

And so it came that the bold idea of extending the railway line from London to New York was made at the railway board meeting. Guppy, aged thirty-seven and Brunel, aged twenty-nine, sat debating into the night and came up with a plan for a transatlantic steamship. After the lengthy and enthusiastic debate, Brunel and Guppy now needed additional support. They took their ideas to three other members of the railway board. Robert Scott and Thomas Pycroft both came from Bath and Robert Bright was a leading Bristol merchant. These men became the nucleus of a proposed steamship company and recruited one more member, 'a practical seafaring man' well known to both Guppy and Brunel, Captain Christopher Claxton.[43]

At forty-four, Claxton was a little older than the other two but had plenty of nautical experience. He was born in 1791 in Bristol. His father, Robert, was a West India merchant who died in 1813, leaving £3,000 each to his sons Christopher, Robert, William and Phillip.[44] Christopher's father wanted him to be a barrister, but Britain was at war and Christopher was more interested in joining the Navy. He joined as a midshipman in 1804 and as a teenager saw plenty of action during to the Napoleonic Wars. He was in naval actions off the coast of Portugal and in North America. He became a lieutenant in December 1810 and four years later, during the war with the United States, he led a group of men in an attack on Baltimore. With peace in 1815 he returned home to England, and with so many men now surplus to requirements he was fortunate to get the command of a revenue cutter out of Yarmouth. He spent four years chasing smugglers, and when that came to an end he, like other men in his position, turned his attention to the mercantile marine world and spent six years crossing the Atlantic in a fast-sailing West Indiaman.[45]

The fact that he was a half-pay lieutenant and not a captain rankled, but he admitted he probably had himself to blame. In 1816 he had anonymously published a book, *The Naval Monitor*, in which he gave his views on the education and public and private conduct of 'the young gentlemen'. It was aimed at midshipmen, their parents and the Navy hierarchy. In his introduction in a republished edition in 1833, he was open about his disappointment. But he also admitted his own limitations. 'Modesty and diffidence,' he wrote, 'are said to be the surest signs of worth and merit. The author cannot lay claim to either the one or the other.'[46]

It is many years. since he published his first edition, and he is compelled to publish the second without having the power of prefacing his name with any higher title to the one in which he originally wrote. He feels to how much more weight would have been attached to a naval monitor had it been headed by the rank of captain of His Majesty's Navy, as its author. Everybody knows since the peace, the mass of interest that has been necessary to attend the promotion; and the author acknowledges with thanks much that was made for himself, at the same time he regrets that it was not sufficient.

But, as he said, he had 'long, very long, ceased to covet that rank, which in a war with other nations would have had charms that a long peace, and increasing years, have entirely robbed it of in his eyes'.[47] He was protesting too much, and status would remain an important part of his ambition in the world. Although in the Royal Navy's eyes he was a lieutenant, he was very happy to assume the courtesy title of captain, which was used for masters of merchant ships.

The Navy's system at the time was essentially one of part-time employment. Once there was no need for their active service, officers of the rank of lieutenant and above were on a system of half pay. In the event of war they could be called into action, but meanwhile they were free to take up other employment outside the service. Promotion still happened, but only as those above fell away. With 1,500 lieutenants on half pay and the 'great block', as it was called, above him, Claxton was at a distinct disadvantage in getting any further.[48] He witnessed those junior to him on the list becoming commanders, but he knew that he had himself to blame. 'I was aware that my language was the language of truth, but also how dangerous and impolitic it is for professional men, particularly subordinate ones, always to speak it.'[49] He would continue his outspoken ways.

Claxton was, like Brunel, a man of action and did not hesitate in an emergency. In August 1837 the local newspaper reported that Lieutenant Claxton had thrown off his coat and jumped in to rescue a man who fell into the harbour, 'we have heard this is the 3rd or 4th instance in which Mr Claxton has been instrumental in saving persons from a very watery grave'.[50] Claxton modestly mentioned in his book 'the saving of many persons' lives by swimming in the different ships in which I served as well as in my cutter. The Humane Society honoured me with a medal.'[51]

In 1835 Claxton was the quay warden, the harbour master, of Bristol and was well known to Brunel, who had worked with him on the Bristol dock improvements in 1832. The quay warden post was not part of the Bristol Dock Company but was a council appointment, which is how Thomas Guppy knew him and it paid an annual salary of £400. Claxton was a controversial figure in Bristol, evoking both high praise or strong criticism. He was not a man who did anything by half measures. Nothing he did was in the background, he led from the front. At five feet tall, he was a bundle of energy and a constant writer of letters to the press, frequently expressing his strongly held views and correcting what he saw as wrongful assumptions or errors of omission.[52] Brunel's biographer notes that Brunel remained slightly guarded in his relations with Claxton and his description of him was 'a warm friend but changeable and capable of being a devil of an opponent'.[53]

Guppy and Brunel consulted Claxton in 1835 and enlisted him.[54] Claxton assisted in forming and running the Great Western Steam Ship Company and he would become its managing director. Thomas Guppy became a director and Isambard Brunel invested his money in the scheme and offered his services as an engineer for free. These three, together with William Patterson, a local shipbuilder, formed the building committee on behalf of the then embryo company (it was officially formed in June 1836). Their task was to organise the successful building of a ship that would establish the first service by steam across the Atlantic.

2

Building the *Great Western*

In their report to shareholders in 1838, the directors of the Great Western Steam Ship Company looked back at the building of the ship. They carefully explained that they had 'spared no expense to render her a truly magnificent vessel, worthy of trading between two such great and powerful nations as England and America; they have been exceedingly judicious and cautious in selecting all the parties in any way connected with her build'.[1] There was still some way to go to complete the funding so the report was to reassure existing shareholders and encourage new ones that due care and attention had been taken in this great scheme.

An early and speedy decision had been the selection of the shipbuilder, William Patterson. There were plenty of shipbuilders from which to choose. With a tradition of being one of the major ports in Britain, Bristol was a well-established shipbuilding centre. The output from Bristol shipbuilders was extensive, from small craft, yachts, trows and river barges to large sailing ships for international trade like West Indiamen, East Indiamen and whalers. Any steamship in the Atlantic would need to be strong and Bristol's builders had a good reputation for building ships for military purposes such as warships and privateers. Hilhouse built twelve warships; the largest, *Nassau*, was 1,384 tons. Bristol shipbuilders, as we have seen, were already familiar with steam, having been early adopters of the technology for towing ships along the Avon. In 1822 their first seagoing steam vessels were built; the *George IV* and *Palmerston* were both Irish steam packets.[2]

William Patterson was from London and had served his apprenticeship to Trufitt, a Rotherhithe shipwright, and in due course Patterson became foreman to a well-known steamship builder, William Evans. In 1822 circumstances left Patterson in charge of the yard and he agreed to complete the contract for the Post Office steam packet, *Dasher*. The engineering experience was valuable, but a financial disaster as he had to accept a low contract rate for the hull. Following this Patterson moved to Bristol, probably in 1823, married a local girl and became an assistant to William Scott. Scott, a connection of the Greenock shipbuilding family, had previously been in the timber trade. Now, with Patterson's technical support, he was entering shipbuilding. He soon moved to the Wapping dry-dock in Bristol, recently vacated by Hilhouse.[3]

Scott was not financially successful, and on his bankruptcy in 1830 Patterson went into business with John Mercer, of whom little is known. Mercer could just have been the financial partner and not necessarily a fellow shipwright. Wooden shipbuilders, for whom the craft had been handed down for centuries, overall had something of a reputation as being conservative in their views. This was not the case with Patterson. He was a good designer of ships and his elegant lines impressed the community. The local newspaper was full of praise when reporting the launch of a 'fine pair of steam packets – *Lady Charlotte*, finished in superior manner and certainly one of the handsomest modelled vessels of her class', and the *Mountaineer*. It was, they wrote, 'an improvement in the style of nautical architecture which must be hailed by everyone with satisfaction'.[4] Claxton later reported that Patterson was known as a man 'open to conviction and not prejudiced in favour of either quantity or old-fashioned notions in shipbuilding'.[5]

Patterson joined the building committee and, together with Claxton and Guppy, set off on a tour of the British shipbuilding ports. More information was needed about the current state of marine steam and they travelled on 'every steam line' and inspected every large steamer they could find, noting the rapid improvements being made, 'more particularly observable in the Clyde than elsewhere'.[6] As Claxton later described, 'whenever railway business called Mr. Brunel to Bristol which at this time was at least once in every week the committee and Mr. Patterson used to meet at the office or Captain Claxton or Mr. Guppy's house and sat far into the night discussing the details of the design of the ship'.[7]

From their observations and their debates, the committee provided a detailed set of recommendations on 1 January 1836 to the company. The report included a recommendation from Brunel about the dimensions of the ship and its engines.[8] The original plan had been to build smaller steam vessels, but the report now advocated a larger steamship 'for purposes of carrying cargoes as well as passengers, the most speedy and certain passage, the greatest economy of power, and the best assurance of a profitable return for the capital invested, will require a vessel of at least 1,200 tons'.[9] Fuel was a major debate and the cross examination of engineers and the detailed tracking of other steam vessels clearly demonstrated that the type of fuel was important. However, they noted that most trials had been done in London while in Bristol it was felt that Welsh coal was the best.[10]

The report was a plea for thorough funding, making the case for not stinting on the comfort of passengers. 'Accommodations for passengers should be at least equal to those of the present first-rate sailing vessels, otherwise prejudice would be raised against the steamers which would blight at once every prospect of success; this can best be effected by vessels of much greater dimensions than the largest steamers now in use.'[11] Finally, Brunel added an important point about the significance of the size of the vessel and the consumption of fuel in ensuring success.[12]

Even before the official report there had been much open discussion among the shipowning community locally, and questions were raised about the practicalities of the project. Claxton took the step of writing to the newspaper to address the various rumours even before the final decisions had been made. Queries had been raised over fuel consumption estimates, the cost of obtaining coal in New York, and the challenges posed by the narrowness of the locks in the Bristol harbour. As the secretary to the new venture, Claxton strove to answer all the queries. In his responses he was remarkably optimistic about the company's potential ability to persuade the Dock Company to widen their locks.[13]

The whole project was widely reported and the *Bristol Mercury*, which was closely connected with Guppy's mother Sarah, applauded the 'deep research into all matters connected with the subject as well as the knowledge of nautical affairs generally'. Shares, they announced, had already been taken up and the target was to raise capital of £250,000 in £100 shares. The value of such investments would be positive as it was projected to give a 15 per cent return. This assumed that the fares, from a modest estimate of fifty passengers in the first cabins and fifty in second cabins, would equal the running costs and even allow for a reserve of £10,000 per year for contingencies. With a proposed full ship of one hundred first cabins and eighty second cabins, the prospective investor was to be reassured. In addition, the ships – two were planned – could carry up to 200 tons of freight. So, if the minimum of passengers was met the rewards would be reaped. 'On every ton of freight, there will be an additional receipt of £2, on each first cabin passenger over 50, £28 15s, and on every second passenger over thirty, £16, – the charges being the same as by sailing packets.'[14]

The plan was for two identical ships, estimated to cost £35,000 each, with engines of 300 horsepower, to each make six voyages both ways in the year so that one would be regularly dispatched from each port every month. What investor could possibly ignore such a wonderful opportunity? Like all such well-crafted marketing tools, this prospectus had certainly impressed at least one newspaper. Conscious of the competition from other ports for a steam link across the Atlantic, the newspaper promoted the advantages of Bristol as the nearest port to America, and with the possibility that 'a rapid communication with the metropolis, as well as with northern and western provinces, will, in a few years, be established by the means of the Great Western and other railways'. Finally, the *Bristol Mercury* underlined the 'numerous body of our leading merchants and capitalists' who had taken up the project with such spirit.[15]

The provisional committee of the Great Western Steam Ship Company drew up a handwritten prospectus from which the newspaper had taken its information. Just six copies of the prospectus were produced and it attracted limited, rather parochial interest, subscribers mainly coming from Bristol and Bath. Possibly, they felt they had no need to publish widely and just having handwritten copies limited outside knowledge of the Bristol project, which would have been a positive considering concerns over rival schemes.[16]

John Junius Smith, an American businessman who spent most of his time in London, was a regular user of the transatlantic sailing packets both as passenger and for his goods. In 1833 his journey had taken some fifty-four days westbound and thirty-two days eastbound. He found this extremely exasperating and an immense waste of time, and tried to get existing companies interested in steam packets. He envisaged four at £30,000 each and he wanted to have two British and two American ships. Existing companies were unenthusiastic, so he decided he would raise funds for the two British ships and his nephew in New York would get investors there for the American ships. There was no positive response on the American side but he had more success in Liverpool and London, where his initial prospectus was published in June 1835. By November 1835 the British and American Steam Navigation Company had its first meeting.[17] There was much interest in engineering circles about the plans, which were for two ships of 1,500 tons with engines of 460 horsepower.

There is a curious link between the two rival schemes. Macgregor Laird was both an investor and the company secretary of the British and American Steam Navigation Company and was charged with getting the first ship built. The Laird family were friends and allies of Robert Stephenson, 'often taking his advice in engineering matters', and Stephenson was a close friend of Brunel – it has been suggested that Brunel was therefore privy to the plans.[18] In this light, the secrecy in which the first Bristol prospectus was shrouded becomes understandable. It is also equally possible that the Bristol and Bath group did not feel they needed to advertise widely as they had many prominent and wealthy men already involved, largely thanks to the Great Western Railway and their connections. The project was certainly very well promoted in the press. The company was established as a partnership with a Deed of Settlement in June 1836.[19] This type of company avoided the expensive option of being a public company, which at that time required parliamentary approval and the need for public meetings. In the end, due to the low-key nature of the share offer, at the first annual general meeting of the Great Western Steam Ship Company only 1,500 of the 2,500 shares at £100 each had been allocated.

The next task of the building committee was the crucial choice of the firm to build and fit the engines. Before the advent of iron ships, it was quite normal to have a separation between the those building the ship and those building the engine. Shipbuilding was an ancient craft, and it would be the introduction of iron shipbuilding that really changed the industry. There were plenty of shipbuilders, but marine engineering firms capable of handling this big task were in short supply, with only three great centres of engineering. One was Glasgow, where the cousins David and Robert Napier had a shipbuilding yard. David moved away, but Robert remained in Glasgow and encouraged many other talented engineers who would later become great names such as William Denny, John Elder, James and George Thomson and A. C. Kirk. David moved to London in 1836, where he was in good company. Already well established there were Maudslay, Sons and Field, and John Penn and Sons. Finally, in the Midlands was the well-established firm of Bolton and Watt.

The building committee left the selection of the engineer to Brunel, who sent out invitations to tender. It should be asked why it went out to tender, as the choice of shipbuilder had been a quick and easy decision without any tender process. The reason may be in the three firms who tendered for the chance. Winwood was a small Bristol firm, Fawcett was based in Liverpool and Maudslay, Sons and Field was at Lambeth. It is evident from later reports that the company wished to see the project as firmly Bristol based and was under pressure to use a Bristol engineering company.

The Bristol-based firm, Winwood, were not experienced in building large marine engines. They advertised as 'Iron Boiler Maker, Iron Manufacturers & Engineers, Steam Engine Manufacturers' based at Cheese Lane, St Philips. In 1826 they had built the engines for the 60-ton steam passenger boat *Wye*, built by William Scott, and so would have been known to Patterson. The largest engine they built was 180 horsepower for the 400-ton *City of Bristol* in 1828.[20] The firm became Winwood, Bush and Beddoes in 1836. The second engineering firm, Fawcett, was an early pioneer of marine engines based in Liverpool. They built the engines of *Etna* in 1817. This firm would later make the engines of the *President*, the largest Atlantic steamer, in 1840 for the British and American

Steam Navigation Company.[21] Neither Bolton and Watt nor Napier, the other great names in marine engines, appear to have been asked to submit tenders.

There is no great surprise that the winners of the tendering process were Maudslay, Sons and Field. In a carefully written report to the Great Western Steam Ship Company, Brunel made the strong case for them. They were, in his view, the outstanding candidates, and indeed they were. Woolwich was the main naval yard for fitting out steam engines, and by 1835 Maudslay were the dominant suppliers to the Navy of engines and boilers.[22] Henry Maudslay is first mentioned in 1800 when he had a workshop in Westminster. There he met Marc Brunel and was involved in the making of the machines for Marc's block-making machinery, which took eighty men some six years to complete. Joshua Field, the partner, came from Portsmouth, where he had worked in the naval dockyard and he joined Maudslay in 1805. Maudslay's first marine engine was in 1814 for a Thames steamer, *Richmond* and the *Regent* was built in 1815. By the 1830s Maudslay, Sons and Field were the only Thames firm winning Admiralty contracts. Henry died in 1831 and his son, Thomas, took over, later assisted by his brother, Joseph, who had been an apprentice to Thomas Pitcher of Northfleet. Maudslay had built river steamers for the East India Company in 1832.[23]

It was probably their involvement with the oceangoing steamship *Enterprize* that attracted the most attention as this was the earliest attempt to steam eastward to India. The authorities in Calcutta had offered a £10,000 prize for the first steamship to establish a line to India. In 1823, a shipowner named William Jolliffe created a steam vessel company to attempt to win the prize. In view of the state of marine technology at the time it was a very tough challenge, but such a valuable prize was worth the attempt. The ship was built in London and the engines and machinery were supplied by Maudslay. Among the owners of the ship were Charles David Gordon, shipbuilder, and Henry Maudslay of Lambeth, engineer, both were trustees of the steam packet company.[24] Henry is said to have personally invested £2,000. Coal was shipped to the Cape and to Calcutta and the ship set sail from London on 2 August 1825, heading for her first scheduled stop at Falmouth. Maudslay's partner, Joshua Field, was on board for three days between the Thames and Falmouth monitoring the efficiency of the boilers and engines. After many stops and several incidents, including a fire on board, she sailed into Calcutta in December 1825.[25]

There were other, more personal reasons for choosing Maudslay. The engine and the paddle wheels were crucial factors for the success of the whole project. There were plenty of shipbuilders, but there were few skilled marine engineers in a field that was still pushing boundaries. What was needed was a firm with a reputation for innovation but also the ability to work with a man as demanding of high standards as Brunel. The connections between the Brunels and Thomas Guppy with Maudslay's firm were strong. Marc Brunel had worked with them for some years, and there is no doubt that Isambard Brunel knew them just as well. Although no evidence has been found that Brunel as a young man was actually apprenticed to Maudslay, he did have a very close working relationship with them. This is made plain in a letter he wrote to Henry Maudslay's son many years later in which he referred to 'your firm, with which all my early recollections of engineering are so closely connected and in whose manufactory I probably acquired all my early knowledge of mechanics'.[26]

Personal preferences aside, Maudslay, Sons and Field were the outstanding contenders, but at least the process had allowed a Bristol firm to make a bid; Winwoods were later used for other work for the Great Western Steam Ship Company. Brunel's firm conclusion to his report left no doubt.

Of all three parties tendering Messrs Maudslay have made by far the largest number, and have for some years led the way in the introduction of the largest armed steamboats; and that can be no question as to the fact they are the oldest manufacturers of marine engines, that they are themselves the originators of the greatest number of the improvements of the day, but they have made the largest engines yet made, and the greatest number of large engines of all sizes; and, lastly, that they have the principal supplier engines for the launch warships now used for the navy ... The price is, I think, moderate.[27]

Later advertisements from the Great Western Steam Ship Company did request tenders from sailmakers and rope makers of Bristol for the supply of sails:

> ... for the first ship of the company specifying the price per yard according to the numbers of the canvas that will be decided upon. The quality will be the best bleached Coker, single thread manufacture. Also for the CORDAGE of the same ship specifying the price per ton the quality be the best clean Russian hemp, the yarns to be finely spun and tightly saturated with tar. Note: The tenders to be sealed. Directors will not by themselves take the lowest estimate.[28]

Both Patterson and Maudslay had to be flexible as changes were made on a regular basis. One of the first changes was the size of the ship. The report in January 1836 and the prospectus had proposed two 1,200-ton steamships of 300 horsepower; each ship was projected to cost £35,000 pounds. This changed to a single ship of 1,400 tons, which would enable more powerful engines of 400 horsepower. Brunel and the rest of the building committee understood the need for a hull capable of withstanding the severe pressures of an Atlantic crossing.[29]

The keel was laid with little publicity or ceremony in June 1836. The great backbone of the ship, from which the ribs extended, this keel was at the time the longest in the world – so if this was laid without any ceremony then the next stage, the raising of the stern section, would be well reported. The rather unusual move to celebrate this stage could have been Claxton's idea, as he was now the managing director. The company had apparently not planned to make the raising of the stern a public event and had thought to restrict it to the owners and a few notables, but as it was mentioned in the newspapers a very large crowd gathered. The lengthy, detailed and well-informed report in the *Bristol Mercury* described the scene. The reporter found all the vessels in the immediate location decorated with flags. The *St George*, belonging to steamship director Acramans, was moored in front of their warehouse and decorated with the flags all nations, and nearby was moored a 'well known West Indiaman, also profusely decorated with flags', and this provided the accommodation for the directors and their friends.

With military precision, at precisely half past three, Claxton gave the word and the stern frame, which weighed several tons, was raised and fixed into position as cannons were discharged. The band played 'Rule Britannia' and Claxton led a series of cheers. The directors and friends then moved to the yard loft for a celebratory meal. As was the custom, numerous toasts were proposed and drunk. Thomas Guppy replied on behalf of the town council and referred to the honour the venture would bring to Bristol, praised the venture, claimed the keel as the longest in the world (to which there were loud cheers) and reminded them all of the importance of the connection between Bristol and New York.[30]

Claxton, in his address, was keen to point out that Bristol was ahead of everyone else. He referred to a similar project being proposed in Liverpool but declared himself proud to say that Bristol had the lead. No other ship that planned to cross the Atlantic was as yet in build. He also took a swipe at the doubters who did not believe that such a large vessel could get down the tortuous run of the River Avon, and caused much laughter when he told the audience that the shipwrights had started a rumour that the ship would be made with a joint in the middle. An important aspect of the various toasts was that it was not just about prosperity for Bristol, but also, with a nod to the several investors from Bath, the prosperity of the West of England and the United States of America. Mr Denison, the American consul for the port of Bristol, was present and he emphasised the importance of the Great Western Railway and the cotton trade. So, on went the speeches and toasts, all carefully noted by the press reporter. The Chamber of Commerce was thanked, as was the Society of Merchant Venturers, who had widened their dock to provide accommodation for larger vessels. Brunel was the subject of a particularly warm toast for his professional expertise and as the person who had assisted 'very materially with his advice' and who was superintending the construction of the engines. Brunel was not present – he was getting married – but a Mr Tait replied on his behalf. Every organisation, with the notable exception of the Bristol Dock Committee, was named, including the Trustees of the Clifton Suspension Bridge and the gentlemen of the press. Mr Summerton, editor of the *Bristol Mercury* and partner of Mrs Sarah Guppy, replied to the latter. Claxton then made what he hoped was an important announcement. Bristol, for the first time, was to have the honour of a visit by a body of the most scientific men in Europe, and he proposed a toast to the committee of the British Association for the Advancement of Science. Christopher's brother William Claxton, a member of the Society of Merchant Venturers, who had issued the invitation, replied to that one. Indeed, such a scientific venture as the *Great Western* steamship would surely impress these notable scientists. Claxton was then himself thanked for his admirable management of the event and he again paid tribute to his colleagues:

> I do pin my faith on men of first rate experience in mechanics in the United Kingdom; Mr. Guppy is one of them, but I allude principally to Mr. Brunel, on whose advice we have constantly relied; indeed, such is the intelligence of that gentleman that I believe him fully competent to direct the building of a ship.[31]

With that the grand celebration disbanded and Claxton, ever the Navy man, headed to the Bathurst Hotel where the shipwrights were having their party and being entertained by the band. He was greeted by loud cheers as the men contemplated a rosy future and 'an order was instantly given for extra amounts of strong beer'.[32]

After this oddly timed celebration, which served to publicise the ship and encourage investment, the shipwrights went back to work and building progressed steadily on traditional lines. The difference to all previous projects was one of scale. A long hull such as this was thought to be a particular risk. Using wood to build a ship had its limitations: wooden ships were prone to sag in the middle if built too large, and it was not until iron and steam were used that ships would reach much larger sizes. Joints between the wood were the weakness, and constant working in heavy seas could open up the joints, allow in water and weaken the ship. This had long been a challenge for the Navy, who needed large, heavy ships capable of carrying heavy armament and withstanding heavy seas and bombardment from the enemy. Sir Robert Seppings, a previous Surveyor of the Navy, had invented diagonal cross bracing as a way of strengthening wooden hulls. By the 1830s his system was well used and he was recommending it for merchant ships, although few, with the exception of the *Great Western*, were built in this way.[33] The company acknowledged the considerable assistance they had from the Royal Navy. Most of the key players had good connections there: Marc Brunel had many contacts, and Claxton saw Sir Thomas Masterman Hardy as one of his Navy mentors, having served with him. Hardy was First Lord of the Navy from 1830 to 1834 and had been a great supporter of steam warships. Maudslay were, of course, major suppliers of engines to the Navy and worked with them at Woolwich.[34] The contact with the Royal Navy was to be of great value. Sir William Symons, the Surveyor of the Navy, and Oliver Lang, Master Shipwright at Woolwich, provided plans, drawings, calculations and much advice. In the eyes of the Great Western Steam Ship Company it was almost an official government seal of approval.[35]

True to his word, Brunel was keeping an eye on progress in London and inspected the engines at Maudslay's yard in April 1837. Pleased with what he saw, but aware of the scale of the project and the many elements left to manage, he wrote, 'I cannot help still feeling some hopes that we may effect that most important object of performing the voyage across the Atlantic this autumn.'[36] Keen as they were to see the ship in action, there was still much to do before the ship could have her engines fitted. As time elapsed, it was sensibly decided not to risk a late-season voyage across the Atlantic.

The many other practical matters to consider fell to Claxton as the managing director. Advertising was required for passengers and freight, and it was necessary to arrange a system for purchasing tickets, which meant arrangements with agents in different cities. Crucially, Claxton needed to select a master for the ship, and his choice fell on James Hosken, another half-pay lieutenant. Hosken's job was to work with Patterson and make suitable arrangements for the ship, getting the sail plan right and attending to other sailing matters, and finally to engage crew members. Arrangements needed to be made for the ship in New York, and berthing facilities needed to be found in the busy harbour so that maintenance and coaling could be carried out and supplies of coal laid in. This was to be a regular line, not just a one-off experiment, and so agents had to be employed to handle ticketing at the other end and advertise the eastbound crossings. Later, Hosken would personally go out in the American packet *Garrick* to make the various preliminary arrangements. The company noted with pride just how much interest was already shown in the ship among the columns of the New York press.[37]

In July 1837 came a hoped-for announcement for the public:

Notice is hereby given that the time for issuing cards for the intended ENTERTAINMENT after the LAUNCH, is extended to 3 o'clock on SATURDAY, the 15th inst. Further applications for admission cards to the Booth and premises will be useless as the number is completed and the time as per advertisement expired. Parties coming from Clifton or from that side of the country as well as from the Somersetshire side who have the entree are recommended to come by the new cut and Bathurst basin. By order of the board, C. Claxton, Great Western Steam Ship Company.[38]

A ship launch was always a big celebration, attracting large crowds of people who were either curious, supportive or just hoping for excitement, and this was a hotly anticipated day. The *Bristol Mercury* was there, as usual, and devoted many column inches to the ship they nicknamed 'the great leviathan of the deep', a name later used at the launch of the *Great Eastern*. By eight o'clock crowds had already congregated; every spot, every ship, every rooftop that could command a view was occupied. On the water were the ships the *Saint George* and *Clifton* (both East Indiamen), the *Stedfast* (and other West Indiamen), and the *Benledi* and *Torridge* steamers. The ship began launching at 10.00, and as she moved, Mrs Miles, the wife of the local MP, 'dashed a decanter of Madeira and named it the *Great Western*', while at the same time Claxton broke a six-gallon bottle, also of Madeira, on the figurehead of Neptune, repeating the name. The ship launched fully without incident and the crowds took in her magnificence as she floated on the waters, looming over all other vessels. She was 236 feet long and 58 feet wide and her registered tonnage was

1,340 tons. Apart from her size, she looked much like any other wooden ship at this stage, as the funnel and paddle wheels would be fitted in London. She was well decorated, and the Neptune figurehead against which Claxton had dashed so much Madeira had a gilded trident, imitation bronze dolphins and other gilded mouldings on each side.[39]

The invited guests then headed aboard the floating vessel. The plan had been for 270 guests, but such was the interest that 300 were present. Chairman Peter Maze presided and had the Member of Parliament, William Miles, and the Mayor of Bristol seated in places of honour beside of him. The listed names reflected 'every distinguished family in the city': Colonel Whetham, Majors Worrall and Kington, Captains Canville and Shute, Messrs Walker, Bailey, Worrall, Acraman, King, Savage, Claxton, Guppy, Gibbs, Hicketts, Osborne, Robinson, Jacques and their respective ladies. Brunel was present, as were various unnamed naval officers. The consul to Alexandria, the American consul Mr Denison and Mr J. B. Clarke from the cotton factory joined the throng.

William Miles MP, in his address, saw the ship as a link in the great commercial chain which would connect America and Great Britain. He referred directly to the cotton factory and the Great Western Railway, then still inching its way to Bristol, as not only beneficial to Bristol but 'likely to place it in a most pre-eminent station, forming an era in the commercial history of the country'. The chairman, Mr Maze, referred to the Atlantic race, and while commenting briefly that 'another ship of the kind was building at Liverpool and one at London', he was pleased to say that 'neither was so forward as that built and now launched in Bristol'. Local benefits had included wages in excess of £8,000 for the building of the vessel, providing employment for 180 workmen.

The deputy chairman, Mr Kington, paid warm tribute to Christopher Claxton, calling him the 'mainspring and sheet-anchor of their concern'. Claxton then replied with warm tribute to Mr Patterson, whom he said had 'particular merit of not being bigoted to his own opinion; whenever any improvement was suggested to him, he considered it, and, and if approved of, adopted it'. A principle of the company, he said, was to order all they could from Bristol, excepting some work from Bath, where one-fourth of their shareholders resided. The engines were not from Bristol; although 'Mr. Winwood's engines were most excellent', they had chosen Maudslay as they had 'manufactured upwards of 200 engines'. Brunel was duly toasted and thanked for his 'most efficient services for having volunteered gratuitously to superintend the construction of their engines'. Brunel rose to reply and proposed 'success to the undertaking', as did Joshua Field of Maudslay, who invited the audience to a similar event on the Thames when the engines were completed.[40]

The assembled company could now see the finished ship, and there were plenty of representatives on hand to extol its virtues. Claxton had referred in his speech to the building committee and placed himself as the practical nautical man of the four. His example for this was that Brunel had expressed a wish to have the cabin windows in the stern look more like drawing-room windows, with glass down to the floor. Brunel thought this would be more pleasing to passengers, creating a different atmosphere, and it was typical of his attention to detail and concern for the passenger experience. Guppy also thought this was a good idea, but Claxton and the experienced shipbuilder Patterson reminded them that this might not be the most practical arrangement during an Atlantic storm. It was decided to stay with the usual small, nautical windows.[41]

The newspapers reported the ship's details as provided by the company, who wished to emphasise the strength and solid workmanship:

Her floors are of great length, and overrun each other; they are firmly dowelled and bolted, first in pairs, and then together, by means of 1½ inch bolts, about 24 feet in length, driven in four parallel rows, scarfing about four feet. The scantling is equal in size to that of our line-of-battle ships; it is filled in solid, and was caulked within and without up to the first futtock heads previously to planking, and all to above this height of English Oak. She is most firmly and closely trussed with iron and wooden diagonals and shelf-pieces, which, with the whole of her upper works, are fastened with screws and nuts, to a much greater extent than has hitherto been put into practice ... Such of the timbers as may be exposed to alternations of dryness and moisture, have been prepared by

Kyan's patent process; and every effort has been made to combine the various points of naval architecture and engineering, so as to render them most effectual in a service requiring speed, strength, and accommodation, and in which she will have to compete with the finest sailing passenger-vessels in the world.'[42]

English oak was, naturally, featured, and together with the reference to line-of-battle ships gave the image of true British strength and solidity. Tempting as it is to think that ships were mainly built of oak, they were largely built of pine from Dantzic (now Gdansk in Poland). Patterson confirmed this in a letter to a later parliamentary enquiry. 'All the upper timbers of the frame of the *Great Western* were of Dantzic pine, all the outside plank, with the exception of the flat of the bottom, two shear strakes, and two strakes of the bends, were of Dantzic pine, and the whole of the ceiling, beams, shelves, waterways, and decks were of pine.'[43]

The spacious ship could stow 800 tons of coal, or coal and cargo combined, and could carry sufficient fresh water for 300 people. There was plenty of space for the sixty officers and crew, plus state rooms for 128 first-class passengers and twenty good secondary berths. With an eye to expansion, 'should it eventually be found advisable to forgo cargo space all together' 100 more sleeping berths could be provided.[44]

The *Great Western* headed off to the open sea on her first passage, sailing for London, and carried on board was the Bristol contribution to the machinery: the two paddle shafts manufactured by Acramans. She was accompanied by the little 120 horsepower steamer *Benledi*, which was on hand to provide towage when needed. The great ship sailed most of the way, and at times left the *Benledi* in her wake. She arrived at Gravesend on 22 August and was towed into the East India docks. Built in 1802 to accommodate the massive East India ships, a steam wharf known as the Brunswick wharf had been opened in 1832 and was mainly used by the General Steam Navigation Company. Here Maudslay berthed a hulk (an old ship without its masts) and used her as a workshop for fitting out steam vessels. An advantage of the site was the masting machine, mainly used for stepping masts but also very handy for lifting boilers in and out of ships.[45]

Once she was in London, the engineers got their chance to work on her. If Brunel had been the main contact between the building committee and Maudslay, keeping a regular check on progress and authorising stage payments, Patterson and Maudslay must also have been in close contact.[46] Indeed the *Great Western*'s design was altered when the boilers and funnel were placed forward of the engines and paddle wheels. In a letter to John Scott Russell in November 1840, Patterson explained the need for extra weight (ballast) in the stern of the ship to restore her trim and thus ensure that the ship's performance in both head seas and following seas was not compromised. 'The iron ballast carried in the *Great Western* was not for the purpose of correcting any deficiency in her stability but for the purpose of correcting her trim which had been greatly deranged by Messrs Maudslay's new plan of putting the boiler before the engines.'[47] There is sense of disapproval from Patterson, and a wish to defend his shipbuilding ability.

If the ship was large, the engines were the wonder of the day and 'justly eminent for the superiority of their workmanship':

> ... they are the two largest marine engineering engines that have been made and are equal to 450 horse power. The boilers are constructed with several adaptations for the economy of steam and fuel, on an entirely new principal, which has greatly economized space, and, it is believed, will very much lessen the consumption of coal. They consist of two linked and independent boilers, so that the engineer can work such number only as circumstances may require; while, by means of passages reserved between them, he can cool, examine, repair, and clean those not in use. The wheels have the cycloidal paddles, which are of Iron, and possess decided advantages.[48]

While much attention was focused on the engines, paddle wheels and boilers, the requirement for attractive and comfortable passenger accommodation was also in hand. With just one class of passenger – 'superior class' was the term used, rather than 'first class' – luxury was the watchword. The newspapers were happy to repeat Claxton's enthusiastic description of the interior and the assertion that the directors had 'attentively studied comfort and convenience with appropriate decoration'. The decorators were the London-based Jackson and Sons of Rathbone Place, who advertised themselves as 'Composition – ornament and Papier Machee manufacturers', and the artist was Edward Thomas Parris of 17 Grafton Street, Bond Street.[49] As the biggest social space on the ship, where passengers would congregate and dine together, the saloon was designed to impress. Around the saloon were the upper cabins.

> The saloon, which, in size and splendour, is not exceeded by any British steam vessel, is 75 feet in length, and 21 inches breadth, exclusive of the recesses on each side, where the breadth is 34 feet, and 9 feet high in clear of the beam, which is increased by the lantern light; each side, except where the recesses intervene, being occupied with state cabins.

At the lower end there was a small compartment exclusively for lady passengers, fitted with sofas and draperies. On the opposite side was the stewards' room and the staircase that led to the lower cabin, which was fitted up with sleeping berths for gentlemen. The main saloon was painted in salmon pink with gold ornamentation. The columns imitated palm trees and they resembled pier glasses, with frames that looked like Dresden China.

> The front of the small cabins are divided into six compartments, with panels about five feet high, and one and a half foot to two feet wide. These are painted in the gay, pleasing style of Watteau or Boucher, by E.T. Parris, Esq., R.A., and historical painter to Her Majesty. The panels are 50 in number: the large ones represent rural scenery, agriculture, music, the Arts and Sciences, interior views and landscapes, and parties grouped, or engaged in elegant sports and amusements; the smaller panels, over the doors, etc., contain beautifully pencil paintings of Cupid, Psyche another aerial figures, which can considerably heighten the appearance of the saloon. The ceiling, and such parts of a saloon as are not occupied with Mr Parris's pictures, are painted by Mr Crace, of Wigmore Street, of a warm and delicate tint, with the mouldings and enrichments, picked in a light colour, and relieved in gold;

but so kept under as not to encroach upon the principal pictorial embellishments of the apartment. In subjects of this class, Mr Parris is scarcely excelled by any contemporary; Stanfield, we remember, painted a few panels with maritime scenery, a few years since for the Duke of Sutherland; and such distinguished patronage has rendered the style of decoration very fashionable. At this moment, Mr Parris is employed in ornamenting the United Services Club House in a more finished and classical style than that of the embellishments of the steam ship.[50]

It reflected the latest fashion, which was in a state of flux, and as ever at this time the reference point was royalty. This was a most exciting moment for fashion. Gone were the elderly kings, George and William; in June 1837 Queen Victoria, aged eighteen, had succeeded to the throne, ushering in new possibilities in fashion. 'We can only add that the effect of the saloon is altogether of a palatial character in point of decoration; yet not, like the state departments of our last new Palace, overloaded with ornament.' This was a reference to the extravagance and gaudy taste of the late George IV in his restyled and vastly expensive Buckingham Palace. 'The general styles of the mouldings, framework, etc., is that of Louis Quatorze, somewhat curtailed of its luxuriance, so as to please, but not fatigue the eye with its graceful curves and harmonious proportions.'[51]

It is not obvious who on the building committee influenced this choice of style, but the fact that the main decorators were from London, the capital of fashion, rather than Bristol suggests that Brunel's view might have been a factor. He had acquired his London house in fashionable Duke Street just before his marriage in 1836. Here he applied his eye for detail to the decoration of his marital home; his sketchbooks show his designs for wall fittings, and plans to commission works of art from contemporary artists. The property was richly decorated and opulently furnished.[52] In later years, he kept a keen eye on the details of the interior decorations of the *Great Eastern*: 'To complete her in time, the mirrors, gilded pillars, painted panels, carved walnut and Utrecht select furnishing, crimson silks *portieres*, pile carpets, and cut-glass "moderator" chandeliers, had to be hurried forward and not a detail escaped his attention.'[53]

With engines and paddle wheels fitted, the ship could now commence her sea trials, which would be conducted in the full glare of publicity.

> On Saturday last the first experimental excursion of this magnificent vessel was made on the Thames with the most complete success. The engineers were engaged during the whole of the week in getting ready her stupendous machinery and paddle-wheels, and the fires were lighted and the steam got up on Thursday and Friday, while the vessel was at her moorings. The working of the engines and the revolutions of the wheels having more than answered the expectations of her owners, on Saturday morning, at 11 o'clock, she got under way, and started from Blackwell on her first steam trip.[54]

There was much excitement as news spread about this first trial voyage. It was a useful occasion for entrepreneurs to make money, since shopkeepers, innkeepers and those running river excursions all stood to benefit. Steam they were used to – there were many small steamers plying the River Thames – but this was on a different scale, dwarfing other vessels. The river banks were therefore crowded with spectators, who gave out a great cheer when, after the steam had been sufficiently raised, the large paddle wheels at last moved. As the newspaper columns excitedly informed those readers who were not present to witness the occasion, 'Our readers have only to fancy a large man-of-war of 80 guns, without her usual warlike appearance, moved by the power of steam, and they will form some idea of the size of the *Great Western*, the largest vessel propelled by steam which has yet made her appearance on the waters in Europe.'[55] Her registered dimensions were given as 1,604 tons, 234 feet long, 58 feet at her widest across the paddle boxes, and with engines and machinery of 450 horsepower.[56]

The river pilot, Mr Grundy, was described as an able man. He saw that just one steersman was insufficient to control the vessel, possibly due to the vibration of the brand-new machinery, and a second man was put on the helm so that 'she answered to the helm as well as any steamship in Her Majesty's service and soon began to cut through the waters at a spanking rate'.

She was accompanied down the river by a well-known steamer, *Comet*, which was 'always considered a very fast-going vessel' and 'appearing a mere pigmy' beside the *Great Western*. At 158 tons, the *Comet* was literally one-tenth of the size. Not to be outdone, the *Comet* cut well inshore and endeavoured to use every means to stay in the race, to the delight of onlookers. She did not gain, but watched as the *Great Western* increased the gap between them. Crowds continued to appear along the river. At Gravesend, 'the town-quay, Terrace-hill and every spot commanding a view of the river were crowded with people'. As the ship passed, they cheered loudly. She made 12 knots and proceeded to 3 miles below Gravesend, where the next test came: turning the great ship. But this too was 'accomplished without difficulty' and the ship returned to her mooring at Blackwall just before four o'clock. Here the crowds still waited patiently to cheer her return.[57] It was reported that 'a number of engineers, shipbuilders and scientific persons accompanied the *Great Western* on her trial, and all expressed their perfect satisfaction at the result'. There was constant checking, measuring and testing by Brunel with Maudslay and Field.[58]

There was one minor incident in the crowded river. Most of the river users were not under steam and were small sailing craft, barges and rowing boats. Slower and less manoeuvrable, they were also less able to judge the speed of the new mammoth in the river.

> In going down river a large sailing barge crossed her bows, and to prevent the barge being run down, in which case the three men in her must inevitably have perished, the engines were stopped and reversed, when she ran foul of a ship lying at anchor on her larboard side, and carried away the starboard quarter of the vessel, besides doing other damage. The *Great Western* sustained no injury.[59]

Still the visitors came to see the ship on her moorings, and one of the first was Lord Sandon, MP for Liverpool, where rival ships were in plan. The visitors arrived in such numbers – among them many members of the House of Commons and House of Lords – that the hapless clerk who had been instructed to take down the names of the visitors gave up in despair and simply wrote, 'The people began to flock in shoals, and four men and as many books would be unable to take down their names and addresses.'[60] The public were fascinated, assisted by enthusiastic news reports of this 'long talked of project of navigating the Atlantic Ocean by steam'. There were reports of the interest of commercial communities in Liverpool, New York, London and 'old Bristol herself'. As the reporter of one London newspaper put it, 'The buzz of excitement yesterday, reached even the secluded walls of our own study. We rushed down to Blackwall, *pell mell*, in an omnibus like all the rest, to see, not the *Sirius* but the *Great Western*, which the papers have told us so much about for the past month.'[61]

The reference to the *Sirius* was in relation to the British and American Steam Navigation Company. All along the *Great Western* had been in the lead, ahead of its main rival. Junius Smith's first ship had been contracted to Curling and Young of Limehouse, in the east of London, and its keel laid down in October 1836, four months after that of the *Great Western*. This ship was given the working name of *Victoria* – it would later be launched as the *British Queen* – and the engines were being built by Claude Girdwood and Company of Glasgow. Unfortunately, Girdwood had overstretched themselves. They went into liquidation, so a speedy change of marine engine builder had to be found. Robert Napier of Clydeside agreed to take it on, but, given their other work for existing customers, matters slowed down the plans so the *Great Western* was now well in the lead.[62] Junius Smith and his fellow directors were not to be outdone and decided they would attempt the Atlantic in another ship. Two directors were Joseph Robinson Pim and William Laird, who had the majority shareholding and management of the St George Steam Packet Company. This company ran steam packets across the Irish Sea between Liverpool and Dublin. Their 703-ton ship *Sirius* was registered in 1837. Despite its small size at 208 feet long and 28 feet wide, with engines of 320 horsepower, she was hired by Smith, who brought the small paddle steamer to London to be its flagbearer across the Atlantic.[63]

It was, however, the *Great Western* which was the big draw. People had been flocking to see it, 1,000 in one day by the estimate of a happily employed waterman. In the cabin album were written the names of nobility and gentry, headed by His Grace the Duke of

Wellington. The Lord Mayor of London arrived in style in his gold state carriage with four footmen to see the ship.[64] There was no sign of Queen Victoria, however, as it would be Prince Albert who later encouraged her to take an interest in technology. The work on the internal fittings and decoration was still ongoing, and there were more than 100 workmen on board endeavouring to complete their tasks while excited onlookers peered over their shoulders and got in the way. The newspaper commented on the four masts, declaring that these were the 'most remarkable thing about her' as they were there for use when the engines were not running and 'as they are somewhat lower than the masts of other vessels of similar dimensions, will offer less resistance to the wind when they are adverse'.[65]

At the invitation of 'Captain Hoskins [sic] RN, the commander, Mr Patterson the builder and C Claxton, Esq, RN the managing director', visitors could view the engine room. Here they looked on in awe 'although the heat was insufferable, the novelty of the thing superseding all other considerations'. The four boilers had space between them for ease of access and were reported as weighing about 96 tons and holding 80 tons of water. Added to the 200 tons of potential cargo, space for 150 passengers and 60 crew and many tons of coal, this testified to the strength requirements of the hull.[66] The *Great Western* was partly coaled on the Thames, holding 470 tons, and she was to be recoaled at Bristol with another shipload of 400 tons. The newspaper also reported, incorrectly, that the 'coal tanks would be filled with seawater as they emptied to keep a continual ballast'.[67]

The warmth of the reception and the intense interest boded well for the company. The *Sirius* they did not regard as a threat as it was not built for the Atlantic, but there was one debate hanging over the congratulations and it was one that would linger for many years to come. At the celebration for the raising of the stern, there had been much pride that the distinguished body of scientists belonging to the British Association for the Advancement of Science were to visit Bristol in the autumn. The anticipated visit turned out to be a trial of strength of views between one speaker, Dr Lardner, whose views on the impossibility of steam navigation across the Atlantic were already well publicised, and Brunel.

Dr Lardner was for a time Professor of Natural Philosophy and Astronomy at University College London. A leading member of the British Association for the Advancement of Science and a well-known authority on the steam engine, he spoke on the railways and steam navigation. In his view the best route of transatlantic voyage without an intermediate stop at the Azores was direct from Valentia Island off the coast of Kerry, Ireland to Newfoundland as this was the shortest great circle route. This was, in his view, the only possible way. He was quoted in the *Liverpool Albion* in December 1835 as commenting that to go by a steamship direct from Great Britain to New York was 'perfectly chimerical' and that it was as likely to succeed as a voyage from Liverpool to the moon. It was these rather sensational statements that caused astonishment and concern in some quarters, and they would continue to haunt his career long after his theory had been disproved.[68]

Lardner's report had included a table based on the logs of some naval packet ships, including one belonging to the Post Office and one private packet. This showed the coal consumption, rate of sailing and the number of miles averaged. As an example, in his calculation a ton of coal per horsepower had been required for the *Africa* to cover 1,000 miles. His concern was that the vessels simply could not carry sufficient coal. In his opinion, unless coaling stations were provided at Cork and Halifax, no vessel could be made large enough to carry sufficient fuel for the voyage, and even then he seemed to be of the opinion that it would be useless to attempt to compete with the existing packet ships, which made a voyage in such short periods. The time for sailing packets on the eastbound crossing could be as fast as fifteen days with a good wind and fair weather. With respect to the communication to India by steam, he seemed to think more favourably of the project, especially with the lines and stations fixed upon.[69]

The British Association for the Advancement of Science held its meeting in Bristol on 25 August 1836 and Dr Lardner, it was announced, would speak on transatlantic steam navigation. He was still of the opinion, based on his coal consumption calculations, that if a ship could be found large enough to carry the coal he estimated was required for the voyage, there was no engine possibly big enough to achieve the result. It was a large meeting, and Brunel was present. Lardner again spoke against the project. He had slightly amended his views but still insisted that 'if the first attempt failed it would cast a damp upon the enterprise and prevent a repetition of the attempt'. Brunel then stood up and pointed out his calculations were based on an erroneous assumption.[70] In Brunel's view:

> The resistance of vessels in the water does not increase in direct proportion to their tonnage. This is easily explained; the tonnage increases as the cubes of their dimensions, while the resistance increases about as their squares; so, the vessel of double the tonnage of another, capable of containing an engine of twice the power, does not really meet with double the resistance. Speed therefore will be greater with the large vessel, or the proportionate power of the engine and the consumption of fuel may be reduced.[71]

Brunel 'exposed several errors in Dr Lardner's calculations, but failed to produce any effect upon the majority of those present, who were powerfully impressed by the lecturer's dogmatic assertions'.[72] Lardner was a charismatic and effective speaker, and as an established scientist and academic his words carried weight.[73] Brunel was not the only one to challenge Lardner. Macgregor Laird, of the British and American Steam Ship Company, wrote anonymously to the *Liverpool Albion* and pointed out that Lardner had based his data on Admiralty boats whose performance had since been surpassed. The Valentia route meant a journey would involve travelling by multiple stages just to get to the ship, which would result in at least six changes of conveyance before getting to New York. Laird conjured up a vision of the daunting prospect for a family, laden with luggage, travelling by stages from London to Ireland and pointed out that there was no railway between Dublin and Valentia Island.[74]

The whole debate was also being followed closely in New York. The newspapers there had naturally been interested in the scheme for some time, regularly repeating announcements from the British newspapers. In February 1836, the *Morning Herald* of New York announced that 'in connection with a London and Bristol railroad, a steam packet line is to be established to New York and the vessels are now building'. In January 1837 they put forward their view of the proceedings of the British Association meeting in Liverpool, and they were not impressed with Lardner's statement that navigation would be possible to India but not to the United States. There was, they decided, a perceived bias in Liverpool against the scheme. Bristol, they noted, had been the chief port for American vessels about half a century ago. The increasing trade from the Midlands and better transportation from Liverpool caused the rise of that port. But since then there had been many changes, and the railway was due to open between Bristol and London. The newspaper felt that there was some strong opposition in Liverpool to steam navigation, and since Dr Lardner was closely connected with the interests of Liverpool he 'takes as a matter of course the same ground that she does'.[75]

Despite the controversy and perhaps even because of it, public interest remained intense. In London, finally, the engineers, painters and decorators had all done their job and the ship was ready to head back to Bristol. At 4 p.m. the day before starting, Claxton asked if there was a fire engine on board. Realising the serious omission, Captain Hosken rushed back into London and bought a small Merryweather. Moses Merryweather's firm was based at Lambeth near Maudslay, Sons and Field and specialised in firefighting equipment.[76] The equipment arrived on board by midnight. On Saturday 31 March, the great steamship headed downriver towards the English Channel. On board were Sir Marc Isambard Brunel and several other distinguished visitors. Engine tests continued on the way. Some visitors, including Sir Marc, disembarked at Gravesend, and shortly after this came a famous incident. There was a smell of burning and smoke and flames were seen at the base of the funnel. Quick thinking by the master James Hosken and the pilot put the *Great Western* on a mud flat. At considerable risk, Pearne, the chief engineer, took a deep breath and dived into the engine room, which was full of smoke and partially on fire. He adjusted the water supply to the boilers to prevent explosion, thus saving the ship and everyone on board. Meanwhile, on deck, the small fire engine was being operated by Claxton and the chief officer, and they descended with a hose at great personal risk into the stokehold and got the fire under control. Brunel, in his classically impetuous style, also rushed to assist, but when going down to inspect stepped on broken rungs and fell 20 feet into the hold. Luckily for him he landed on Claxton, who broke his fall. Brunel had landed face downwards in water, and quickly Claxton pulled him clear and called for assistance. Brunel appeared to be seriously injured and was taken ashore. Claxton's quick thinking had saved Brunel's life. It was later discovered that Brunel was not severely injured, and three days later he was able to write one of his classically detailed letters to Claxton.[77] Joshua Field and Joseph Maudslay inspected the damage to the ship and declared all was well; the cause had been some felt, held in place with oil and red lead, that had overheated close to the funnel.[78]

In Hosken's view 'there was a marked providence in the want of a fire engine being discovered before starting, else the *Great Western* would in all probability have been destroyed'.[79] Very true, but it was not mere chance as at least one person on board had experienced a very similar mishap. When the *Enterprize* set sail from London in 1825, Joshua Field was on board to keep an eye on the early performance of the engines, just as he did with the *Great Western*. The *Enterprize* left Deptford on 2 August, and just off Beachy Head the alarm was raised when a fire broke out around the funnel. Due to the large amount of coal required for the voyage, every vacant space had been used, including between the top of the boiler and the deck. The engine was working at very high pressure as the ship laboured against wind and tide. The boiler became so hot that the coals ignited and fire broke out around the funnel and issued through the deck. There was considerable panic, but eventually the fire was brought under control 'with the aid of a force pump worked by the engines'. The captain, Lieutenant Johnston, not surprisingly made light of the incident, saying that it was 'got under [control] in ten minutes, doing very little damage'. Joshua Field remained on board for three days between the Thames and Falmouth monitoring the efficiency of the boilers and the engines.[80] His firm was fully alive to the dangers of fire. Henry Maudslay had filed a patent in 1812, together with Robert Dickinson, for a pump that would clean water by forcing a stream of air through tainted water. The pump tube and nozzle, it was pointed out, could also be used to fight a fire.[81] It is more than likely that it was Field who was the instigator of the enquiry about the presence of a fire engine.

Meanwhile, the *Great Western* was floated off the mud on the next tide and the ship continued on its way without Brunel, but with Joshua Field, Joseph Maudslay and George Pearne keeping a close eye on the engine performance. They were short of men, since several stokers on hearing the explosion had got into a boat and headed for the shore. The paddle ship headed down the English Channel and reached the mouth of the Avon early on Monday 2 April. Despite the shortage of hands, she made a creditable average speed of 13 knots and exceeded expectations.[82] Her next big adventure was about to begin.

3

The First Record-Breaking Voyage

The *Great Western* anchored at Kingroad at the mouth of the River Avon into the Bristol Channel. Here, as in London, there was a clamour to see the newly decorated ship and her engines. Bristol visitors would need to take the trip downriver, a three-hour passage, and then get on board. Given the awareness of the strength of demand, and the ability to keep some control as the ship was moored mid-river, a ticketing system was introduced. Wednesday was allocated for the owners and their friends, and nearly 1,000 people went on board after being delivered by steamers and other boats. Many of the most distinguished families in the neighbourhood were among the company. William Miles, MP for East Somerset, was accompanied by a large party from Leigh Court and Kingsweston. On Thursday and Friday the general public were admitted by ticket and nearly 3,000 people eagerly availed themselves of the opportunity to inspect the vessel. The Bristol newspapers had repeated the glowing London descriptions of the interior and now were able to confirm to those who had not been among the visitors at Kingroad that the reports of the luxury were not exaggerated.[1]

There was still much to be done before she could take on her first passengers. Some of the furniture and upholstery had been supplied in London, but now the firm of Stafford of Bath, who were providing much of the cabin furniture, needed to get their items on board. Additional coal had to be taken on and fresh provisions, including livestock, accommodated. While the crew rushed to be ready to welcome the prospective passengers, there were still plenty of curious visitors wanting to get on board to examine the ship before it left.

The company was keen to promote the ship's merits and advantages over other vessels when advertising for passengers. She was described as 'strongly built, coppered and copper fastened, with engines of the very best construction, by Maudslay, Sons and Field'. In a nod to their competitors they added, 'and expressly adapted for the Bristol and New York station', so not just a hired coastal or cross-Channel steamer – this one was expressly designed for the Atlantic, and she would not need to stop at Cork for fuel. There was just one class of cabin, all berths were at 35 guineas, and tickets could be obtained from a variety of offices. In London customers could go to the offices of the Great Western Railway in Princes Street; in Liverpool the agents were Messrs Gibbs and Bright & Company; in Glasgow it was Messrs Hamilton, Brothers and Company; in Cork, Mr Robert Hall; and, of course, tickets could be purchased direct from the Bristol offices of the Great Western Steam Ship Company, courtesy of Mr C. Claxton, managing director, at 19 Trinity Street, Bristol.

Concessions were offered to officers on duty in Her Majesty's service and their families, and an unspecified allowance was to be made for their travelling expenses to Bristol. Those from the depot at Cork (a major Army base) were offered their passage money by the regular steamers to Bristol. Families could get a reduction in proportion to the numbers and the berths they required. Children under twelve and servants were half price. The final reassurance was the coal, bearing in mind the many sceptics who were convinced the voyage was not possible. 'Ship has coal stowage for twenty-five days constant steaming and therefore will not require to touch at Cork for coal.'[2]

After five days of visitors and frantic activity, the crew was ready to receive passengers and freight. A thirty-one-year-old merchant from Philadelphia was booked on this first passage. W. Foster arrived on Saturday 7 April 1838 and reached the *Great Western* at 5 p.m. after embarking on a small steamer, 'a twaddling little thing', at Cumberland Basin in order to travel down the Avon to the ship. 'So strongly had curiosity been excited by this vessel, that we, who had now come to take our departure by her; were obliged to wait whilst a small steamer, thronged with eager visitants, left her side to make room for us.'[3]

As they stepped on deck all appeared to be in chaos. This did not unduly concern Foster, since he was well accustomed to the departure scenes on sailing ships. As he described it there were 'spars, boards, boxes, barrels, sails, cordage, seemingly without number, stirred well together, coals for the ground work, baggage to infinity; captain scolding, mates bawling, men growling and passengers in the midst of all, in the way of everything and everybody'. Captain Hosken needed to employ twelve local labourers to assist the crew in restoring order to the deck. But at last the various passengers found their berths and 'so each installing himself in his little castle, found enough to do in the arrangement of it to amuse him for the evening, and all, I believe, found an early bed made welcome by a day of fatigue'.[4]

Captain Hosken decided to wait for one more night due to poor weather conditions as there was storm due, and, wisely, he decided to let it blow over. This may seem surprising in view of the well-known intentions of the *Sirius* to beat the *Great Western* to New York, but caution was the watchword. The company did not see it as a race; they were in it for the long haul, intending to establish a regular liner service between Bristol and New York, and no advantage would be conferred by sending the ship and passengers into a wild night. The company had issued clear instructions to Captain Hosken that he should 'endeavour to accomplish his voyage more with an eye to a discreet use of fuel, than to the constant attainment of maximum speed, through extreme consumption'. The aim of the promoters, it went on to add, was 'not so much the mere accomplishment of the voyage, as to bring its time within definable computation, and to fix that time as less than sailing packet would require under almost any circumstances'.[5]

Foster's description of the chaos created on the deck by a multiplicity of luggage, packages, parcels and stores might appear to show that the ship was full. There had indeed been a goodly number of reservations taken up, but when it came to time many cancelled, not helped by the news of the fire on board as it left

London. In the end there remained just six men and one woman, who were all outnumbered by the crew, including the waiting staff and steward. Foster was joined by another American merchant, James Welman, aged thirty-one. There was a British Army officer, Colonel Vernon Graham, aged fifty-five, and two other merchants: John Gordon, aged twenty-five, and the wonderfully named Cornelius Birch Bagster from Canada, aged twenty-five. Cornelius Bagster had an interest in the newly emerging science of photography. His work would later be displayed in an 1852 exhibition organised by the Society of Arts in London. This exhibition led to the creation of the Photographic Society in 1853.[6] Unfortunately for us it would be a year before the first effective photograph was announced by Fox Talbot.[7] Charles Tate or Tait, aged twenty-five, was a Yorkshireman, a civil engineer and quite possibly Brunel's protégé who had represented him at celebrations of the raising of the ship's stern the previous year. While it is doubtful that Brunel himself had planned to travel with the ship, it is very likely that he would have wanted one of his men on board to check on progress and observe.[8] So it was a mixture of those who had business to conduct and those who were there for the grand experiment. The odd one out was Miss Eliza Cross, single, aged twenty and travelling alone.[9] She has been described as a 'proprietress of stay, straw and millinery warerooms in Bristol'.[10]

The next morning at 8 a.m. the passengers woke to the sound of the furnaces being fired, and by nine o'clock steam was up. Captain Hosken ordered the deck crew to man the windlass to weigh anchor, which caused an unexpected delay since it took nearly two hours to achieve. This was 'unavoidable by reason of the great scope of chain out, and everything being new the windlass worked stiffly'.[11] Foster noted excitedly in his journal that 'we are of the first to make the great adventure'. In the later publication of the journal together with the ship's logs this statement would be corrected by the punctilious Captain Claxton, who noted the crossing under part steam and sail of the *Savannah* in 1819.[12]

And so the steamer headed off. The public in her home port of Bristol, and those interested in London and elsewhere, would now have to contain their impatience and wait some weeks for the news of her safe arrival to (hopefully) reach Britain. The speediest way in which news returned to Britain was via home-bound vessels encountered en route. Two ships noted sightings of the *Great Western* but were not close enough to exchange any communication. It was not until the *Henry Brougham* sailed into London docks that the first real news arrived, and, as was the way with news then, it was widely repeated word for word in regional newspapers:

> By the arrival in the London docks, on Friday afternoon of the *Henry Brougham*, Captain Wilkin, from Laguna de Terminoa, we learn that the captain of that vessel spoke the *Great Western* on the 15 April on her passage to New York, in latitude 45, 40 longitude 37, 59. The *Great Western* since her departure from Bristol, has been seen twice by homeward vessels to the port of London; but the *Henry Brougham* has been the first vessel to speak with the Great Leviathan. It is fully expected that the next intelligence of the *Great Western* will be her safe arrival in the western world. Captain Wilkin, we are informed did not see or hear anything of the *Sirius*, which sailed from Cork for New York, several days prior to the departure of the *Great Western* from Bristol. Both vessels are first rate, and are doubtless at this moment surprising Jonathan [Americans] in the port of New York.[13]

A few days later a London newspaper reported another sighting of the *Great Western*. 'This vessel from Bristol to New York was spoken with on the 15th in latitude 46.26, longitude 33.13. This gives her an advantage over the *Sirius*; but the *Great Western*, sailing four days later, had not encountered the heavy gales with which the *Sirius* had to contend.'[14]

Meanwhile, on board the *Great Western*, the passengers and the crew were entering an isolated bubble, with no contact with the outside world save for the occasional glimpse of another vessel. They left at noon, and Foster admitted some apprehension present among the passengers, but there was reassurance. 'Such stability, such power, such provision against every probable or barely possible contingency, and such order presented itself everywhere on board as was sufficient to allay all fear.' It could not, however provide protection from seasickness as they crossed into the deeper ocean. On Tuesday 10th, as the ship pitched in the waves in a head wind, the figurehead of Neptune lost his trident and the steward and his team were soon in great demand to assist the seasick. For those strong enough to go on deck there was the first sighting of another vessel, an American packet ship of the Black Ball line. They exchanged greetings by way of flags, and Foster was deeply admiring of the beauty of the packet ship under full sail in a fresh breeze. Hosken brought his steamer up beside the packet and Foster could see the passengers packed on the deck to glimpse this new wonder. Noting the two ladies on the sailing ship, he commented with pride on the one female who was 'a sharer in the venture of our voyage'.[15]

On Wednesday, four days out from Bristol, the seas were calm and there was, an unexpected and mysterious surprise. On one of the cabin tables there appeared an arrangement of fresh flowers: 'Hyacinths, daffodils, violets and primroses at sea! It were vain to enquire whence they came.'[16] The incident became a challenge and the passengers vowed to maintain the flowers and endeavour to keep them alive until New York. While most days passed much the same as every other, Sunday at sea was quite different. The decks had been holystoned (scrubbed with stones) on Saturday, an indescribable din according to Foster, to whom it was a form of torture. Sunday, however, was quiet, with 'swept decks, clean clothes, smooth chins and no work among the crew ... as distinct from the everyday complexion of the sea life as are closed shops smart dresses and a quiet air, from the weekday bustle of a crowded city'. A mid-morning service was held in the upper saloon, and Captain Hosken led the prayers.

While the passengers tried to amuse away the hours, life was quite different below decks in the engine room. Foster was fascinated, if bemused, by it all and noted the experiments on power ratio and coal consumption as careful notes were taken. He observed the men below. 'The paper and lead pencil in such hands, and the close observation of be-smutted engineers, might verily be said to bear some resemblance to the intercourse of imps with an incarcerated devil.' Chief Engineer Pearne was indeed watching over every part of the engine and wheels like an anxious parent. His detailed notes were taken in clear knowledge of the experimental aspects of the voyage. Three days out the engine had to be stopped to tighten up a connecting rod, and seven days out it was stopped again, this time to tighten bolts in the wheels. Every squeak, every bit of coal consumed, plus the temperature, speed and hourly revolutions were noted.[17] A London reporter had spotted a neat gadget that assisted the noting of performance:

> Affixed to the framework of the engine is a clock or index by which the number of strokes performed by the machinery, and the rate of their performance, is shown with the greatest accuracy; and we were told that, without requiring to be again wound up, it would mark as many strokes as will suffice for the whole voyage to New York and is the most ingenious, and we believe, novel invention.[18]

Coaling was challenging. As the *Enterprise*, had found on her ocean passage, a decade before, fuelling the boilers was a constant and consuming task. It was not just a matter of getting the coal to the fires; the remaining coal had to be trimmed to ensure stability and access. It was such a large ship, with large coal supplies, and Pearne was finding coal consumption greater than planned. On Thursday 12th he put the stokers and trimmers into two twelve-hour watches of eight men, with the addition of a sailor who was drafted in to help. This was an unpopular move; watches were usually eight hours, and Pearne had to take them before the captain to give them specific orders. This need to get Hosken involved is also an indication of men who were not accustomed to on-board discipline. The carpenter was employed to make a platform for coal passage, possibly to make access easier.[19] One trimmer, Scully, was slightly injured by a coil of rope hitting him. The heat was intense and the stokers could get little rest in their berths, so the carpenter was brought in to provide a grating in the bulkhead. The same had been true of the *Enterprize* on its first voyage; the heat of the boiler had made some of the men and boys unwell, and one man fainted. They were fortunate in being able to engage extra labour at St Thomas (Sao Tome) off coast of Africa, when thirty-two local men were engaged to trim the coal bunkers.[20]

On 14 April, Pearne noted the stokers were overly tired from lack of sleep and the heat. He reported the engines were 'all that can be desired', but the men who fuelled them were exhausted and there were simply not enough hands to do the work. Not only did the coal have to be brought to the fires, but there was also the constant job of removing the ashes. There were problems maintaining steam 'by reason the coal cannot be got from ends of the ship and brought to the furnaces fast enough for consumption'. Heavy Atlantic swells made the task of pushing wheelbarrows laden with coal ever harder. By Friday all hands, including extra seamen, were trimming coal from the extreme ends of the ship and the muttering continued.[21] The seamen were also pressed into service to help with the removal of the ashes and their disposal overboard. One stoker, Crooks, found it was all too much and got drunk. He did not turn up for duty and was abusive to Pearne and Captain Hosken. Hosken had him confined but Crooks got free and this time compounded his behaviour by attempting to throw Hosken overboard. Crooks was confined again but the engine room hands rebelled in his support and he was released. Crooks later complained of being ill and was given medicine and retired to bed. The ship's surgeon no doubt had a useful selection of potions.[22]

When not dealing with recalcitrant stokers, Hosken's attention was on the whole ship and he spent much of his time on deck. The passengers were considerably less of a challenge, as there were only six. Hosken kept an eye on progress across the Atlantic with the assistance of a special chart. Brunel's attention to detail extended to the charts prepared.

> When we started the *Great Western* to New York, I had a chart drawn and engraved of the sea (that is the lines of latitude and longitude, and the bearings of the compass and the coast and soundings) on a cylindrical projection of the great circle from Bristol to New York; and we found it very useful for the captain to see his great circle sailing, and see how much he was deviating from it.[23]

The small number of passengers amused themselves as best they could, taking an interest in shipboard activities, the weather and tending the vase of mysterious flowers which, unfortunately, did not make it across the seas after one rather stormy night. The motion of a steamer was unique, and Foster noted how much smoother it was; with paddle wheels in the centre of the ship and the help of sails, each plunge into the sea was less severe. He also noted the other difference in the *Great Western*: the 'lack of motion or jar from her engines', arising, he believed, from the quality of the engines and the strength of the ship.

On Monday 23 April, the pace changed as the crew got ready to enter port. At ten o'clock they stopped the engines for five minutes to receive the pilot, who brought news to a ship of people who had heard nothing from the outside world since leaving Bristol. The news included the less welcome, but anticipated, information that they had just – only just – been beaten by the *Sirius* in crossing the Atlantic by steam. With all flags flying, the *Great Western* entered New York harbour, saluted on all sides by guns firing and crowds cheering. 'It was an exciting moment – a moment of triumph! Experiment had ceased – certainty was attained – our voyage was accomplished!'[24] From the deck, the diarist Foster viewed his countrymen and women: 'Myriads were collected, boats were gathered in countless confusion, flags were flying, guns were firing, cheering from the shore, the boats and all round, loudly and gloriously, as though it would never have done. It was an exciting moment, a moment of triumph.'[25]

With not just one ocean steamship in the harbour but two at once, New York went wild with excitement, augmented by relief at their safe arrival. Knowing the planned departure dates from Cork and Bristol, there had been some anxiety as watchers, aware of the weather conditions mid-Atlantic, had scanned the horizon. Now they were both safely arrived. The *Herald* was a newcomer to the New York press, established with 500 dollars just three years previously by a forty-year-old Scotsman, James Gordon Bennett. Bennett's reporting style was very different to that of the other, more traditionally staid newspapers. Even before the arrival of the *Great Western* Bennett wrote, 'We will take several days before we get over our delirium and think soberly.'[26] With the arrival of the second ocean steamship, his headline went into overdrive: 'Triumph of steam – the *Sirius* and *Great Western* – the passage of the Atlantic in 14 days!'[27]

The *Herald* conveyed the joyous enthusiasm and excitement of the crowds in witnessing such a momentous event:

> The excitement yesterday was tremendous; from an early hour in the morning until dark myriads of person's crowded the battery to have glimpse of the first vessel to cross the Atlantic on the British isles. The approach of the *Great Western* was most magnificent. It was about 4:00 yesterday afternoon. The sky was clear- the crowds immense. Below, on the broad blue water, appeared this huge thing of life, with four masts, and emitting volumes of smoke. She looked black and blackguard – as all that the British steamer is generally are – rakish, cool, reckless, fierce, and forbidding in their sombre colours to an extreme. As she neared the *Sirius* she slackened the movements, and took a sweep around forming a sort of half circle. At this moment the whole battery sent forth a tumultuous shout of delight, at the revelation of her magnificent proportions. After making another turn towards Staten Island, she made another sweep, and shot towards the East River with extraordinary speed.[28]

Philp Hone, a wealthy New York auctioneer and diarist, described the city as being in a ferment: 'The Battery and adjacent streets were crowded with curious spectators and the water covered with boats conveying obtrusive visitors on board.' He was no stranger to Atlantic crossing by packet line and noted:

> The Passengers on board the two vessels speak in the highest terms of the convenience, steadiness and apparently safety of the new mode of conveyance across the ocean. Everybody is so enamored of it that for a while it will supersede the New York packets – the noblest vessels that ever floated in the Merchant service. Our countrymen 'studious of change and pleased with novelty' will rush forward to visit the shores of Europe instead of resorting to Virginia or Saratoga Springs; and steamers will continue to be the fashion until some more dashing adventurer of the go ahead tribe will demonstrate the practicability of balloon navigation and gratify the impatient by a voyage over and not upon the Blue Waters in two days instead of as many weeks.[29]

The *Herald* hailed the bold expedition and also looked ahead to 'the results to business, commerce, manners, arts, social life, and the moral approximation of the two hemispheres'.[30] Colonel Webb, editor of the *Courier and Enquirer*, wrote:

> What may be the ultimate fate of this excitement – whether or not the expenses of equipment and fuel will admit of the employment of these vessels in the ordinary packet service – we cannot pretend to form an opinion ; but of the entire feasibility of the passage of the Atlantic by steam, as far as regards safety, comfort and despatch, even in the roughest and most boisterous weather, the most skeptical must now cease to doubt.[31]

The intrepid passengers were interviewed and Captain Roberts of the *Sirius* was spoken of in the most complimentary terms by the ladies. 'They should,' they said, 'have been dreadfully alarmed by the bad weather but they felt quite safe when they thought they were under Captain Roberts' charge whose celebrity as a steam navigator was proverbial.' The cook, noted as 'an authority in such matters', described the rolling of the vessel as 'very trifling, and not so heavy as in a sailing vessel'.[32] On the *Great Western* the seven heroic passengers described their voyage as having been, on the whole, pleasant, but 'for the vibration and smell of machinery and their continual dread that she was going to blow up'.[33]

Before the arrival, the corporation of the city had appointed a joint committee to receive and visit the ships. The New York papers had eagerly printed what news they could of the potential arrival date of the ships. Hone noted drily, 'They will probably make a jollification on the occasion.' Indeed they did, and New Yorkers were relentless in celebrating the achievement of the two steamers. The plans included a collation on the *Sirius*, a banquet on the *Great Western* and an all-day party on Blackwell's Island for the commanders of both ships.[34] On the day of arrival, both captains were invited to a banquet at Carlton House hosted by the committee of the Saint George Society and Hosken, who arrived late, was conducted to a seat next to the president of the society while 'my friend Lieutenant Richard Roberts was seated on his other side'.[35]

Philip Hone noted on 24 April that the committee of arrangements of the corporation had organised for the politicians and distinguished friends to visit 'the *Sirius*, where the collation will be prepared for them on which occasion the commander Lieutenant Roberts is to receive the Freedom of the City'. The food and wine on board the *Sirius* was said to have cost $1,000 and was served up by Downing of 5 Broad Street. The mayor and corporation were well entertained.[36]

Despite the stream of visitors, both ships while in port needed to make repairs and clean up for the return passage. On 24 April there was a tragic accident on board *Great Western*. Chief engineer Pearne, assisted by his deputy, Roberts, was blowing off the boilers, emptying them to allow them to be fully inspected. In the process, something went wrong and Pearne, an experienced man, was severely scalded. Medical help was sought, the on-board surgeon presumably being elsewhere now the ship was in port, and Pearne was taken to New York City Hospital on the 26th, where he died. He died from excessive vomiting; with such severe burns, his body had gone into shock.[37] Pearne was an experienced engineer with a thorough knowledge of his engines. Claxton referred to his 'zealous prosecution of his duties in an enervating and heated atmosphere for fifteen days on succession'. If the stokers had worked hard in terrible conditions, Pearne had not spared himself. Whether his tiredness had been a factor or whether the disaster was the result of another's action there is no way of knowing, but it was a grave tragedy in the midst of such celebrations. He was a well-liked man for both his knowledge and his kindness.[38]

The public show had to go on, and after a couple of days to rest their stomachs the dignitaries paid their next visit, on 27 April, to the *Great Western* – for such, wrote Philip Hone, 'is the rather awkward name of this noble steamer'.[39] This time Hone was with them. He assembled with the rest of the dignitaries at the mayor's office at one o'clock. In addition to the corporation there were judges, members of the legislature, Mr Daniel Webster, Governor Mason of Michigan, Mr Bradish, the speaker and newspaper editors. They processed on foot to Beekman Street, where about twenty barges, each commanded by an officer in full uniform and bearing the American flag, were arrayed. They formed a procession led by a barge carrying musicians, and, under the command of Captain Stringham of the United States Navy, they were rowed out to the *Great Western*, which was moored just up the East River off Pike Street. They were met by Captain Hosken and his officers and given a tour of the 'stupendous machinery of the great vessel' before being escorted to the saloon and seated. The food, 'arranged in excellent taste', was washed down with oceans of champagne. Speeches were given, toasts were drunk and 'Captains Hosken of the *Great Western* and Roberts of the *Sirius* appeared to be as happy as they said they were'.[40] Everyone felt happy, all had gone well, the weather was fine and the ship showed off its best side, even when crammed with visitors. The normally cynical observer Philip Hone was pleasantly surprised:

> The vessel exceeds my expectation, the accommodations for passengers in the best possible taste; the principal saloon is surrounded by staterooms, sufficiently capacious. The ornaments are of the quaint old-fashioned style and the panels are decorated by exquisite paintings. One of the greatest advantages which this saloon has over the cabins of the packets consist in the height of the ceiling, which affords light and air equal to a well-proportioned dining room.

Brunel would have been delighted if he had heard the comparison. However, Hone expressed a common cautionary view by adding, 'All that is now wanting to confine to the steam vessels the patronage of all the passengers going to Europe is the assurance of safety and that would be obtained by one or two more passages across the Atlantic.'[41]

Meanwhile, the people of New York were desperate to get on board. The newspapers recorded the reactions. The saloon was 'splendid beyond all description', the ladies' boudoir was 'a love of a spot, and a bijou of a place'. The stewardess who presided over the ladies' boudoir was described as a pretty girl who was horrified by the possibility of dirty feet coming into 'this *sanctum sanctorum* of the vessel'. The pantry was 'admirably arranged', the lower saloon 'neat and commodious', the cuddy 'a nice snuggery on deck, the only part of the ship which is to be profaned by tobacco'.

The kitchen was the 'most admirable contrivance we ever saw' and the engine 'awful to behold so immense is it'. Such was the crush of people that a close eye had to be kept on the paintwork and the carpets needed to be protected by matting. A rumour went around that less enlightened visitors were spitting on the carpets and chipping off pieces of deck and furniture as souvenirs, at which the 'pretty stewardess' almost fainted.[42]

Saturday 28th was set aside exclusively for ladies, who were invited to visit between the hours of eleven and four. Captain Hosken's request in the newspapers was that no gentleman visit the ship on that day, 'except those in attendance on the ladies'. He suggested not more than one gentleman to three ladies would give 'more of the latter an opportunity of seeing the ship'.[43] That evening it was his turn to be invited again, this time to a reception at Astor House. The three men who arranged the reception for both captains were prominent New Yorkers. Samuel Swartwout was the Collector of the Port of New York, Charles Livingston was a politician and had been the speaker of the New York Assembly, and James Murray was a businessman and leading member of New York society.[44]

The location for the reception was one of New York's own palaces, a luxury hotel built by millionaire John Jacob Astor. It had opened in 1836 and was an impressive and very large structure in the Greek revival style. Five stories of granite around a central courtyard contained 309 rooms that could house up to 800 guests. It had gas lighting and on each floor there were bathing and toilet facilities – so many facilities were something of a novelty lacking in most other elegant boarding houses, many of which sent their clients to public baths. The food was lavish and offered another novelty: *table d'hote*.[45]

During the continuing and lavish celebrations, one small cloud was caused by a newspaper spat. James Watson Webb, editor of the *Courier and Enquirer*, and James Gordon Bennett of the *Herald* were in a frantic race to get the very latest news from Europe. Webb hired a boat to intercept the *Sirius* and scooped the European news with newspapers from London and Cork. But the greater prize lay in those papers carried by the *Great Western* as these were the most up-to-date; London newspapers dated 6 April and Bristol newspapers from the 7th. Knowing the arrival of the *Great Western* was imminent, Webb got a man on board the pilot boat and again managed to grab the first set of newspapers. Unfortunately, in his enthusiasm the man also grabbed the mailbags, much to the fury of the authorities as mailbags were sacrosanct. Bennett, livid at being beaten to the post and not a man to let a slight go unnoticed or a conspiracy unpublished, took umbrage and retaliated in print.[46] Bennett's journalistic contemporary Charles A. Dana wrote that he was

> ... in many respects the most brilliant, original, and independent journalist I have ever known. Cynical in disposition, regarding every institution, every man, and every party with a degree of satirical disrespect, living through his protracted career in this city with very few friends, and those generally of a mental caliber inferior to his own, ready to affront alike the interests, the prejudices, and the passions of powerful individuals, or imposing parties with a judgment always inclining to be eccentric, and a lawless humor for which nothing was sacred except his own independence, he yet possessed such fresh and peculiar wit, such originality of style, such resources of out-of-the-way reading and learning, such unexpected and surprising views of every subject, such comprehensive notions about news, and such ability to direct the collection of news, and to employ those able to organize and push that business, that he made himself the most influential journalist of his day; and in spite of enmities and animosities and contempt such as I have never seen equalled towards any man, he built up the *Herald* to be the leading newspaper of this country, and indeed, one of the great and characteristic journals of modern times.[47]

From being an enthusiastic supporter of both ships, Bennett now made snide remarks about the *Great Western* and Captain Hosken in his newspaper. Supporters of the *Great Western* retaliated, and tall tales were circulated, among which were the stories that the *Sirius* had to burn all its furniture to complete the passage (including a child's doll) and a near mutiny of stokers on board.[48] American supporters of the *Great Western* inserted a notice to the public in the *Evening Post* defending the 'gentlemanly treatment' received from all the officers of the *Great Western* steamship and their disgust at an article, in what was described as a 'vile two-penny print', which had attacked the conduct and character of the men. They wished to offer 'unqualified praise of the commander and his subaltern officers' and their praise for his 'courteous, obliging, and hospitable reception of *all*' who have visited his 'magnificently fitted out and well-tried floating palace'.[49]

Webb remained a supporter of the *Great Western* and noted that the ship 'was literally run down with thousands of all classes, eager to look upon this eighth wonder of the world, this steam leviathan ... We knew too that the *Sirius* was very generally looked upon as kind of interloper, chartered for the purpose of snatching honours from those to whom they justly belonged.'[50] Throughout this rivalry in the press and in subsequent reports Hosken and Claxton were always generous and complimentary about their fellow naval officer, Lieutenant Richard Roberts of the *Sirius*.

It was eventually time for the return to England. The *Sirius* was the first to depart, on 1 May, observed by Philip Hone. She sailed at one o'clock and passed the packets; the 'weather being pleasant and the sea calm [she] was soon out of sight ahead'. The *Sirius* departed with nearly fifty passengers and was loaded with 400 tons of coal which made her sit deeply in the water. 'She went off however in good style, several musicians took passage in her, part of a band who will return.'[51] She could not take any freight as she needed all her space for coal. On board she carried twenty-six passengers in first class – including Colonel Vernon Graham, who had come out on the *Great Western* – and twenty-one passengers in steerage.[52] But on the same day came shocking news that underlined the sometimes precarious nature of travel by steamboat. At Cincinnati on 25 April, the steamboat *Moselle*, on a voyage down the river, caused a horrific and dreadful disaster when its boilers burst. It was a scene of carnage. There were 280 passengers on board and only ninety were saved. 'The papers are filled with the details of this shocking catastrophe which cannot be read without shuddering.'[53]

On 7 May, one week after the departure of the *Sirius*, it was the turn of the *Great Western* to leave New York. It was an ideal day, with light winds and fair weather. At 11 a.m. the engines were started, and at half past they cast off from Pike wharf and headed downriver to No. 1 Quay, North River, to receive the passengers and their luggage. Even for this short trip the engineer's log noted 'immense multitudes of people assembled to cheer us, which we returned, also the United States frigate *Macedonia*'.[54]

Just after two o'clock they finally cast off and headed for home. The send-off was even greater than that for the *Sirius* as New York said goodbye to the Leviathan that promised regular fast passage between their port and Britain. Colonel Webb saw 'the crowd on the Battery, the roofs of houses, and the piers, that continued constantly to augment until nearly two o'clock, while at the same time the number of steamers had increased to thirteen – the smaller craft being absolutely innumerable'. When they reached the narrows, 9 miles out and escorted still by multitudes of craft, the steamer stopped to let all the distinguished guests disembark. They included His Excellency William Marcy, the Governor of the State of New York, and Mr Bradish, the Speaker of the House of Assembly, and many other distinguished citizens. It must have been dangerously crowded on board as the additional citizens numbered '200 or 300 friends of passengers who had accompanied us thus far on a voyage'.[55] It was an opportunity yet again for the commercially minded – the steamboat *Highlander*, commanded by Captain Wardropp, promised 'an uncommon fine opportunity' of witnessing the speed of the *Great Western* and working of her engines.[56]

The *Great Western* carried more passengers this time – sixty-eight in total – than the *Sirius*, but still not a full complement. Possibly the very recent tragic accident on the *Moselle* was still in the minds of some. Among the passengers was Colonel James Watson Webb; his rival, Bennett, had elected to travel on the *Sirius*. It was rumoured that Bennett, a bachelor, had sold off his furniture to pay for his trip to Europe. Both gentlemen were apparently travelling in order to make arrangements for 'availing themselves of the new facilities for correspondence afforded by the commencement of steam navigation between England and the States'.[57] Bennett said he intended to go over to London for the coronation and, while there, establish agents in Europe and also purchase a press 'like that used by the London *Times*, capable of throwing off 5,000 sheets in an hour'.[58]

On board the *Great Western* was the Dodworth band of music 'to keep the passengers in harmony and to pass away the time'.[59] Also loaded were fresh provisions, including an 'ample supply of first rate Yankee beef and poultry supplied by Daniel Winship of Fulton market'. The hope expressed was that if she made a fast passage then the English 'will be able to taste some of our fresh beef'. There were many dreams of new markets for New York produce due to the speed of the ship, even if the ice house on board was unlikely to be able to store much more than was needed for its own consumption and the number of live cattle on board for milk was equally limited.[60]

Her freight included one trunk of clothes, ninety bales of cotton, six packages of cochineal, thirteen cases of indigo, two barrels of apples, twenty-six bales or cases, contents unknown, and over 20,000 letters.[61] The crew had their own happy memories of New York and several had souvenirs. Among the many items presented to him, Hosken had a painting: 'An American painted a picture of our arrival and commissioned me to bring it home as a present to the queen. I have a copy of it and among private papers I have a copy of a letter to the queen sent with the painting.'[62]

At five o'clock they dropped the pilot and then stopped briefly one hour later to receive some letters from the ship *Wellington*, which had left Portsmouth on 11 April. As the ship headed out into the Atlantic, the crew continued the normal tasks on board. All hands were employed clearing decks of passenger luggage and various stores, lashing spars and water casks, taking in and making sail as required. The tradesmen were busy securing tables and seats and fitting shelves in passengers' berths. The carpenter repaired an accommodation ladder and the joiner was making glass stands for cabin tables. The ship's cook, however, was sick and remained so for five days. This was the crew cook, as there was a separate cook for passengers. Several other crew members were also off duty sick. As before, seamen were drafted in to help the coal trimmers and one depressing task was to make an inventory of Mr Pearne's effects for his family.

After a good passage across, they anchored in Kingroad at a quarter past eleven in the morning on 22 May. The timing of their arrival had been anticipated since the arrival of the *Sirius* in Falmouth. The *Sirius* took eighteen days to return compared to the *Great Western*'s fourteen days and seventeen hours.[63] The *Great Western*'s arrival was announced by the firing of guns, and when she came to anchor the American band on board played 'Old England Forever'. Church bells rang out and yet more guns were fired. Her foremast carried the American ensign, from the second hung a streamer with the ship's name and from her fourth mast she flew the English ensign. She looked as fresh as when she had been launched. The passengers, who 'are well, and in excellent spirits', transferred to the little steamer, *Cambrian*, to take the passengers and luggage up the river. There had been cheers on board when Captain Hosken announced to the passengers that it had been arranged that they should be landed at Rownham to be met by Customs officers, which was far more convenient for their hotel, without having to go onwards into Bristol to the Customhouse.[64] The passengers and their luggage reached Hotwells about half past two. 'They expressed themselves much pleased with the urbanity and civility of the Custom House officers', which rather suggests this politeness was not the normal state of affairs. The Bristol authorities were doing what they could to make everyone feel welcome.

A large number of the passengers then headed for Ivatt's Royal Gloucester Hotel at Clifton. Newspaper reports singled out forty-three of the passengers by name. Considered worthy of note were Lord James Butler, Judge Crane, Colonel Webb and several married couples and many single males. Miss Eliza Cross does not get a mention in any reports despite being the first woman to voyage to and from New York on a steamship.[65]

There was enormous pride in the achievement and the behaviour of the 'officers and crews of the *Sirius* and *Great Western*, their extreme urbanity have won for them a greater share of popular approbation than ever attended the successful efforts of the directors of similar expeditions'. The joyful news of her arrival was said to be felt across all classes, and it was compared to the tidings from the 'Nile, Trafalgar bay, and the Plains of Waterloo'.[66] Later fifty-three of the passengers signed an open letter to Captain Hosken, expressing their grateful thanks for the satisfaction and comfort they had experienced and for his kindness to them and for the 'vigilance with which he had watched over their safety during a residence of fourteen days on board of her on the bosom of the Atlantic'.[67] It was, said the newspapers, as if they were 'relating a fairy tale. Our readers will, we are sure, to a great extent, partake in this sensation, and say to themselves, can this be real, or a wandering of the imagination?'[68]

In London the news was similarly greeted with great enthusiasm, particularly in commercial quarters. The *Taunton Courier* gave a report from its London correspondent, who wrote from the North and South American Coffee House, which was a key gathering place for many merchants and captains. Writing just two days after the ship's arrival, he reported that there had been only one topic of conversation there in the London journals and in the coffee houses: 'the mighty stride which steam navigation has just taken'. The latest American newspapers were summarised with extensive reports on the reception of the ship in New York.[69]

The London correspondent saw that this new era would also have a political effect, noting the New York journals that referred to the thousands of people who had come from Boston and Philadelphia for the purpose of seeing the *Great Western*. All disputes were put into the past as 'New York at all events will henceforth be the fast friend of old England'. The timing of the steamship had also coincided with another event that was causing great speculation in New York: the eagerly anticipated coronation of England's queen, which partly explained the good take-up of cabins. 'Among our fashionable circles, this approaching event is beginning to create a deep sensation. The arrival of the two British steamers, both of which will return in time for that celebration, has given additional impulse to this feeling.' The packet ships were already carrying passengers to England for the event, but now a 'fresh and more brilliant opportunity presents itself, in the return voyage of the steamer as all fashionable people are almost beside themselves; and these sentiments a widened and deepened by the singular feelings of enthusiasm developed in New York towards the youthful British queen'.[70] Meanwhile, the return of the ship to Bristol and the news that she had carried fresh beef and poultry from New York in her ice house on board convinced American merchants based in London 'that we shall have Covent Garden market supplied with watermelons and other fruits from the States before the end of this present summer. Such are among the minor effects of the mighty power now brought into action, a power by which "distance is annihilated and the ends of the earth brought together".'[71]

In Bristol the ship was yet again subject to eager visitors, but this time the company, in trying to manage crowds, charged a fee – a fact that did not go down well with one section of the public, who felt most aggrieved and indignantly wrote to the editor of the *Bristol Mercury*.

> Sir – I wish you would inform me what the ladies of Bristol have done that they should hold so unworthy a place in the opinions of the proprietors of the 'Great Western' steam-ship? I suppose we are not so handsome, or are less polite than the American ladies, that we are to be charged five shillings for a peep at the cabins, while they were absolutely pressed to come and had a splendid *dejeuner a la fourchette* into the bargain. If you or any of your readers can solve the enigma you will oblige a whole host of young ladies, and more particularly yours,
>
> Eliza
31 May, Clifton

The editor added that they had received many similar letters and, while conceding it was wholly a decision for the directors, felt the fee was neither wise nor prudent considering the excessive interest in the ship.[72]

With the undoubted and brilliant success of the voyage, pressure now came from the press and from the town council (several of whom were directors of the Great Western Steam Ship Company) to follow up the advantage gained and build a sister ship for the *Great Western* as soon as possible.

4

Masters and Crew

The *Great Western* carried a large crew across three departments within the ship. A deck crew was needed to handle sails, ropes and mooring. Another group of men were there for the engineer's department, some with highly specialised skills and others simply to shift the coal. Within a dedicated passenger ship, the hospitality section was very important and required land-based professions such as steward, cook and waiter. Over all of these were the officers, headed by the captain. Managing a team with such different tasks and skills on a long steam voyage carrying demanding passengers was in itself a new challenge, and there were some early lessons for the master and the company. Naturally, the company was keen to show they had the best men for the roles. 'In the appointment of officers your Directors have been careful to obtain the strongest testimonials, and have exercised their best judgement,' they announced in their first report.[1] Indeed, the officers, especially the master, would be a critical factor for the whole project.

The first and longest-serving master of the *Great Western* was Lieutenant James Hosken, who made sixty-six passages on the ship. He was a Royal Navy officer like Claxton, and had been out of commission since 1832. He was born in Devonport, Plymouth, to Cornish parents, his father serving in the Navy at the time.[2] James followed his father, entering the Navy at the age of twelve as a midshipman in 1808, and so saw service in the Napoleonic Wars, although much of it involved the very tedious role of blockading enemy ships in their ports. He served in both West India and home stations. The largest vessel on which he served was HMS *Bulwark*, a seventy-four-gun under Captain Dundas based at Plymouth. After the war his most exciting role was in a revenue cutter, *Scout*, chasing smugglers off the East Anglia coast. This was a more lucrative posting since prize money for captures was distributed among the crew. He gained the coveted promotion to lieutenant in 1828.[3] He then had command of a bomb vessel, *Aetna*, after which he moved into the merchant service. In 1832 he was the commander of the packet ships *Princess Elizabeth* and the *Tyrian*. His command took him across the Atlantic, carrying mail and a few passengers to Brazil. These packets were based at Falmouth, where his family was settled. In 1833 he took command of a merchant ship, *Richard Watson*, which traded between Liverpool and Brazil, and he and his family moved to Liverpool for three years. In 1837 they moved again, this time to Bristol, where he turned his attention to steam navigation.[4] What is not clear is whether he heard about the ship and moved or if the offer came first.

At sea, the task of keeping the passengers content, especially the important ones, was an essential part of the captain's role. Hosken frequently dined with them when duties permitted, and from most passenger accounts he was highly regarded. Elizabeth Dixon was very warm in her comments: 'Last but not least comes the pleasantest kindest most gentleman like of captains, James Hosken, he seemed to take quite a fancy for me. And every day the fat boy came with the captain's compliments to take wine with Mrs. Dixon and always on his way he had some pretty speech for me when I was able to go on deck and try to amuse me if he was near.' He teased her about not getting her sea legs and said he would tell her father when he saw him that she drank too much wine and could not stand on board the ship. His attentiveness extended to the evenings when his own chair was brought out for her and placed near the piano so she could enjoy the music. Mrs Dixon was a very rich woman from a very well-placed and influential American family so she was a passenger worth cultivating.[5]

The master of a ship such as the *Great Western* met many people, and certainly in the early years it carried the rich, wealthy and influential, such as Mr and Mrs Dixon. This had benefits for Hosken, giving him contacts in several parts of the

USA, a country he was keen to explore. From 1841, once he felt matters were well organised and settled in the early New York runs, Hosken took the opportunity to go sightseeing leaving his second in command, Mathews, with the ship. Hosken took a week or ten days away from the ship and travelled as far as he could. He visited Philadelphia and Boston, went up the Hudson River to West Point and saw the Military College, to the Mohawk Valley and the lakes. He was impressed by the beauty of Saratoga on Lake George: 'This lake is very beautiful and studded with islands.' He got as far as Buffalo Lake, Ontario, and walked behind the waterfalls at Niagara and 'on all these excursions I received great kindness and hospitality from authorities and individuals'.[6]

In late November 1841 he visited Richmond, going by way of Fredericksburg and returning by James River and Chesapeake Bay. It was late in the year and the weather turned for the worse. Coming up the bay in the first week of December from Portsmouth, Virginia, to Baltimore, there was a snowstorm and heavy gale. They reached Baltimore and then took the train to Philadelphia and onwards to New York, but the snow was very heavy and the train could not get through. Good fortune smiled on him as he was by now very concerned to get back to the ship. 'The conductor in charge of the mails knowing me said I should go on with him if he could get a sleigh.' This they succeeded in doing, eventually reaching Bordentown, Burlington County, just before dark. All hotels were fully booked but he remembered that 'I had been repeatedly invited to Bordentown by Mr Joachim Murat, afterwards Prince Murat. I sent in my card and in a very short time he came to a hotel with a sleigh and pair and took me to his house where I was most hospitably entertained until the next day.' There is no mention of the fate of the helpful train conductor. Eventually Hosken made it to New York and arrived at the ship on the planned departure date. But he knew some passengers were likely to be detained at Philadelphia by the snow and so, after discussion with the agent in New York, it was agreed to delay departure by one day. This was not something they had done before as they had a reputation for punctuality to keep, but it was a lesson in North American winter conditions.[7]

The master's role involved considerable diplomacy in a ship, with passengers from different countries and those from the same country with different opinions. In Britain the slave trade was outlawed in 1807, and slavery itself was abolished across the British Empire in 1833. In the northern states in America slavery was abolished, although segregation remained.

It was in 1841 or 1842 when the following incident occurred. Just before starting in the *Great Western* from Liverpool, when the agent Mr Bright was leaving the ship, I observed a black man among the passengers, and I asked Mr Bright what I should do with him, he shrugged his shoulders and turning away said 'the best you can'.

The next morning early as I took my usual walk on deck, a gentleman joined me and complained about his fellow occupant. Each cabin was arranged for the accommodation of two passengers. I told him that the black man had paid the first class fare and was entitled to the full privileges. But I found another berth for the complainant and the other had the cabin to himself. The latter behaved very well and gave no cause of offence and the others soon left off annoying him. He afterwards wrote me a letter of thanks for what he was pleased to consider my courtesy.[8]

An alternative view was taken by a Cunard agent. In 1845 the Cunard office in Boston refused a first-class cabin for the black American abolitionist Frederick Douglass, who was forced to travel steerage. Douglass was told that other American passengers would object to his presence. Two years later the Liverpool agent took his fare but gave him a cabin by himself on the understanding that he was not to mingle with saloon passengers. The British newspapers went to town in high dudgeon and fulminated over the 'intrusion of peculiar American racial mores on a Royal mail ship'. Samuel Cunard responded with his personal regrets about 'the unpleasant circumstances respecting Mr Douglass' passage, but I can assure you that nothing of the kind will again take place in the steamships with which I am connected'.[9]

In port the captain was the ambassador for both the ship and the company. Hosken was the ideal man for this job as his handling of the New York reception showed. He also smoothed the prickly editor of the *Herald*, James Gordon Bennett, who had been so incensed by his rival's grabbing of the first newspapers to arrive by steam. On the next visit to New York, 'by the politeness of Captain Hoskin [*sic*], our news collector was allowed to board her in the bay about four o'clock in the morning, and before six all our copies of English files were on our table'.[10] Realising the potential of the speedy transmission of news, Bennett had quickly buried the hatchet.

By August of that year, on the ship's third arrival in New York, Hosken hosted another reception on board. The mayor and various members of the corporation were invited and the mayor gave him a presentation copy of the original British charter of the city of New York.[11] Hosken continued to be highly regarded. After tremendous gales on a winter passage several 'testimonials were presented to him by the passengers, all tending to add to the fame which he has already attained'. The company applauded his work on their behalf as the public face of the ship: 'He has nobly sustained the reputation won by the first achievement of the regular and continued transatlantic Steam Navigation, and the high testimonials of his passengers attest to the general esteem in which he is held.'[12]

Testimonials from passengers made for good publicity if they were in the form of letters to newspapers:

It is not the intention of the under signed passengers in the *Great Western* from New York to Bristol, merely to compliment the Commander, but to perform a duty that they owe to themselves, to their friends, and to the public generally, to declare their high sense of gratification at the attention of Captain Hosken to the comfort and safety of all on aboard. We return our sincere thanks to him and strongly recommend him and his noble ship to all persons making the voyage between England and the United States.[13]

Such letters were not unusual; they were written about masters of other ships, particularly if the ship had come through bad storms. Gifts were also a regular way of thanking the captain, and were a perk of the job; passenger memorials often came in silver. Such warm expressions of gratitude from various quarters made Hosken something of a minor celebrity in the early days of transatlantic steam, which he enjoyed.

> ... many valuable pieces of plate were presented to me from time to time, as well as other tokens of regard and appreciation in various kinds. The last of these was a present of 100 guineas from the underwriters at Lloyd's who had insured the Great Western. With a part of this I purchased a valuable watch, inside which they had the following testimonial engraved: 'In testimony of the high opinion entertained by the underwriters at Lloyd's, of the nautical skill of Capt. Hosken in having successfully navigated the Great Western steamship, 64 passages between England and America from the 8th of April 1838 the 1st of November 1843.' Mr. Thornton the principal underwriter afterwards gave me a white bait dinner to which he invited a large company of gentlemen to meet me.[14]

Hosken's lack of direct steamship command may have been seen as a limitation upon his appointment to head the *Great Western*, although in the eyes of Claxton, a fellow officer, his naval career no doubt more than made up for that. It was still early days in steam navigation and the number of masters with experience was few. To balance this perceived lack, the company's selection of his second-in-command was equally careful. In smaller sailing ships under the traditional shared ownership system it was left to the master to select his crew, but a ship owned by a company with a prestigious reputation to make meant a greater degree of concern, particularly over the selection of officers.

Hosken's chief officer was a Cornishman born in Penzance. Barnard Mathews' sea career began at the very young age of nine in a coastal vessel of 120 tons. He worked his time on several sailing ships, including the London-based 240-ton *Harriet*, which was sailing to Newfoundland, until he got a position as an apprentice on the 360-ton *Valiant*, which was in the Jamaica trade. This was owned by Henry Fletcher, a shipbuilder based at Limehouse who was among the early builders of steamships.[15] Mathews remained working for Fletcher, moving up to the position of chief mate. His captain, James Tilley, provided a testimonial to his excellent abilities as a second-in-command, finding him 'sober, zealous, and attentive to his duty ... The confidence I placed in him was never shaken on any one instance.' Eventually, in 1831 he gained his first command on the sailing ship *Maria Louisa*. His employer recommended him 'as in every respect qualified to command a ship to any part of the world and a man of integrity worthy of confidence'.[16]

He then moved to Bristol, where he had his first command of a steamer, and was employed by Thomas Guppy to be the master of his *County of Pembroke* steamer. This ship was chartered to the Portuguese government, whose naval commander was Count Cape di Vincent (Sir Charles Napier). Mathews subsequently returned to Bristol with the steamer and was then in charge of her for two years before becoming a master of the *Benledi* in 1835.

The *Benledi* was a 120 horsepower steamship and steamed across the Bristol Channel, serving the ports of Tenby, Milford, Pembroke Dock and Haverfordwest. Described in an advertisement as 'this splendid and Powerful steamer [which] performs her voyages with great rapidity and punctuality', it carried goods and passengers, and naturally the saloon and cabins were described as being of a 'very superior style of Elegance'. Refreshments were provided at a fixed price and there was a female attendant.[17] So, Mathews had plenty of passenger experience, although no doubt the trips across the Bristol Channel attracted a different clientele to the superior class targeted by the *Great Western*'s owners. It was Guppy who personally recommended Mathews as the chief officer to support Hosken, and he was appointed in June 1837.[18]

In addition to the chief mate (later described as second officer), there were second, third and fourth officers and a purser. In merchant shipping, there was no system of qualifications. Reputation and service were the main recommendations and testimonials, verbal or written, from previous shipowners or masters were essential. There was no government system of examinations for merchant service. State involvement in shipping was limited at the beginning of the nineteenth century and strongly resisted by ship owners. There were private schools of navigation available to the seaman if he had time on shore and could afford them. As their name indicates, they taught the science of navigation and not the practical seamanship skills – these were acquired through experience. Some philanthropists set up marine schools specifically to remedy this lack, but they were never widespread enough to make a real difference. This is why the surplus of trained naval officers post war was attractive to high-profile ships such as the *Great Western* and the rival ships, although existing merchant mariners might have been unimpressed, even if the merchant fleet was growing rapidly and the demand for mariners was high.

The combination of a trained naval officer as captain and a highly experienced merchant mariner as his chief officer looks like a very good decision by the company when considered against a background of concern by the public about safety at sea. While the *Great Western* was being built, and after several high-profile shipwrecks, public pressure grew for action. Safety at sea was not a government priority and it took a determined Member of Parliament to persuade the government to investigate the causes. The 1836 Select Committee on Shipwrecks was set up at the end of a parliamentary session. Although its recommendations were ignored by the sitting government, its report was to have a far-reaching impact and it included the vexed issue of the variable standards of navigation and seamanship among masters of the merchant marine.[19] It owed its existence to James Silk Buckingham. He had been the Member of Parliament for Sheffield since 1832 and was a persistent, determined and effective lobbyist. Described as an 'active and reformist parliamentarian', he was a promoter of the creation of parks, museums and libraries for the fast-growing industrial towns and was a temperance supporter. But as a seasoned traveller, his passion for maritime reform was his greatest legacy.[20]

Once Buckingham had successfully gained his select committee he worked with drive and energy. The committee met twelve times in July and early August and the report, with its 400 pages of evidence, was presented to Parliament on 15 August 1836. The report heavily criticised some masters and officers for incompetence, citing evidence of appalling ineptitude and utter ignorance of navigational skill and techniques. Drunkenness was established as a further cause of shipwreck. Among the suggested remedies was the establishment of a mercantile marine board to oversee a wide range of measures including nautical schools for seamen and the examination of officers. No action was taken, and Buckingham shortly stepped down as an MP and continued his life as a traveller, writer and reform supporter. He travelled out to New York from London in October 1837 on board the 468-ton *President*, an American-owned packet ship, with his wife and son a few months before the steam service began.[21] If Buckingham was disappointed by the lack of any immediate action following the work of his committee, he could rightly be proud of its legacy. All the 1836 proposals did eventually find their way into law by 1862. A voluntary scheme of certification by examination was introduced for masters and mates in 1846 but was not widely adopted. Mathews and a few other *Great Western* officers would later apply for certificates of service in 1850, when the compulsory scheme was introduced by the Marine Act of 1850. Mathews came under the scheme in 1850 and was granted a certificate of service.[22]

The chief engineer on the first passage to New York was Pearne, and his tragic death at the end of that pioneering voyage has already been noted. His was a major loss to the nascent profession of marine engineer. In 1839 the limited pool of experienced engineers was identified as a cause of steamboat accidents. Edward Gibson, a witness before the select committee on steamboat accidents in 1839, gave his view. Steam technology, he said,

> ... has advanced more rapidly than men of experience and knowledge can be found to conduct it; hence, we often find in the river packets men advanced to the post of engineer who are mere automatons, ignorant of the first principles of the machinery over which they preside who, in case of any derangement, do from ignorance of the result the very thing which they ought to have avoided, creating rather than averting danger or accident.[23]

The demand for engineers grew with the increasingly complex and innovative machinery.[24] It was not as if the roles of railway engineer and marine engineer could be easily interchanged. A railway engineer might require just a basic knowledge. In Brunel's view, he was prepared to recruit a man who was illiterate if he could be trained to do the basic job on a train. A railway engineer was never far away from a station, advice or engineering support. On the other hand, a ship engineer had to be able to carry out running repairs and attend to routine maintenance many miles from any land-based expertise. Engines at sea presented new challenges. Engineers had to work the engines to maximum efficiency, and this meant close attention to every aspect, from boilers, gauges and metalwork to the right type of coal. If the engine or wheels broke down mid-Atlantic, the engineers had to rely on their own ingenuity and skill, often in dangerous conditions. Being near shore brought its own dangers; the *City of Glasgow* was wrecked at the entrance to Douglas harbour on the Isle of Man when its engines stopped in 1825.[25]

In a ship carrying superior-class passengers and with the reputation of the company at stake, the engineers would be hand-picked men from the start. The chief engineer would be recommended by the engine makers, and he would bring his own team with him, but in the early days, such as on the *Great Western*, these men are unlikely to have had much experience of the sea or life on board.[26] Most engineers had four to five years' experience gained on land before going to sea.[27] On the *Great Western* there was a large crew, and although uncongenial it was better paid than deck work. Under normal, full-crew conditions the watches were four hours on, eight hours off, unlike four on/four off on deck. However, as they discovered on the first voyage, this watch system was not always workable and much was learned about crewing in the first voyages of the ship.[28] There were other compensations in addition to better pay. The regular liner offered the prospects of steady employment and it brought career opportunities as men might move from fireman to engineer and upwards.[29] The eventual introduction of the second ship, the *Great Britain*, offered career development opportunities: junior engineer to chief engineer to superintendent of a fleet.[30]

Certificates of competence and certificates of service rules laid out in the Merchant Shipping Act 1854 were amended in 1862 to include certificates of engineers, which seems a rather late regulation of a crucial role on board.[31] Specialisation was slow as the term engineer in the early nineteenth century covered a wide range, as the careers of Brunel and other prominent engineers demonstrate. The Institution of Civil Engineers was founded in 1818 and Joshua Field was an early president; the Institution of Mechanical Engineers was founded in Birmingham 1847; but the Institute of Marine Engineers was not founded until 1888. *Lloyd's Register of Shipping*, however, appointed engineers from 1834 as 'surveying engineers'.[32]

Supporting the engineers were the firemen and trimmers. As we have seen, the fireman shovelled coal into the furnace, levelled the coals in there and removed the ashes and clinker. It was a skilled job; the correct firing and cleaning of the fire was critical, as while fuel burned, 'ash and clinker clogged the fire, gradually reducing the heat output'.[33] One of the key skills the fireman needed to acquire was to judge the state of the fire from its colour to anticipate the fall in boiler pressure. His other skills involved a combination of judgment, physical strength and dexterity in both placing the coals evenly on the fire and removing and disposing of the ash and clinker. There were ever-present dangers from boilers, faulty machinery or high pressure as demonstrated in the death of the highly trained and experienced chief officer, Pearne.[34]

Trimmers were constantly at the beck and call of the firemen, supplying the firemen with coal from the bunkers, and constant fuelling was essential to maintain steam. The coals were shovelled into wheelbarrows and taken to the stokehold – a comparatively straightforward if brutal task at the beginning of a voyage, but as it progressed the coal was further away and trimmers could be pushing wheelbarrows in dark, narrow passages at all times of day or night in rough or calm weather. Apart from the great physical demands of the job in dark and dusty spaces, there were other dangers to the basic task. Coal in confined spaces gave off a gas which drove out oxygen, and it was explosive and prone to spontaneous combustion.[35] Particularly in the early days of experimentation, there was much to learn about different coals and the problems of regular supply of the right type of coal. It was not just in its burn properties that the quality of coal was a consideration, as trimmers often had to deal with lumps of coal up to 3 feet in size by breaking them up with a sledgehammer.[36]

Many trimmers had no sea experience and were simply brought in as labourers. Seasickness meant others, such as seamen, had to be drafted in to assist, which was the cause of considerable resentment.[37]

The *Great Western* was a four-masted sailing ship, and without her paddle wheels had sailed well on her first passage from Bristol to London. Adding paddle wheels, a heavy engine and tons of coal considerably changed the ship and the way in which she moved through the water. The sails were there mainly as support to the engine and could help in reducing fuel needs, but sailing a hybrid ship like this also required plenty of sailing skills. In 1838 there were thirteen seamen on board, and by 1846 this had increased to fourteen able seamen and three ordinary seamen. In addition, there was a carpenter, a carpenter's mate and a painter, and they would also be working in the passenger areas.[38]

Sea duties for the deck team were standard. While on the first crossing to New York several seamen had to be drafted in to assist the trimmers and stokers, on the return to Bristol there is no such mention as the ship was able to pick up additional men in New York. On the return passage from New York in May 1838, the log gives the weather as light winds and cloudy. The watch was employed clearing passenger luggage and stores off the deck and stowing them below. Once these were off the deck, other items had to be tied down safely, and then the regular task of taking in and making sail as required across four masts. The tradesmen were employed fixing tables and seats and making fittings in passenger berths.[39] There were occasional accidents, such as the fall suffered by McKallin, a seaman, who was said to have fallen from the top of the long boat head-first on to the deck and injured himself.[40] The seamen tended not to mix with the engineering crew; each worked, slept and ate in their own quarters, while the officers were in separate accommodation and also messed separately.[41]

The 1839 report to the *Great Western*'s shareholders was pleased to report that experience after the first season has shown the 'benefit arising to your service, and to Steam navigation generally, from the introduction of young Gentlemen into your employ as Cadets'.[42] This was an aspect on which Claxton himself was very keen. The cadets were to be instructed in navigation, arithmetic, mathematics and steam engineering; Pearne himself took a great interest in their schooling on board on the first passage. Three were quickly appointed, and there were several applications for the fourth position. They would be apprenticed for four years at a cost of £200 each. The introduction of cadets has all the hallmarks of Claxton. Both he and Hosken were products of the naval midshipman system, and Claxton was an enthusiastic supporter. His book *The Naval Monitor*, published in 1816 and reissued in 1833, contained 'many useful hints, for both the public and private conduct of the young gentlemen, on entering that profession in all its branches'. He also included recommendations for improving the naval system for midshipmen, and he even itemised the clothing and other items that each 'Middy' should take on board.[43]

Ships were required by law to carry apprentices; the first law on apprenticeship was passed in 1703, largely as a measure to assist with the Poor Law. A second Act in 1823 regulated the number of apprentices to be taken on board British merchant vessels, and the number of apprentices was in proportion to the size of the ship. By the time of the *Great Western* any vessel 700 tons and above was required to take a minimum of five apprentices. Normally these were apprentice seamen brought in at the youngest possible age to train on deck. Most apprentices came from parishes where the Guardians of the Poor Law took the opportunity to place pauper children on board ships. This was at a time in the 1830s when employers such as those in the textile trades were reluctant to take them due the now extensive legislation limiting the hours of work and controlling their working conditions.[44] The government also saw enforcement of apprenticeship in the merchant marine as aiding the 'nursery of seamen' for the Royal Navy, an aspect that met with Claxton's approval. However, the financial burden of apprenticeship was a constant refrain from shipowners in evidence to the select committees in the 1840s, and by then no group of employers other than shipowners were subject to apprenticeship regulation. The shipowners opposed the system, including the contractual obligation to provide food, washing, lodgings, medicine, etc., whether at sea or on shore. Shipowners could keep costs down by laying off all labour in a port and retaining the master and perhaps a couple of other officers for continuity, but apprentices could not be discharged.[45]

As one shipowner put it:

> After a long voyage a ship may be laid up for two or three months
> and the owner has five apprentices to keep during that time. It
> is a hardship … to maintain these apprentices in idleness, to pay
> for their board three or four months; it amounts to a great deal
> of money 12 shillings or 14 shillings a week for the maintenance
> of each lad.[46]

The *Great Western* scheme was different, designed not to be a
burden on the company; instead it would be an asset, while still
meeting the legal requirements. The cadets were not poor children
destined for deck crew but cadets to be trained as officers. The
company saw the *Great Western* as a potential supply of officers
trained in steam navigation to provide future officers for their
ambition of a transatlantic steam line. Claxton claimed it was a
novel system, and there may have been some new ideas in there,
but other foreign-going trade operators such as Wigram and Green
of London and Brocklebank of Liverpool had similar schemes for
youths 'earmarked as future officers'. These schemes came from the
quasi-naval East India Company. The legal requirement to carry
apprentices was repealed in 1850.[47]

The *Great Western* cadets had a smart semi-naval uniform
with buttons stamped with the initials GW.[48] These were not
young children: Claxton was a firm believer that boys should
remain in school and not be sent to sea before the age of
thirteen.[49] At sea, in addition to various duties, they had formal
lessons from the ship's accountant, who was recruited as part
purser and part teacher.[50] In the first group of apprentices there
were Thomas Tidcombe from Shepton Mallet, William Henry
Peach from Bath and one G. M. Whitehead. Two were French,
Cedrick Stafford and Felix Letrosne, both born in Paris – perhaps
some influence here from the half-French Brunel. All of these
were on the very first crossing, and remained with the ship to
complete their apprenticeship when a new group was taken on.[51]
Of these, only one went on to get formal qualifications as a mate.
Stafford served as third mate on the *Great Western* and gained
his certificate in 1853.[52]

'In no department has more difficulty been encountered than that of the Steward, arising from an under estimate of the space required for the conduct of its various branches, and from the novelty of preparations on Ship-board of unequalled extent and variety.' This was a big lesson learned in the first season.[53] The *Great Western* was setting new standards in hospitality at sea, as a group of passengers attested in December 1838 when referring to the new steamers as 'magnificent floating hotels'.[54] As an early luxury steamship which prided itself on looking after its passengers, the hospitality section was crucial. By 1880 the catering departments, the stewards and kitchen crew, would form the biggest occupational group on transatlantic liners and by 1911 the *Carmania* had 70 men on deck, 144 in the engine room and 271 in the catering dept.[55]

The steward's position was a good one, with plenty of prospects for tips and some additional earning on the side.[56] For instance, the passengers' fare included the food but not wine and spirits, and this bill was settled direct with the steward.[57] Initially all wine had been included, but there had been claims from some well-placed passengers that this led to intemperance and they recommended in an open letter that the wine should be paid additionally, as was the custom in hotels and in steamships on the rivers and lakes of America.[58] This excellent idea of charging additionally for wines and spirits was quickly put in place.

By 1846 William Crawford, aged forty-two, was head steward, plus George Richards as second steward, and there was a head pantryman, and two storekeepers. In July 1846 on the Liverpool to New York run there were thirteen waiters, two porters, three cooks, a pastry cook, a butcher, a baker, a boy and a dishwasher.[59] Stewards and their staff working in the saloon needed to be able to manage the dangers of cooking and preparation of meat and vegetables at sea. Cooking and serving food in a luxury floating hotel at sea was not easy. A list of the number of dishes produced to serve eighty-seven passengers provides an idea.

Breakfast: 6 dishes boiled ham, six additions fish six dishes mutton chops 100 eggs in omelets, six dishes devilled legs of poultry, six dishes Indian meal

Dinner: 6 tureens of mock turtle soup, two dishes venison, four roasted turkeys, four couple of ducks, four dishes roast beef, four dishes cod fish, four couple of chickens, 6 dishes fried oysters, 4 dishes stewed oysters, four dishes boiled mutton, 4 dishes macaroni
Vegetables: 6 dishes baked mashed potatoes, 6 dishes mashed turnips, six dishes parsnips, six dishes plain potatoes
Pastry: six plum puddings, six custard puddings, six raspberry pies, six apple pies, six cranberry pies, two cherry pies
Wines in abundance[60]

A Canadian judge, Haliburton, had an alter ego, Sam Slick, and this was the pseudonym under which he wrote several humorous books. He was an early passenger on the *Great Western* crossing in 1839. As a result, he wrote a book, *The Letter Bag of the Great Western*, with a series of fictional and amusing letters from different personalities on board reflecting the variety of people and occupations. Several were from crew members and, while fictional, they are based on real situations. In the fictitious letter from the butcher, he refers to the well-built head steward, who obviously lived well, with 'five inches of fat on his ribs'. The butcher's job was to tend to the livestock on board, with cows and chickens for fresh milk, eggs and fresh meat.

A dissatisfied passenger in 1845 saw the power of the steward, 'serious complaints were made about the ship including the steward who seemed wholly independent of the captain'.[61] Smith complained that mealtimes were crowded, 'cold and unsatisfactory and the service insufficient'. This contrasts with Mrs Dixon's more benevolent view of the attentions of the steward and waiters, but Smith was a librarian from Philadelphia and Mr and Mrs Dixon were a wealthy couple from Connecticut and had the ear of the captain. Haliburton shows this in his fictional account of a travelling Army man, Captain Haltfront, who had great difficulty in attracting the attention of the steward – 'Have it in a moment sir – I am waiting on a *gentleman*' – while the fictional letter from the steward admits to ignoring many male passengers as 'very few are superfine gentlemen'.[62]

The majority of the *Great Western*'s crews in both the engineering and deck departments were British, which was fairly standard for a British ship at this time, and while they came from across Britain and Ireland there were many from areas local to Bristol. Shipowners were required by law to engage British seaman for at least three-quarters of the crew, but this ceased to be enforced long before it was removed from statute books.[63] The hospitality department, in contrast, seemed to be staffed with Americans.

Almost from the beginning of steam excursions, advertisements referred to women employed on board. In 1815 the paddle steamer *Thames*, then working between London and Margate, announced, 'For the express purpose of combining delicacy with comfort a female servant attends upon the ladies.' A few years later the *Talbot*, a cross-Channel steamer with overnight accommodation, especially on potentially rough crossings, had the reassuring message that 'ladies will have a female steward to wait on them'.[64] In Bristol, in the very bouncy Bristol Channel, the small 30 horsepower steamboat *Charlotte*, plying between Cardiff and Bristol, had a female steward to attend the ladies' cabins.[65]

The superior class of lady passenger on the *Great Western* might have their own servant to look after their needs, but this was not the case for all women. There were also women travelling alone and, of course, the servants were just as prone to seasickness. A female steward on the Atlantic was essential as male stewards could not be of assistance in the sanctuary of a lady's berth or the ladies' separate boudoir. The stewardess looked after women and children, helped in ladies' cabins, tended the seasick and served meals in their cabins. Mrs Dixon refers to Margaret seeing off the passengers at Bristol.[66] 'Taking care of the linen was another responsibility gendered as female, and the linen store was the responsibility of a stewardess.' According to Cunard's rules, 'when the ship is lying at any foreign port, the stewardesses are to be constantly employed, and every opportunity must be taken by them to keep the ship's linen in order'. Charles Dickens travelled to America in 1842 on the *Britannia*, which carried a stewardess. He wrote of her tasks in *American Notes*: 'There was a stewardess, too, actively engaged in producing clean sheets and tablecloths from the very entrails of the sofas.'[67]

These staff, as with all hospitality staff, do not appear on the early crew lists. It takes until 1846 before they are shown. The need for a female steward may answer a puzzle. Eliza Cross is listed as one of the intrepid group of six who crossed on the first voyage. Described as the owner of a 'stay, straw and millinery wareroom', she appears in the list of passengers arriving at New York, but she does not remain there and comes straight back on the return passage. She was young, just twenty-five, and travelling alone in the company of several single young men. Was she hoping to do business in New York? How could she afford such an expensive two-way passage just for a few days there? Or was she provided with free passage to act as a lady companion and steward to potential lady passengers?

The *Great Western* also advertised the benefit of a surgeon who 'is permanently engaged in the ship and every provision made for the comfort and security all the passengers'.[68] The first was a Mr McKenna, 'a gentleman of high professional character and great experience, (having practiced in India)'.[69] Another was George Macready, an Army surgeon, 31st Regiment, who earned the thanks of passengers. He was presented with a gold snuff box as a token by grateful passengers after a 'horrid crossing' from New York in March 1839. Another named surgeon was John Courtenay, aged thirty-four in 1846.[70]

But again, like the stewardesses, these do not show on the crew lists until 1846, and these categories are not alone. There were a number of supernumeraries on board at various times whose presence can only be detected in other sources as they do not appear in either the crew agreements or those passenger lists that survive. I have suggested that Charles Maitland Tate on the first passage may have been working for Brunel. Brunel put on board another of his assistants, Berkeley Claxton, who was Claxton's son. Brunel, as always, wanted detailed and specific observations on the working of the ship. He sent Berkeley on no less than six voyages to obtain 'reliable information on many points'. His job was to note the amount of rolling and pitching, the exact performance of her engines and the consumption of fuel. These reports all furnished Brunel with essential detailed information and calculations as he considered the next ship for the company and the big decision over paddle wheels or screw propulsion.[71] But he does not feature on any lists.

Another group who are mentioned in newspapers and occasionally in traveller diaries, but nowhere else, are the on-board entertainers. For the return voyage of the *Great Western* the Dodworth band had been engaged. The New York-based Dodworth family were first rate performers, versatile on all band instruments and originally from England. In 1842 they became founding members of the New York Philharmonic Society.[72] Bands continued to be taken on some passages – Mrs Dixon recalls the band striking up as she left the ship in 1840. Such entertainers might get a free passage or be paid a nominal fee and food on board in the hope of attracting other paid bookings on shore.

For the crew who signed on, a regular liner service (and the possibility of the addition of a second ship in the company) meant reasonably secure employment. The rise in rival steam services also provided additional opportunities. Second engineer William Roberts took over after the death of Pearne on the first voyage and remained with the ship for some years. He was thirty-three in 1838 and came from Glasgow, the home of some excellent marine engineers. Joseph Williams took the second engineer role vacated by Roberts. He was aged twenty-four and from Neath in Wales and he had his opportunity as chief engineer in 1846.[73] Thomas Guillam from Bristol remained as officer for several years, from 1838 to 1846, when he became second officer to Barnard Mathews.[74] Hosken had been moved on to the *Great Britain*, so Mathews had his big chance as master of the *Great Western*. He had many of the same crew who had crossed the Atlantic with him.

Crew members might also be discharged if found unsuitable, or they might make their own decision and leave. New York was an attractive proposition for those hoping for a new life or trying to avoid something in their past, so there were desertions. In May 1841 six young seamen deserted in New York, three from Bristol, one from Exeter and one each from Cardigan and Cardiff. The attractions of the port presented difficulties for some; three coal trimmers, Joe Mahoney, aged twenty-eight, and Andrew Taylor, aged twenty-one, both from Cork, together with A. Macintosh, age thirty-seven, from Aberdeen, were all late back and did not get on board in November 1839. The following year William Evans of

Bristol, aged nineteen, ran away in New York, and in 1842 it was the turn of the cook's mate, Bowden.[75]

Such desertions were not unusual, and their reasons were various. On a ship in the middle of an ocean the crew are never off duty. They can be called into service at any moment in the ship's needs. The ship is their place of work, their home and a place of occasional leisure. For seamen slack time typically came with the weather – calm seas or doldrums meant little activity, time for some fishing perhaps – but there was no slack time on a steamship. The pace was relentless for the whole crew as the engineers, firemen and trimmers tended the fires.

It was all about teamwork, and two passengers with very different attitudes, at different times and in different circumstances, were witness to the working of the master and crew on the *Great Western* in moments of great danger. Among the many Atlantic weather challenges faced by the passengers and crew were fog and ice. James Hosken recalled two particular occasions. In April 1840 they were near the banks of Newfoundland when they came across light field ice; they went through 30 or 40 miles of it until they cleared it about midnight. The following year, at the same time, they came across a similar field one evening. Hoping to do the same as the previous year, they continued but were forced to turn back and had some difficulty in getting clear. They coasted the ice and by sunrise saw a large field of ice and icebergs as far as the eye could see, with four or five ships in it.

> It was a splendid sight! I took a sketch and afterwards had it painted. The greater part of the night the thermometer of the water stood at 25 to 28 and the air from 28 to 30. I remained on the paddleboard all night and did not put on a great coat until four a.m. My servant repeatedly asked me to do so, but I did not feel the cold, anxiety kept me warm.[76]

From Hosken's brief description of the event it is only the final few words that convey the danger of the moment. This is, however, clearly shown in another account of the same incident when the danger was obvious to all passengers. On board on that occasion was Lydia Sigourney, a writer and poet. She had boarded the *Great*

Western with some trepidation at Bristol and here is her descriptive passage from her travel publication:

At 9, from the sentinels stationed at different points of observation, a cry was made of 'ice ahead! ice starboard! ice leeward!' and we found ourselves suddenly embedded in field ice. To turn was impossible; so a path was laboriously cut up with the paddles, through which a steamer was propelled, stern foremost, not without peril, changing her course due south, in the teeth of a driving blast.

When we were once more in an open sea, the captain, not concealing from the Passengers their danger, advised them to retire. This we did a little before midnight, if not to sleep, at least to seek that rest which might aid in preparing us for future trials. At three we were aroused by harsh grating, and occasional concussions, which caused the strong timbers of the ship to tremble. This was from a floating mass of ice, by which, after having skirted an expanse of field ice 50 miles in extent, we were surrounded. It varied from two to five feet in thickness, rising from 8 inches to a foot and a half above the water, and interspersed with icebergs, some of them comparatively small, and others of portentous size and an altitude. By the Divine blessing upon nautical skill and presence of mind, we were a second time extricated from these besieging and paralysing foes; but our paths still lay through clusters and hosts of icebergs which covered the whole sea around us. The captain, who had not left his post of responsibility during the night, reported between 3 and 400 distinct ones, visible to the naked eye. There they were, of all forms and sizes, careering in every direction. The general aspect was vitreous, or of a silvery whiteness, except when a sunbeam pierced the mist; then they loomed up, and radiated with every hue of the rainbow, striking out turrets, and columns, and arches, like solid pearl and diamond, till we were transfixed with wonder at the terribly beautiful architecture of the northern deep.

The engine of the *Great Western* accommodated itself every moment, like a living and intelligent thing, to the command of the captain. 'Half a stroke!' and its tumultuous action was controlled; 'a quarter of a stroke!' and its breath seemed suspended; 'stand still!' and our huge hulk lay motionless upon the waters, till two or three of the icy squadron drifted by us; 'let her go!' and with the velocity of lightning we darted by another detachment of our deadly foes. It was then that we were made sensible of the advantages of steam, to whose agency, many of us had committed ourselves with extreme reluctance. Yet a vessel more under the dominion of the winds, and beleaguered as we were amid walls of ice, in a rough sea, must inevitably have been destroyed.[77]

It was a dramatic way in which to learn the advantages of steam. Lydia Sigourney also made a sketch of the unforgettable sight, reproduced in this book, showing the ice field and icebergs, the route, the temperature and the navigational position. She wrote two poems; one was part of her book on her travels, *Pleasant Travels in Pleasant Lands*, and the other was commissioned for *Godey's Lady's Book*. This second poem is in the tradition of poetry in that period and blends drama, romanticism and sentimentality.[78]

Regardless of passenger views or crew complaints, above all they were fellow travellers in a wooden ship in the middle of potentially dangerous seas and it was at times of danger that the crew, whatever their personal views, needed to work as one and follow the captain's lead. A later voyage in 1844, under the command of Captain Mathews, was to encounter one of the worst storms the ship had experienced halfway into its passage. The passengers, many of whom described what happened in an article in the *New York Tribune*, were terrified and convinced the ship could not survive. Final prayers were said and thoughts turned to families on shore. The gales continued, the port paddle box was demolished and a piece of timber knocked Mathews overboard; he was fortunately saved by netting. The storm raged throughout the night, and the next day a severe squall forced the ship onto her side, but the wheels continued to turn and the ship survived. A passenger, John Jay Smith, who had not been happy at all with the ship – it was overcrowded and dirty in his view – left his cabin in the night to see what was happening. His admiration of the teamwork of the crew was sincere, but he was less than impressed with the limited options for saving life in the event of abandoning the ship:

Every officer of the vessel was on duty the whole night; descending to the engine room, I was practically astonished to see the accuracy with which the machinery operated under such unfavourable circumstances. But one moment the starboard wheel was nearly submerged; at the next the larboard, and yet the engine worked with the regularity of a clock. There was no confusion among the crew; every man stood at his post without uttering unnecessary words; one had a hammer in his hand to adjust any bolt that might get out of position; and these hardy, picked men, were an example of disciplined attention which might be imitated to advantage.

This scene in the depths of the enormous ship amid the powerful, the gigantic machinery, was one which I never can forget; had a valve or a crank given out the vessel would have been at the mercy of winds and waves; most probably none of us would have reached land; the boats provided in case of ship wreck, were of such construction as made it out of the question that they could survive in such a sea; and, moreover, they were not of sufficient capacity to hold more than half the number of passengers and crew, that being about 240 in all.[79]

Mathews took his ship, crew and profoundly grateful passengers into New York on 30 September. The passengers arranged a collection of £200 for distribution between the whole crew. Mathews thanked them and, after saying it was the worst storm of his long experience, expressed his view that had it not been for the 'good qualities of my noble ship, under the direction of God, she could not have weathered it'. The passengers additionally collected nearly $600 to establish a fund to be called the Great Western Fund for the relief of families of men who had been lost at sea.[80]

The masters and crew of the *Great Western* had much to learn, often the hard way, about the management of a first-class passenger steamship across the Atlantic. In this she was also a pioneer. The ship carried more passengers than the existing sailing packet lines, and passenger expectations were high, driven by glowing advertisements and press reports. But it was not just the staff on board who dealt with demanding passengers – there were also staff handling bookings on shore, and this was not an easy task.

5

Looking after the Passengers

The passengers were the key element in the success of the enterprise. They were also the most unpredictable. The company needed office staff on shore to manage the administration and one vital role was handling bookings. Until 1842 these were all coordinated via the Bristol office. The other permanent office was in London at the Great Western Railway offices, where Mr Thomas Ward was based. His letter book from 1841 to 1843 has survived and gives a good view of the problems in dealing with the superior class of passengers that was the target market for the *Great Western*.[1]

With agents in many different places and the company's headquarters in Bristol, there was always a risk of confusion and double booking. The system allocated specific numbered berths to each office and there was constant correspondence between them to ensure no overlap. The London office might write to request additional berths if all their location was taken, or the reverse might occur. The office also handled requests for freight and the despatch of letters and newspapers via the ship.

Ward was responsible for ensuring the very latest London newspapers reached the ship in time; they had to go from London to Bristol and arrive before the ship sailed. This might mean him having a very early start, as in April 1840 when there was also an important package to go with them. Claxton had ordered the rather expensive copy of Thomas Tredgold's book on steam navigation. Recently republished, the new edition cost £2 5s and included mention of the *Great Western*. Ward collected and packed the papers by half past five in the morning and then caught an early train from Paddington, arriving in Reading, which was as far as it went in 1840, at half past seven. He then personally gave the parcel to the post boy, 'having previously written the instructions in accordance with Mr Claxton's letter to me'. On another later occasion Mr Ward had to apologise when the newspapers did not arrive in time before the ship sailed. 'It was occasioned by the late publication of *The Times*. I will take care however in future that they go by the proper train or they shall not be paid for.'[2]

Requests for freight might range from samples, boxes of books or an enquiry from the Morton company about the cost of shipping rocking chairs. High-value items such as gold or specie were handled and such valuables would be the personal responsibility of the master. Melhurst and Gray had £700 in specie to go out in May 1840, Barings regularly shipped gold, while, coming eastward, Brown and Shipley were anxious to check that their box of bullion destined for the Bank of England had arrived safely.[3]

Passengers often sought a better deal; a frequent request was to try to get a whole cabin for the price of one berth, or one family might want to pay three and a half fares for two cabins to themselves. One gentleman wanted a partition erected in his cabin, while one Mr Frederick Tarrant was determined to have the whole of cabin nineteen to himself but was only prepared to pay one passenger fare. Ward wrote in exasperation after several dealings with Mr Tarrant that he had let the cabin to him but could not get him to pay more than one fare 'and the condition on which I received his Passage Money is that he shall not be doubled upon unless the ship is quite full of passengers'.[4] Tarrant knew how to play the system to ensure his own comfort.

Other passengers had somewhat unrealistic requests. Mr Austin, who had booked berth 116, was an invalid and 'very much dislikes noises'. He wished to be removed 'if possible to a better position than that of the fore saloon'. Any passage on a steamship was unlikely to be a quiet one. The well-travelled passenger requested cabins midships, which was a good position in some respects but also put them closer to the engines and paddle wheels. The cabin with berths 1 and 2 was sought after for ladies as it was next door to the ladies' boudoir, with its private facilities. Servants were accommodated in less salubrious berths, and one French minister insisted that his three servants were all berthed together. Ward was well organised and kept an up-to-date list of who had which cabin under his control, but was not helped by those who caused unintentional problems by reselling their ticket. He discovered by accident that Mr Bates' wife was unwell and that he might have resold his ticket to a Colonel Lascelles but omitted to mention this change to the office. Ward only resolved the name confusion by making enquiries at the North and South American Coffee House.[5]

Managing difficult and demanding passengers was all part of the job, but just occasionally there is a hint of desperation in Ward's correspondence. Ward had written to Bristol as a Mrs Arno had wanted a cabin all to herself and it had to be the best possible. He chased them up with a second letter to know if Bristol had allocated a cabin, but could they advise him '*by return* as she will call on Thursday morning'. Clearly a woman not to be easily put off. Then there was passenger luggage to be dealt with. There were those passengers who sent their luggage ahead and joined the ship at the last possible moment and those who had more than just a couple of trunks. There were, for instance, a lady and gentleman who were thinking of going out and wanted to know whether they could take a van load of furniture 'of the usual description and a pony and chaise and also a spaniel'.[6]

Some passengers caused difficulties of another kind. Ward wrote to Mr Bennett, the secretary in Bristol, requesting his help for Mr Carl Ghega and two friends and two servants 'who are I believe entirely unacquainted with the English language. They will put up at the Bush and will feel greatly obliged by any attention you can offer them during their short stay in Bristol.'[7] Some employers were making bookings for staff: 'Messrs Barings are very anxious to secure for two gentlemen the same room in the cuddy that was occupied by Mr Andrew Foster in September and suggests it was 64/65.' Another employer was sending out an overseer of a mine but only wanted to pay half fare for him, and 'he is willing the man should rough it in respect of provisions etc., but will prefer his having a Berth in the fore saloon'.[8]

Such were the trials of dealing with the public, and Thomas Ward performed his duty well, but he was not impressed on suddenly receiving a letter from Gibbs, Bright and Company of Liverpool which requested him to advise them in future of all changes of all berths with other agencies. He wrote a short, stiff letter to Bennett at Bristol. 'I conclude this is not contrary to your wishes but I think it best to take my instructions on all such points from the *head* office. Perhaps you will favour me with a line.' The full effect of the move to Liverpool had not been communicated to Mr Ward and he was not happy.[9]

Finally, after dealing with all the enquires and issuing tickets, Ward could send off the list of passengers for the ship. So what was the experience for passengers joining the *Great Western*? If setting out from London, their journey meant a train ride to Bristol, or part train and part coach if they travelled before the line fully opened in 1841. In Bristol they transferred to small steamer which might take three or four hours depending on the tidal conditions in the Avon before stepping on board. In New York and Liverpool, it was a question of getting to the right wharf or dock and getting straight on board.

When a passenger goes on board, the first action after waving goodbye is to settle into the cabin which will be their home for the duration of the passage. Elizabeth Dixon and her husband, James, were on their honeymoon trip on board the *Great Western* from New York to Europe in October 1840. They remained on deck waving until they could no longer see their relatives and then went into their cabin, which had berths 3 and 4.

> We made our abiding place as pleasant as possible. The sounding of a gong at four made us aware that we must prepare for dinner and as that took but a small portion of my time, we proceeded to arrange our luggage to the best advantage. My hat took the place assigned it behind the door. Near the looking glass hung the life preservers which James got one of the Waiters to blow up – for it is a pretty exhausting affair to blow one's self up.[10]

The life preservers were saturated with turpentine, and although the Dixons understood the good reasons for keeping them close at hand, the smell was all pervading and so they were put into close confinement and assigned to a bureau.[11] The cabins were small, just 7 feet by 8 feet, with the berths one above the other and 'so arranged that in the daytime they may be turned up against the side of the vessel, and conceal all the bedding, thereby forming a small sitting room'.[12] The cabins were directly off the main saloon, which was the main public room and used for dining and leisure. A report in 1846 described the saloon as being 60 feet long, with a double rank of tables the whole length and four stern windows. In addition, there was a ladies' saloon, a small drawing room 'very tastefully fitted up by the upholsterer' with a water closet, which provided them with some additional privacy and was often close to staterooms reserved for women. Male smokers were typically allocated a deckhouse shelter for smoking, which was not allowed below decks.[13]

After settling in their cabin, they then went into the saloon to find their places for dinner and to assess their fellow voyagers. There were both upper and lower cabins on two decks linked by companionways, and the dining saloon on the main deck remained the unrivalled social centre.[14] This central saloon perforce mingled all passengers, and while British and American society in the nineteenth century was highly stratified by class, wealth, ethnicity, race, nationality and religion, these distinctions did not survive on the ship. The normal rules that defined encounters with other members of the populace were broken down by the simple ability to pay the fare on the *Great Western*. 'Steam is the great democratic power of our age,' wrote an optimistic American, Samuel Laing, after steaming to Europe in 1848, 'annihilating the conventional distinctions, differences, and social distance between man and a man.'[15] Not everyone saw it in quite the same progressive light. John Jay Smith, the librarian from Philadelphia, described the mixed nature of his fellow passengers on board the ship in 1845:

We had ministers of the gospel, and ministers from John Tyler whose missions were over, – preachers and players – painters and physicians, – artists and amateurs – mechanics and musicians – merchants and merry-andrews, – singers and sewers – patentees and plaster venders, – booksellers and basket makers, – picture dealers and portrait painters, – barbers and bakers, – Irish, Italians, Germans, Swiss, French, English and Scotch. – young newly married people and newly married old people, – men older than their wives and women older than their husbands, and rather remarkably so, – women who would neither walk nor talk, and women who did too much of both, – ladies and gentlemen, and people who were neither, – and not to be tedious, we had a smart sprinkling of British consuls, one of whom was by far the most consequential and least considered person on board, if we except a very noisy parrot, whose quarters were shifted each morning as successive complaints were made of her disturbance ... Then to crown our catalogue, we had a real member of parliament coming out to take a peep at Brother Jonathan and see its small country in six weeks![16]

Added to this mix was the nature of a journey on a steamer in the mid-Atlantic where everyone was confined and literally tossed together in fair winds or foul for two weeks, often in trying circumstances.[17] Observers such as Judge Haliburton, who travelled across in April 1839, viewed this mix of life on the steamship with equanimity, seeing them as being a good cross section of life in the real world. 'This little community is agitated by the same passions, impelled by the same feelings, and actuated by the same prejudices.'[18] For him, they were excellent material for his humorous books.

Elizabeth Dixon was another observer of people. After exiting their cabin the Dixons looked for their prearranged seats at the table for dinner, but they found that they had been taken by a man she described as a 'dogged Englishman'. Her husband, James, insisted upon their rightful places and the steward, Bill Crawford, persuaded the intruder to move places. The Englishman, Captain Stirling, was of the 73rd Regiment and he had been stationed in Canada and had persuaded his wife to remain at home in England. Mrs Stirling had other ideas, and, 'being of a jealous turn', decided to join him. But then, after just two months in Canada, she made her husband sell his commission and return to England. Mrs Dixon's description of Mrs Stirling was that she was 'extremely plebeian in her appearance and very rude and ill bred'. She wore some elegant rings and always sat with her hands to her face to show them off to advantage. Her rudeness manifested itself in 'torrents of invectives against America'. In Mrs Dixon's view, such rudeness was typical of the middle classes in England, but the English ladies 'are ladies indeed, while the lower classes never expect anything better but the intermediate ones are always pettish and dissatisfied'.[19] Mrs Stirling certainly seems to have done her best to confirm Mrs Dixon's opinion of the English middle-class female.

Among the distinguished passengers travelling with the Dixons on the *Great Western* was Sir Joseph Copley, who was a 'real gentleman' in Elizabeth's eyes. He was accompanied by his nephew and his servant, but was much approved of, and described as unostentatious when he dispensed with his servant's services at table. 'Of course, he made no acquaintance with anyone but was affable to all.' Elizabeth noted he had married Lord Yarborough's daughter and was 'really a nobleman'.[20]

But this mingling did not find favour with all passengers, as in the case of the black American previously noted. The fictional Captain Haltfront is forced to share with a stranger, a man of most unpleasant personal habits who borrows his hairbrushes.[21] John Jay Smith was not impressed by the superior view of one English diplomat who disliked the forced intimacy of the ship and the free and easy manners of the Americans. He was overheard saying, 'I wish these Americans would not talk to me!' and Smith wondered if this was a good or bad policy for a man going to reside in a new country.[22] George Moore was one of the few English diarists on board the ship, and on taking stock of his fellow passengers in 1846 he noted there were 'some of all sorts here' among the 100.[23]

Judge Haliburton's book *The Letter Bag of the Great Western* includes a fictional letter from an experienced passenger that is full of useful advice for the passenger new to the ship. His first piece of advice is to ensure the steward was well tipped at the beginning; then 'you'll get the best dish and it will always be before you and the best attendance from the waiters'. Also, one should see what wine the captain drinks and order the same. Haliburton also describes the narrowness between the tables and the sidewalls as being 'but an ell wide', which is too narrow for two to pass and repass without treading on feet. His letter from a lawyer's clerk refers to the thinness of the partitions between the cabins, where everything can be heard, so private conversations were almost impossible except in a quiet corner on deck if the weather was fine.[24]

Women on average comprised fewer than one in five adult passengers, and a surprising number of women travelled without spouses or male relatives.[25] Some were going to join family members, some were intrepid travellers and occasionally there were businesswomen – Mrs Dixon got talking to a Mrs Durand who was going to England as 'a chief buyer of corn'.[26] Women might, however, travel in a prearranged group for company and support. Lydia Sigourney returned from a trip to Europe on the *Great Western* and she found what she described as pleasant society on board and had her 'more immediate circle composed of Mr Bates, the celebrated banker from London, with his lady, both natives of New England, Miss Jaudon of Philadelphia; Rev Dr Wayland, President of Brown University; Hon Isaac Davis of Worcester; and Sir Joseph de Courcy Laffan, a baronet of Irish extraction'.[27] A lady, notably those travelling alone, had to be aware of the scrutiny of other passengers and *Miss Leslie's Behaviour Book: A Guide and Manual for Ladies*, which was published in 1859 as transatlantic steamships became more plentiful, had this advice:

There are few places where the looks and manners of the company are more minutely scanned than on ship-board; and few where the agreeability of a lady will be more appreciated. There is little or no variety of objects to attract attention. The passengers are brought so closely into contact with each other, and confined to so small a neighbourhood, or rather so many neighbours are crowded into so small a space, that all their sayings and doings are noticed with unusual attention, by those who are well enough to regard anything but themselves.[28]

On the *Great Western* in 1840 the rather vain and conceited Mr Osborne of New York was observed flirting with a Miss Chapman, even though he was known to have a wife and child in England. Then there was the lady passenger who became the laughing stock of the ship by pursuing a handsome Swede. Her behaviour was so odd it was generally concluded that she had a 'bee in her bonnet'. Also on board was Mr Jeffrey, a merchant of

London, and his wife. 'Mrs Jeffrey had evidently been very pretty' and was the daughter of a baronet, 'possibly a poor one', and it was decided that she had married Mr Jeffrey for money as he seemed twenty or thirty years older than she was. 'She was delighted with any attention from a beau and if she had one, seemed determined to retain him.' Major Brooks 'was very polite to her' and one evening they left the table together, which caused eyebrows to be raised.[29]

Women also had a few practical matters to consider, and one of them was their clothing. The ship had been designed by men who had not taken into consideration the clothes of the day. Cabins were small and passages narrow, while the prevailing ladies' fashion was for ever wider and more voluminous skirts supported by an extensive number of petticoats. In 1829 a Liverpool newspaper complained about the trend, but the accession of the young, clothes-loving Queen Victoria continued the fashion. An estimate is that the average dress in 1855 required some 30 yards of material while the petticoats brought the total to 100 yards.[30] Queen Victoria was very fond of voluminous skirts as they accentuated a narrow waist. For those who were also larger than average, getting dressed was a trial. The fictional Mrs Figg, who is clearly a stout party, complained about the difficulty of getting in and out of the berths, as she had to have the upper one in sharing with Mrs Brown. 'I'm obligated to dress in bed, afore I leave it and nobody that hasn't tried to put on their clothes lying down can tell what a task it is.' Lacing her stays behind her back and pulling on her stockings were all great trials, and to do so 'while you are rolling about from side to side is no laughing matter. Yesterday I fastened the pillow to my bustler by mistake.'[31]

In the early steamships the largest group on board were young men, usually single, travelling unaccompanied by family, and this is true of the *Great Western*. These were young merchants in their twenties, attached to some business concern or other, and it was easier for their firm to send them to Europe or to America to do business in person and to learn their way. There were also those who were looking for new opportunities, young men of good background with fortunes to make. Admiral Coffin, who lived in Bath, wrote to his friend Philip Hone in New York asking for his help on behalf of a young man, Mr Cooper, who was the son of his friend. Cooper was determined to travel to America. Coffin reassured Hone that the young man had business knowledge, having been 'brought up in the wine and spirits trade', and literally underlined the information that he was 'not in indigent circumstances'.[32]

It was not long before her trip that Mrs Dixon had been a highly eligible single girl, and on board were several young men of her acquaintance. Frederick Delano she described as always pleasant, always kind and amiable, but 'how different his manners now I was married and he unrestrained, from what he used to be when he tried to look his best before Miss E Cogswell'. He and Richard Ely and Mr Attesbury were three young merchants and very similar. Ely was rather pompous, having 'seen everybody and everything in this world I believe'. In her view he was amiable and polite, though very shallow minded. Mr Attesbury came from two high-society Jersey families, Stockton and Bondinol, and was very handsome, being the 'perfect picture of a Greek'.[33]

Not all the men travelling solo were young businessmen. George Moore was a thirty-eight-year-old English lace merchant who travelled on the *Great Western* across the Atlantic. He had with him a set of introductions to bankers and businessmen in North America and was looking for other opportunities and commodities to expand his business.[34] On Saturday 17 August 1844 he left Liverpool for New York on board the ship with a complement of 138 passengers and a crew of 40, and as they left they headed into a strong gale. After two hours very few passengers were left on deck. At four o'clock the pilot was discharged, and by half past twelve they had passed Holyhead. George says he went to bed rather squeamish at seven.[35]

One historian of steamship travel has pointed out that 'comparatively few had both the motive and the means to make the crossings'.[36] Thomas Ward, the manager of the *Great Western*'s booking office in London, had to deal with those who sought a cheap method of crossing. He wrote in kindly terms to Mr Thomas Huntly of Dover. Ward explained that the passage in the *Great Western* was 45 guineas plus 1 guinea stewards' fee and that 'she carries no steerage or intermediate passengers'. But rather than simply rebuff Mr Huntly, Ward went out of his way to make inquiries and gave him the dates of packet ships leaving from London and from Portsmouth the next month. Ward informed him that steerage was £5 5s and referred him to the North and South American Coffee House in London or to George Wildes & Company, 19 Coleman Street, London, where he could get more information.[37]

The 'superior class' of passengers on the *Great Western*, mixed as they were, became a temporary community and bonded over a shared experience of storm and tempest, food and seasickness. The saloon, the central area, was a place of rest, recreation, dining and entertainment. If weather permitted, walks on deck broke the monotony. Books and travel advice were freely traded on board and useful contacts were made, both social and business. Mrs Dixon noted that 'Mr Ely presented Mr Bindon the consul in Florence, a very gentlemanly Italian, who offered his services to us when we went there saying that he should be "wholly ours"; which of course we took literally.'[38]

The *Great Western*'s progress through the water was quite different to that of the sailing packet. Haliburton described it in lyrical terms:

> How this glorious steamer wallops and gallops, and flounders along! She goes it like mad. Its motion is unlike that of any living thing I know; puffing like porpoise, breasting the waves like a sea-horse, and at times skimming the surface like a bird. It possesses the joint powers of the tenants of the air, land and water and is superior to them all![39]

But not all enjoyed the motion, and some tried to set a shipboard routine. Lydia Sigourney had suffered badly on her outward passage in a sailing ship; now, on her return on the *Great Western*, she was determined not to succumb. Willpower was essential and a 'determination not to yield to the pitiless monster'. Her prescribed system involved 'cheerful society, light reading, walking much in the open air upon deck, when the weather permits, and overcoming the repulsion at the sight of food by brave and regular appearance at the table'. Any setback was met with a determination to 'return to the charge with an invincible courage'. It worked, or the motion of the paddle steamer assisted, as she was proud to gain a reputation for being a 'good sailor'.[40]

George Moore also set himself some rules. Rise at seven thirty, then walk on deck until breakfast. After breakfast, read at least six chapters of the Bible and walk on deck again for an hour until lunch time. In the afternoon he would write, then back on deck again, then read any books he had. Between dinner and tea he would walk and talk, and after tea he would play whist until ten. He was very fortunate, as the weather on his passage remained calm and the sea smooth. Whether self-imposed or not, life on board became routine and was mainly driven by mealtimes. George describes the schedule for each day. The gong sounded at half past seven to rise, for breakfast at nine, and at half past three the passengers dressed for dinner, dining at four o'clock. At half past seven in the evening there was tea and a few took supper at ten o'clock. All candles were put out at eleven sharp and this was strictly enforced to avoid any fire risk.[41] The days revolved around mealtimes for those who were not troubled by illness. The passengers rushed in a herd-like stream when lunch or dinner was called, and the narrow passageways made passing difficult.[42]

When the ship was launched there was an innovation installed for calling the steward:

The arrangement of the bells is deserving of notice, in the steward's room, standing on a shelf, are two small mahogany boxes, about one foot long, and eight inches square, each containing a bell, communicating by means of wires, to every berth, cabin, and other department in the vessel. When the attendance of the steward is required, the passenger pulls the bell rope in his berth, which rings the bell in the small box, and at the same time by means of a small lever, through a slit in the lid, a small tin label, about two inches by one inch, with the number of the room on it requiring the services of the steward, and there remains until the steward has ascertained the number of the room and pushed it down again. Thus, instead, of having an interminable number of bells, one for every department, there are only two. This arrangement which is alike ingenious as it is useful, is deserving of the notice of architects. We understand it is the Invention of a person residing at Greenock.[43]

This is the only time the system was mentioned, and no diary or letter refers to such a bell system. For those who suffered from sickness, the cabin was their place of confinement. Here they were dependent on their spouses or travelling companions and the waiting staff. Elizabeth Dixon had her husband, and on the first voyage in 1838 Foster noted those who succumbed calling out for the steward. It rather seems that the steward may have dispensed with a potentially annoying bell system.

Passengers largely made their own entertainment, reading, conversing and playing games such as whist, loo, chess, drafts and backgammon. Most were light hearted, but George Moore saw some heavy card playing on board and 'imprudent losses' which he much regretted to see.[44] On Mrs Dixon's first passage there was a band on board and a celebrated black singer, John Smith: 'I never saw so complete a specimen of a greenhorn in my life.' But, as John told her, he was convinced he would gain his fortune in England; this suggests an arrangement whereby the musicians got a free or reduced passage in return for entertaining passengers.[45] There was also a young Swedish passenger who played the guitar, and evenings of songs were common and held on deck if the weather was fair. All passengers were encouraged to join in, even the aristocracy. Sir Joseph Copley, Elizabeth noted with approval, took part in everything and when called on for a song gave them '"Old Joe" or something of the kind for he was no singer only tried to oblige'. George Moore also commented on songs and he sang English, Irish and German songs. There were songs to sweethearts, and the ever popular 'Yankee Doodle' was known by everyone.[46]

Topics of conversation could be difficult if they veered into the political arena, and this might include songs. 'Tippecanoe and Tyler' was a campaign song in 1840 promoting the current Whig presidential candidates John Tyler and General William Henry Harrison, hero of the Battle of Tippecanoe in the War of 1812 between the United States and Britain. Their opponent in the presidential race was Martin Van Buren, the sitting US President;

a Democrat, he had been in office since 1837. The song had a catchy tune and it was sung on Elizabeth Dixon's passage to England.

> What has caused this great commotion, motion, motion,
> Our country through?
> It is the ball a rolling on, on.
> *Chorus*
> For Tippecanoe and Tyler too – Tippecanoe and Tyler too.
> And with them we'll beat that little Van, Van, Van.
> Van is a used up man, And with them we'll beat little Van.[47]

The Whig campaign was successful, and Harrison was elected on 4 April 1814; however, he died suddenly four weeks later and Vice-President John Tyler succeeded.

Food was a highlight of the voyage for some, and even John Jay Smith, who felt the ship was overcrowded, could not but admire the range of cuisine on board ship:

> ... yet how it would have astonished the navigators of only 30 years ago, to say nothing of hundreds of years, to see 160 persons in a palace in the middle of the Atlantic, pushing their way through every storm and head wind, and dining off fresh provisions and even grouse, with fresh bread, puddings and pies, and ripe plums daily.[48]

Even another rather strong critic of the ship on that passage was in favour of most of the food, but with limitations. 'Our table is fair, barring three important articles, butter, tea and potatoes which are *abominable*.'[49] George Moore listed the long and impressive menu while Mrs Dixon, who suffered badly from seasickness, seems to have survived on champagne punch and mock turtle soup. This popular soup was standard fare in most hotels and on ships. Palatable drinking water was a challenge as all fresh water had to be carried and took up space. The containers often gave it a strange taste. The steward's room had a supply of fresh water, 'and one of Stirling's filters'.[50] Soda water was also carried for those who did not drink alcohol.

Food was a matter of personal taste, and the American cook was serving several nationalities, although predominately North American and British. Most passengers praised the food, but there was no satisfying some. Mrs Murray, mother to fifteen children and described as a 'pale quiet body', was an individual for whom nothing was right. One day, on complaining that none of the food was well cooked and nothing tasted good, a fellow passenger Mr Riley looked up in exasperation and said, 'Madam, I think your appetite is not very good.'[51]

On board the *Great Western*, the passengers exchanged information, views and advice and the various society strands were mixed. Once on shore, however, the British visitor to New York and the American visitor to Bristol, London or Liverpool instantly noticed the differences in culture, business habits, modes of conveyance and physical surroundings.

Cultural comparisons were inevitable. The visitor to England was particularly struck by the differences in style and the class distinctions. John Jay Smith painted a word picture of the people in a London Street:

The mind is first impressed with the fact that almost every visible thing is different in its form or material from what you have been accustomed to. The houses, carriages, shops, dresses, are all singular and novel. There is a turn-out with livery; the coachman in lace-hat, cuffs, and small-clothes, with a flaming waistcoat; two other liveried, stalwart men, in silk stockings, are behind, bearing gold-headed canes; on the panel is a coronet; the inmate is a lady of some age, or a young mother with children beside her, and a nurse. Yonder another coach has stopped at a shop; the servant in a drab coat and pantaloons, who has let his mistress out, is lounging at the door, ready for instant service when required; the grave coachman, looking sleek as his well-groomed horses, seems pondering on the national debt, though really he is thinking of less momentous affairs; did he make his appearance in your streets, with the prestige of a title, he is sufficiently well dressed to pass for a lord with those who have never seen his class here.[52]

James Gordon Bennett, whose aim for his newspaper was for it to 'exhilarate the breakfast table', knew that society was an excellent topic.[53]

> What a contrast – what a wide gulf exists between the fashionable Society in New York and London! Among other matters I intend to collect all the lineaments and peculiarities of fashionable Society both in London and Paris and describe them as accurately as possible. Such descriptions, properly prepared, may be of some utility to the gay people of New York who are sadly deficient in some points, although tolerable in others. There is a calmness and repose here in good Society, which is only characteristic of those whose rank and position, either in art or arms, are known and admitted. On the other hand there is a great deal of frivolity, form, insincerity, and want of imagination and originality. One of the great elements of English High Society, is expensive and splendid establishments, such as houses, furniture, horses, carriages. The dress and personal decorations are not so gaudy or expensive as ours are in New York. unless on state occasions, the address of gentleman is very simple – so of the ladies with the exception of splendid jewellery.[54]

While Lydia Sigourney knew that her female readers were desperately keen to hear much more about the youthful Queen Victoria. Lydia managed to get a place in the Palace of Westminster to witness the youthful queen, as yet unmarried, opening Parliament.

> The complexion of Victoria is exceeding fair, but her countenance has no decided intellectual expression. It seems remarkable that so young a creature should evince such entire ease and self-possession, nor even betray the slightest consciousness that every eye in that vast assembly was fixed solely on her. This, however, is a part of the Queenly training, in which she has become perfect.[55]

Of the four cities, London was by far the biggest with a population of 1.5 million. New Yorkers, used to streets laid out on a grid pattern, found it confusing: 'The moment the first corner is turned, you are lost. The streets twist about in an extraordinary manner, taking a different name before you know it.' The traffic was heavy and the streets frequently congested, requiring a policeman to untangle the knot and set things moving again. 'The enormous wagons with huge horses greatly impede progress; add to these great busses, carts, brewer's drays, funerals, carriages and outriders.'[56] If it seemed grand on the surface, it was also the city of Charles Dickens. Liverpool was smaller, with a population of 223,000, but what first struck the shipboard visitor were the huge docks lining the sides of the Mersey River. Bristol was very small by comparison, with a population of 64,000 in just over 9,000 inhabited houses.[57] It was small enough to walk across including its suburbs, as it measured no more than 2.5 miles from north to south or 3 miles from east to west.[58]

New York's population in 1840 was 312,710 and was rising with incredible speed. By 1850 it was 515,547 and by 1860 it had risen to 813,669.[59] Much of this was fuelled by immigrants travelling across in steerage in conditions wholly different from the contemporary luxury of the *Great Western*. In 1831, Mrs Trollope visited New York, which she described: 'Situated on an island, which I think it will one day cover, it rises, like Venice, from the sea, and like that fairest of cities in the days of her glory, receives into its lap tribute of the riches of the earth.'[60] Broadway was the great street where you had to be seen and see people such as 'Mr Riley, one of the Broadway dandies who used to promenade up and down every day last winter with an over coat and small cape and crimson vest'.[61] A major fire had engulfed the lower part of the island in 1835 and 13 acres were burnt, but reconstruction was rapid. One American returning home on the *Great Western* noticed near Broadway 'the burnt district still smoking in one part', but the 'remainder already well built up! Evidences, if any were wanting, of a strong contrast between our countrymen and many people we have been to see.'[62] The *Great Western* connected these cities and brought them yet closer together. Each passenger had their own reasons for getting on board, and they were mingled together in one shared experience of a speedy two-week passage across the Atlantic in one of the finest and fastest ships of the day.

6

A Variety of Passengers

The *Great Western* carried businessmen and women, rich travellers and tourists, politicians, military men and celebrities. It was the Concorde of its age, a new, fast and luxurious way to cross the Atlantic. Passenger demand remained higher for the westward crossing of the *Great Western* since the fast sailing packets could still compete on time with a good following wind. Additionally, the packets travelled more frequently and to more locations. For the early years there was little or no competition on the New York steamship route, the most successful being the *British Queen*, which commenced service from London to New York in June 1839.

There was a powerful attraction in the business opportunities presented by a large and rapidly growing market in America and the industrial needs and output of Europe. James Gordon Bennett, editor of the *Herald*, wrote excitedly from London in 1838 about the wonderful possibilities of trade expansion now that steamships had arrived.

The United States now possess a greater influence in the destiny in England that anybody has yet imagined. Last year the decrease of the revenue here equal to two million pounds was caused by the diminution of the American trade principally. Hence the deep interest felt by all parties in the revival of the American trade. London, Bristol and Liverpool have at this moment all started on the new steam enterprise. Then these cities begin a race of commercial intercourse, converging on New York, which in ten years will make our happy island of Manhattan the second greatest commercial capital in the world. There will be no want of capital. Numerous younger branches of commercial houses here, and in other parts of England, are preparing to go out to New York and establish themselves in business. On every hand enquiries are made of me as to the trade, resources and systems of our country.[1]

One business traveller who could afford to pay regularly to travel was Peter Harmony. Of Spanish origin, he was one of several New York millionaires.[2] He was a member of the House of Lords, a social club in New York for 'men of standing', which met on Wall Street every evening. He was a director of the local branch of the Bank of the United States in 1822, owned many ships and was very involved in overseas trade, notably trade between Cuba and Spain. He ran a successful brokerage house in New York, importing and exporting goods, and acting as agent for other merchants. In 1835 he was said to be worth $1.5 million with investments in the United States, Europe, Cuba and Brazil.[3] He travelled each year on the *Great Western* between 1840 and 1843.[4] He was rich enough to book a whole cabin for himself and a separate berth for his nameless servant. Servants are one of the groups on board who remain anonymous in the company records.

The passengers sitting next to one of the Tappan brothers might need to be wary and remain guarded in their conversation – the brothers had a speciality niche in European trade. In 1827 Arthur and Lewis had built up America's largest silk-importing house, using suppliers in England and Italy. They were also prominent abolitionists and strict Calvinists. The panic of 1837 had ushered in a five-year slump which concentrated attention on credit worthiness since business was based on trust and long lines of credit. Lewis Tappan launched the Mercantile agency in 1840. The agency was the first credit rating firm in the United States and was the ancestor of today's Dun and Bradstreet. Tappan established a network of trustworthy informants, recruited from abolitionists, evangelicals and lawyers such as Abraham Lincoln, who forwarded confidential reports on store owners and other businesses. They assessed net worth, liquidity and 'character'. Intemperate habits, sporting interests or associating with 'bad women' went into the reports, which Tappan then sold to subscribers.[5]

New York became the money centre of the United States while London was the great banking centre, and large London banking houses had branches in New York. Among these were Baring Brothers; Mr Bates was a partner in New York, and was a constant traveller on the *Great Western*. Brown, Shipley and Company regularly transported freight and specie and sent many of their agents via the ship.[6] William and James Brown were the Liverpool agents for the Cope Line of Philadelphia that ran scheduled sailing ship services between Philadelphia and New York. They ran one ship per month from each port and took passengers. Steamship competition forced them downmarket to take more steerage passengers.[7]

There were other well-travelled men with a talent for languages, such as Samuel Byerley, who must have made an interesting dinner companion. He was a partner in Byerley, Aspinwall & Co. Born in Staffordshire, his father was a partner of Josiah Wedgwood. A talented linguist who could speak French, Italian, German, Spanish, Latin and Greek, he had been employed carrying dispatches from England to Russia. He had been in Trieste but came to the United States in 1832, where he joined Howland and Aspinwall, eventually taking charge of their vast commercial and shipping interests. He was a well-known figure in New York.[8]

Then there was W. H. Aspinwall, himself, who with his wife and servant returned to New York on 15 November 1838 on the *Great Western*. Aspinwall specialised in the Pacific trade and in importing luxury goods from China. Aspinwall understood speed, financing fast clipper ships such as the famous *Rainbow* and *Sea Witch*, built in 1845. These ships raced from China carrying tea in the well-known tea races, and the *Sea Witch* held the record from Hong Kong to New York. After the 1848 gold rush he went into steam, creating the Pacific Mail steamship company. During the Civil War he was one of two businessmen sent by the United States government to Britain on a secret mission in regard to the construction of ironclad steamers by Laird & Son. In his obituary he was described as one of the 'merchant princes of the age'.[9]

Amos A. Lawrence came from a prominent Boston textile family. He was a merchant and supporter of abolition. He took the *Great Western* to Bristol in November 1839. The company of his fellow passengers was both testing and trying and very different to what he was used to back home in Boston, where there were clear lines of conduct. On the very first day, while walking on deck, 'a bold Italian claimed acquaintance'. While dining, an Englishman laughed at molasses, a Frenchman sang and another Englishman called blessings on the Queen. Then there was the heavy-handed teasing by some of the English of the Americans about republicanism and colonialism. Sir Lionel Smith, a lieutenant general in the British Army, suggested they would soon have a king in the northern states ' as they love royalty and Britain'. 'You love titles in Boston,' said Sir Lionel. 'No, we admire only an aristocracy of merit,' riposted Lawrence. Sir Lionel persisted and urged him to marry an Englishwoman, adding that he must not marry less money than he already had. Lawrence explained, 'I tell him that in America we married for love.' Later that night they toasted the ladies of Great Britain and sang 'Yankee Doodle'.[10]

Rich families from New York, Philadelphia and Boston appear on the *Great Western*'s passenger lists, among them Amory, Coffin, Coolidge, Cushing, Delano, Lyman, Tudor, Van Buren and many others. In November 1843, Henry James and his wife were on board; they were the parents of the novelist Henry James. James Roosevelt was on board in 1844 with his eldest son, James junior. James senior was widowed, and on his second marriage became the father of Franklin Delano Roosevelt.

There were diplomats from various countries: the United States, Canada, Britain, France, Germany, Spain and Italy. Monsieur Pointois, the ambassador from France, was returning home in 1839, and several ambassadors from South America too. There were judges, government officials, Army men and a positive flurry of them all during the Canadian disputes. There was even minor royalty. Hosken, we have noted, had called upon his acquaintance with Prince Murat when stranded in snow outside New York. Murat's full title was Lucien Charles Joseph Napoleon, Prince Francais, Prince of Naples, 2nd Prince of Pontecorvo, 3rd Prince Murat. His mother was the younger sister of Napoleon.

The principality of Naples was created by Napoleon for Marshal Bernadotte, who gave it up on becoming Crown Prince of Sweden, when it passed to the Murats, who lost the principality in 1815. Lucien lived for some years in New Jersey and was a regular traveller to Europe. He tried unsuccessfully to reclaim the throne of Naples in 1838 and 1844, and eventually became a minister under Napoleon III.

Since the end of war in Europe in 1815, continental travel had become fashionable. Mrs Dixon, whose diary has already provided much useful information on shipboard life, was a typical traveller. She was on honeymoon and taking a grand tour of European countries. She was aged twenty-one and had married James in Maine on 1 October 1840. She was connected to many distinguished New England families. As a young girl she had inherited a large fortune, estimated at the time to be around a million dollars. Her husband, James, was a lawyer and was later to become active in politics, becoming a congressman and leading the Whig party. Elizabeth was a friend and neighbour of Lydia Sigourney, who was travelling in Europe at the same time.[11]

Not all American tourists had Mrs Dixon's wealth. John Jay Smith published his book on his return to recoup some of his costs but also filled it with descriptions and useful advice to encourage his fellow countrymen and women to travel outside the United States. He was away for just over five months and travelled extensively across Europe, and in his view $1,000 or $1,200 per person was sufficient and allowed for comfortable conveyances and good hotels. A fellow traveller had visited Rome, Naples, Venice and Switzerland and travelled down the Rhine for just $1,000. Smith's recommendation was to travel out in a sailing ship and back on a steamer.[12]

Lydia Sigourney, the poet and writer, who we have already met, came from a poor family and was largely self-educated. A good marriage, in social terms, moved her into higher social circles in Hartford, Connecticut, but financial problems led her, like her English contemporary Fanny Trollope, to turn to writing in order to support her family. In this she was very successful, writing poetry, books and articles, and she was known for her many poems on the subject of death, especially written as memorials on the deaths of young children. Obituary poems were frequent in this period. Two-thirds of her published work was prose such as *Letters to Young Ladies*, *Letters to Mothers* and *Whispers to a Bride*. She also wrote extensively about the Native Americans to highlight their dilemmas and treatment.[13]

In 1840, due to incipient bronchitis, her doctor recommended travel to England. For Lydia this was a dream realised: 'In early childhood it was my favourite dream to look on the brave old island where our best books come from and our nicest frocks.'[14] Leaving her husband and two young children, she set out on a sailing packet. She went as part of a group that included 'a lady whom I have long admired, her accomplished clerical son, whose mind enriches whatever it contemplates, and a still younger gentleman, the son of esteemed friends, travelling for improvement'. She travelled on the *Europe* with Captain Edward Marshall, a very experienced master. It took seventeen days to reach the Irish coast through bad storm, and then there was a near-fatal calamity in dense fog in St George's Channel.[15] It was not a happy introduction to crossing the Atlantic. She later met up with her friends Elizabeth and James Dixon, and travelled on with them to France, which may have influenced her choice to return on the *Great Western*.

Lydia was not there purely for vacation as she had a commission. As a poet and writer, she was a regular contributor and occasional editor of *Godey's Lady's Book*. Still a relatively new magazine, it was established by Louis Godey of Philadelphia. Mrs Sarah Josepha Hale was the editor. It became the leading women's magazine before the Civil War and was highly influential, reaching a peak circulation of 150,000.[16] It entertained, informed and educated its readers with biographical sketches, recipes and remedies and extensive fashion plates in addition to articles on topics like mineralogy, handcrafts, health and hygiene. Mrs Hale commissioned essays, poetry and short stories from leading authors like Harriet Beecher Stowe, Edgar Allan Poe and Nathaniel Hawthorne.[17] Queen Victoria was seen as a role model of femininity, morality and intellect, and *Godey's* asked Lydia Sigourney to report on the royal activities in London.[18]

One of Godey's contributors was Henry Longfellow, whose fame was growing to the extent that he could consider leaving his teaching post at Harvard and support himself and his family by his writing alone. He travelled home on the *Great Western* in the late autumn of 1842 and it was not a happy passage. Severe storms kept him confined to his berth for twelve of the fifteen days to New York. Through many sleepless nights he lay in his berth composing poems in his head. His cabin was in a poor position forward where all movement was felt. He later wrote it was 'where all the great waves struck and broke with voices of thunder. In the next room to mine, a man died. I was afraid they might throw me over board instead of him.'[19] However, this may have been his fertile imagination as the list of passengers presented to the emigration authorities in New York does not, as it was required to do, list any deaths.

It is tempting to speculate on which poems Longfellow composed in his berth. His well-known *Song of Hiawatha* was not published until 1855, but one book published in 1850, a collection of poems with the title *The Seaside and the Fireside*, does contain two poems with a ship as the subject.[20] Here are the first two verses of one of them, called *The Secret of the Sea*:

Ah! What pleasant visions haunt me
As I gaze upon the sea!
All the old romantic legends,
All my dreams, come back to me.

Sails of silk and ropes of sandal,
Such as gleam in ancient lore;
And the singing of the sailors,
And the answer from the shore![21]

It seems his dreadful passage a few years before had been quite forgotten and the steamship might never have existed. Longfellow did not see the steamship as a subject for his romantic poetry.

Literature and fashion combined in the theatre. Both London and New York had a range of theatres showing everything from Shakespeare to burlesque, variety shows to classical music. The *Great Western* was a favoured ship carrying actors/managers, actresses and musicians between the established London theatres and the emerging New York theatre scene. During the period between 1830 and 1870, London's West End theatres became a mecca for popular entertainment. There were a limited number of theatres, and all theatres and dramatic pieces had to be licensed by the Lord Chamberlain. In 1832 in London those licensed were the Olympic, Adelphi, Drury Lane, King's, Covent Garden and the Haymarket. New York offered more opportunities. The Wallack family were regular passengers on the *Great Western*, and James William Wallack was an English actor/theatre manager who became very well known in New York. He managed theatres in both capitals and Philip Hone, the New York diarist was a regular theatre goer and noted the Wallack family appearances.[22] The speedy transit offered by the *Great Western* attracted many theatrical people.

Noted passengers on board the ship, especially celebrities from the world of entertainment, were announced in the newspapers and written up by diarists. On her third voyage to New York, the *Herald* announced the arrival of James Watson Webb, Tyrone Power, Madame Vestris and Charles Matthews among *Great Western*'s 110 passengers.[23] James Watson Webb was the editor of the *Herald*'s rival newspaper, the *Chronicle*, Tyrone Power was a well-known Irish actor and the other two were better connected than the list suggests.

Madame Vestris was a highly successful leading lady but also a shrewd actor/manager. She was one of many women who played a significant role in the theatre industry. At this time several women achieved success as actress/managers and business entrepreneurs.[24] Vestris managed the London Olympic theatre and staged innovative vaudevilles. The popular works of the time blended elements of ballad opera, operetta and opéra comique, and balanced comedy and sentimentality.[25] Vestris and Charles Matthews, a leading English actor, were lovers. Successful as they both were in London, they arrived to fulfil a disastrous engagement at the Park theatre in New York. Vestris' fame had gone before her and she was expected to sing 'breeches parts'; these were parts sung by young actresses dressed daringly as men. But Vestris was by now forty-one so she sang opera and wisely omitted the 'breech parts', to the disappointment of her audience. But the audience was already inclined to be hostile towards her. James Gordon

Bennett, editor of the New York *Herald* saw her in London in their farewell production before heading for New York and wrote for his paper that 'Madame Vestris is a celebrated woman here both privately and publicly. The history of her life is a love romance.' Sensitive to the rigid standards of morality demanded by American theatregoers, she and Charles Matthews married just before leaving England, but this had the opposite effect and generated some destructive publicity before they arrived. Vestris and Matthews cut short their engagement and returned to England.[26]

Haliburton, the cynical observer, includes a letter in his book from a fictional actress travelling to New York. Aware of the debacle of the Vestris and Mathews visit, she contemplates changing her wardrobe: 'Altered my petticoats, added two inches for Boston puritans, and Philadelphia Quakers, took off two for the fashionables of New York, three for Baltimore and made kilts of them for New Orleans.'[27]

Other acts were more favourably welcomed. On 4 May 1840, J. W. Williams noted excitedly in his diary: 'Arrival of the *Great Western*! This fine steamer arrived at New York Sunday morning May 3 1840 with a goodly number of passengers in 18 days from Bristol England. "Fanny Elssler" the celebrated dancer was a passenger.'[28] Fanny was a very welcome arrival to more than just Williams. Attendance at New York theatres was declining alarmingly, possibly as a reaction to the financial depression. Fanny was a legendary dancer and her arrival temporarily rescued the Park Theatre from disaster. The theatre was crowded with her fans every time she appeared, something of a rarity in a city that was easily bored with repetition. Such was the adulation that her carriage was drawn through the streets by her 'hysterical admirers'.[29]

These were the great celebrities of the day. James Bennett, on his London visit, joined the many admirers of Madame Celeste and provided her with advance publicity in New York:

At the Haymarket Madame Celeste is the principal attraction. Last night she made her appearance in a new line – The tragic drama, and made one of the most decided hits that have been seen here in sometime. The piece was written for her by Mr Jerrold, ... I went to see her debut in the English drama and I never saw excellent

Celeste look to greater advantage. Her pronunciation is slightly tinged with a foreign accent, this I thought only gave additional interest to the scene. At all events her debut as a tragic actress of the highest order has astonished the critics here. Heretofore, she has only been known as a splendid dancer or for pantomime. The discovery of her new Talent will bring a New Era in her life. Her fine figure, her splendid face, her expressive eyes and her classical gestures are all unique.[30]

Such celebrity made her a demanding passenger. She booked on board the *Great Western* in August 1842 and requested a berth for herself and a berth for her female servant, 'provided the latter can occupy the same room as her mistress at the usual servants' fee'. Her father was to travel with her and wished to occupy a cabin to himself.[31]

Whole groups of actors might travel by the ship. On George Moore's passage out to New York he travelled with Mr Anderson, Miss Clara Ellis and Mr Dowsett, who were to play Othello, Desdemona and Iago in a production of *Othello* at the Park Theatre. Moore was not very impressed with the Park Theatre and on the ship he had sat next to the English manager of the theatre, Mr Simpson, 'a worthy man, and much esteemed'.[32]

George was sympathetic to the actors, but the theatrical career was viewed slightly dubiously in London. There were subtle differences in status, a situation that enraged the actor friend of Charles Dickens, George McCready. English society did not see even a leading actor as a gentleman, and the 'mighty difference between the prefix of 'Mr' and the affix 'Esq.' was a particular grievance.' The official list of those who testified before an 1832 parliamentary committee used the affix Esq. for two contractors who specialized in building theatres, while distinguished actors including Macready, Charles Kemble, Edmund Kean, Douglas Jerrold and Charles Matthews were simple Mr. These distinctions mattered a great deal in London but were irrelevant in New York and mattered little on board in the democratic dining saloon of the *Great Western*.[33]

The coming of steamship travel had a marked impact on theatre and music, and this period is viewed as a 'watershed in the evolution of music in the United States'. The introduction of the *Great Western*'s regular service, followed by yet more steamships, encouraged a 'veritable tidal wave of European virtuosos of the highest calibre' who now arrived in America. They could fulfil engagements on both sides of the Atlantic in half the time. In the New World 'an insatiably worshipful public, incited to delirium by a manipulative press, impatiently clamoured to welcome them, deify them and – not least – to shower them with grateful gold'.[34]

This was the growth period for newspapers, which were the main channels of communication to a wide audience. Reports carried in the London newspapers were used verbatim in the numerous provincial newspapers. The *Great Western* was big news and readers wanted to hear about the speed, efficiency and novelty of crossing by steam. On her second return from New York there were excited and enthusiastic, and slightly exaggerated, reports. The ship anchored at Bristol having completed the passage in the amazingly short time of twelve and a half days, which set a record. In total, enthused the report, she had made the round trip between Bristol, New York and back to Bristol in the 'unparalleled short space of thirty-six days, eight of which were spent in New York, which leaves her five weeks of the actual voyage, and which averages as many months by sailing vessels'. The reporter claimed to have the views of all ninety-two passengers, who were keen to share their experience of this phenomenon and expressed themselves. greatly delighted with the 'splendour and comfort of her accommodations'.[35] The motion of this new form of transport was particularly mentioned. Movement had been very slight

> ... on board the vessel throughout the passage even when blowing hard, and during the latter part of the voyage they encountered heavy weather, which gave them some opportunity of judging of the great advantage possessed by the vessel in this respect. A passenger, with whom I had an opportunity of conversing, told me he had several times crossed the Atlantic in sailing packets, and in very similar weather to that experienced on his voyage home in the *Great Western*, and that he should not have believed it possible for such a difference to exist, had he not felt and tested it for himself. Even in toughest weather it seems that passengers

may sit down to dinner without any of the fears or dangers of accident on board sailing vessels. You feel assured that you will not be laid sprawling on the cabin floor by your chair lurching to leeward; or that you will be thought desirous of appropriating to yourself more than your fair share of eatables by getting the contents of half a dozen or more dishes poured wholesale into your lap. None of these or other, somewhat similar, but even more disagreeable accidents so frequent but unavoidable on ship-board, are here felt; in fact, you may sit down and enjoy yourself almost in as much ease as in a drawing room on shore.[36]

Much of this stability and ease of passage through the waves was attributed firmly to her design and the length of her hull, which stopped her wallowing in the waves. The speed of the *Great Western* was reported as nine miles per hour on the outward journey and ten miles per hour homeward.[37] The ship, crew and engines were now well settled in and working well. All of this hyperbole must have been highly gratifying to the building committee of the Great Western Steamship Company where Brunel, Patterson, Guppy and Claxton were now working on plans for the next ship.

Despite such high praise, steam for some was still a worrying mode of transport and there were many anxious passengers. Having travelled on the *Great Western* both ways and on their return passage, Mr and Mrs Dixon considered themselves old hands. They left Bristol on Thursday, 27 May 1841. The first day was beautiful and they made good progress but the second day was rough and Mrs Dixon was very ill and remained in her cabin. The weather continued to grow worse and about half past two in the morning of 31 May they were awoken by the complete absence of noise, the engines had stopped. This was highly alarming to those who had not sailed in the ship before. A passenger's voice awoke Mrs Dixon. Colonel Inland was asking his sister, presumably in her cabin, if she had experienced this before. Mrs Dixon, the seasoned steamship passenger, explained it sometimes happened when the engines were hot. Far from providing reassurance, this further alarmed the colonel who exclaimed about dangerous boilers, dressed and ran on deck. Here all was calm and there was no danger from explosion, although the storm still raged, and indeed the youthful Mrs Dixon was right and the machinery was simply stopped to cool. But the anxiety had spread and the captain himself came down to reassure 'all the trembling ladies'. The storm continued and a short while later there was a tremendous crack as the sails were torn to ribbons in what sounded like an explosion of musketry. This added to the panic of many ladies, meanwhile Hosken, in his tarred coat and hat, was on deck. 'He looked cool but he kept a good look and going down once or twice in to that deep dungeon where the giant engine kept on its iron labour to see that all was right there.' The storm lasted for twenty-four hours and later Captain Hosken confided to his friend, Mrs Dixon, that this was the worst he had ever known. The ship continued at a great rate and bets were laid as to when they would reach New York.[38]

The damage was repaired in New York, and on the next passage home to Bristol a friend of the editor Louis Godey wrote in July 1841 of his journey being foggy for fourteen of the sixteen days. He described the ship as 'the best sea boat I ever saw' and the accommodation and fare as 'first rate'. He compared it favourably with a good hotel and praised some pleasant passengers and wonderful crew.[39] George Moore praised the ship in 1844, and in his view the steamer was 'without exception the easiest and most comfortable I have ever sailed'. The noise of the engines became a background noise and was noticeable when it stopped.[40] Unfortunately a later set of passengers the next year were not so happy with the ship.

John Jay Smith was aged fifty and returning from his European jaunt with his young son. It was his first passage across the Atlantic by steam and had been happily anticipated. His floating palace left Liverpool punctually, but he soon realised there were problems:

At our outset it was evident to all that we were in an overcrowded ship. The *Great Western* is calculated for comfortable conveying about 100, and at the most 120 passengers, we had on board 160, a number purposely decreased in the statement on arrival to 153. Everybody that we have to go was admitted, and sometimes receipts were given twice for the same berths, so that confusion prevailed; the officers, and even the youthful doctor of the ship, were put out of their berths, and the overworked servants slept

on the bare deck; the attendance was insufficient; there were
not seats for all at the table, and in short, so great was the
number, and the settees so crowded with sleepers, that we had
a most comfortless passage; and it turned out too it was a most
boisterous one.[41]

Boisterous was an understatement, and as seen previously it was the
most severe storm the ship had encountered. Together with other
passengers, Smith also complained that the ship was dirty. A letter
of complaint, mainly by American passengers, was written but
there was an opposing one by other passengers who supported the
beleaguered Captain Mathews, who seems to have had difficulty
dealing with the complaints. Standards, it seems, were slipping, and
by 1845 are indicators of wider problems.

While the ship could carry more than Smith suggested, it
was overcrowded – possibly through poor administration. Such
complaints were rare for the *Great Western*, while it was a regular
problem for other companies, with a more cavalier approach to
passenger complaints being common, notably on routes with little
competition. Overcrowding was a constant grievance of P&O
passengers heading to India. William Howard Russell, the famous
war correspondent of the Crimean War, was sent out by *The Times*
in 1858 to cover the Indian mutiny. The journey involved travel
by steamer through the Mediterranean, overland across Egypt and
then by steamer through the Red Sea and onwards to India. On
boarding in Egypt he was approached and asked if he would give
up his cabin for two ladies who should have been on another ship
whose propeller had broken. He was given the surgeon's cabin,
which was the 'the best in the ship'. This, he discovered, was a
severe overstatement. He commented humorously that it may have
been good in the Arctic but in the Red Sea it was exposed to a few
drawbacks: he had a 'commanding view of the steam engine', and
a large pipe that 'rose and hissed' at every throb of the engine.
A stream of passengers visited the ship's library, situated in his
cabin, and he had to fend off those seeking medical advice. The
wine on board was bad – rough wine was passed off as claret and
the port and sherry 'must be made on board as they are never met
with out of ships'. He did spare a thought for the ousted surgeon,

whose berth he imagined was somewhere in the ship's rigging, and noted that officers who were subjected to expulsions received only 'a pecuniary consideration'.[42]

Whether it had been a good or bad experience on the *Great Western*, and most reports were positive, the arrival in port after the crossing was sufficient to cheer the most unhappy of souls. For Foster on the very first crossing to New York it was 'difficult, impossible, justly to describe the expressions which pervade a ship at the moment of first discovering land. It is a look of joy.' His fellow passengers were also thoughtful. '"My country," cried one extending his arms half solemnly, and "There is the road to mine," said another, pointing at the wake stretching back across the sea.' It was time to get ready to be seen on deck, and comfortable clothes worn on board were changed for something smarter: 'The resurrection of "other" clothes, and the exchange of "hats for caps". The rusty jacket has suddenly become the superfine black long-tailed, and the out of elbows of yesterday, sports now, perhaps the finest fleece of the flock.'[43]

In August 1844, George Moore saw land for the first time since leaving Britain and confessed he was 'heartily sick of the Atlantic'. The previous evening there had been a grand last-night dinner and the passengers 'did ample justice to the food'. It was Captain Mathews' first trip as commander and he was presented with a memorial signed by all the passengers to note the occasion. Moore felt that Mathews deserved something more 'substantial as a mark of our regard for his unremitting attentions'. They saw Nantucket at two in the morning and the weather was mild and warm. George paid his wine bill to Crawford, the head steward, and finished his letters to England in the hope of 'catching the Boston steamer which leaves New York at five p.m. on Saturday'. On Saturday morning all the passengers were on deck to greet the pilot. The pilot had come out 160 miles to get the job and lent Moore a New York paper. They were surrounded by an increasing number of other vessels as they neared New York, and there was much confusion and bustle on board as everyone did their packing.

They landed in New York at half past seven; this was too late for customs clearance, and the Boston packet had sailed, so he had missed the chance to get his letters home early. On landing, he found the confusion baffled all description as hundreds of pickpockets were on the lookout. He and companions from the ship headed to the Astor House Hotel where he had a warm bath and retired to rest, happy to be back on solid land. Moore was full of praise for the Astor House Hotel, which was described as the largest hotel in the world: 'They make up 500 beds regularly and can make up 800'. He was most impressed by the large number of staff. He counted sixty waiters, five regular clerks, twenty-one washerwomen, five manglers ('all of which is done by Steam') and twelve cooks. Service was also impressive: 'You never have occasion to ring the bell twice; they have twenty Rotonda men who do nothing else but answer bells and carry out parcels.' And the price of all this for eating and bed was $2 per day including servants.[44]

When Lydia Sigourney arrived in New York she was coming home, grateful to have survived the perils of the ice and looking forward to seeing her young children again. The dangerous times had drawn the on-board community closer despite their different nationalities. 'As we drew near the end of a voyage, we felt how community in danger had endeared those to each other, who, during the sixteen days of their companionship upon the ocean, had been united by the courtesies of kind and friendly intercourse.' She had plenty of material for her book of her travels and for the magazine.[45]

Going eastward, Mrs Dixon was in a different frame of mind on her first arrival in England in 1840. As they got closer to their first approach to land, spirits rose and 'many a song was sung after dinner' amid much cheering. A drink was shared to Nelson's memory in silence. Toasts were drunk to the officers of the ship, who replied with the wish to see all passengers back again. John Smith, the singer on board, surprised everyone with a song in praise of the *Great Western* which had been composed on board. Soon they were arriving and rockets were sent off to hail a pilot. He eventually came on board, a 'busy bustling little body', with letters, newspapers and news. This was the first news they had had of the outside world, and the pilot relished his important role in providing them with the headlines: 'The King of France has been shot at! Danger of war! Ministry all resigned!'

They had an early hot breakfast, and just as the sun rose they left the ship and went on board a small sloop. As they looked back they saw the captain waving his cap, and all along the deck the servants were ranged: 'Fat Billy Crawford the steward and Margaret with her plaid turban straining with the only eye she had to look at us out of sight and Boston's black face and figure in bold relief against the side of the ship like a bronze figure. John Smith and the company struck up "The Western's a good 'un to go" and as the ship receded from our view the song died away.'

The little boat steamer now wound its way slowly up the River Avon, which she described as dark and muddy and bordered by meadows covered with sheep, and the banks of the river grew higher and higher: 'At the highest summit of the rocks and 230 feet high was the suspension bridge in its commencement. When finished it will span 600 feet. It seems like crossing on the clouds from one part of heaven to another.'[46] Lydia Sigourney also noted the pleasant journey down the Avon: 'We saw many elegant mansions in commanding situations, and a suspension bridge in progress, where workmen were crossing by rope and basket at a tremendously dizzy height.'[47] Brunel's bridge was already a wonder and would eventually be finished in 1864.

In Bristol the passengers landed and passed into the customs house, 'a great hall like a church with the two large gates and the blazing fire in each. The trunks were ranged around.'[48] After clearing Customs, the Dixons were then conveyed up the hill to the Royal Hotel in Clifton, a large stone building with the lion and unicorn over the door and facing a beautiful park. They were met at the door by the head waiter and a maid and shown to a room with a bay window overlooking the park. Breakfast soon followed, and a most welcome luxury was to be shown into a fire-lit little dressing room with a small room adjoining in which there was a bath. Mrs Dixon then sent sixty-three pieces to the laundress. The young couple dined at five, and 'never had dinner tasted so good as on this day, so neat, nice and comfortable after the steamboat'.[49]

7

The Great Western Steam Ship Company

After the great success of the first passage across to New York, the company could congratulate themselves on their achievement. The next two voyages established the steady reputation of the ship. On Wednesday 29 August 1838, the *Great Western* arrived at Bristol from New York after her third round trip across the Atlantic. The ship and the crew were now settling in well, and she had made it home in thirteen days and six hours. Her outward crossing had been fourteen and a half days. She arrived with eighty-seven passengers on board from New York. The *Bristol Mercury*, a great supporter of the ship, published a letter addressed to the directors and signed on behalf of the passengers which gave a ringing endorsement to this new method of crossing the Atlantic.

On board the Steam-ship *Great Western* of Bristol
29 August 1838
   Sir:- the undersigned gentlemen having been selected by all their fellow passengers, 87 in number, on board this ship, to testify their entire conviction of the success of the highly important enterprise which the vessel is embarked in, they unhesitatingly declare their fullest confidence in the efficiency of the *Great Western* to navigate the Atlantic Ocean, from the superiority and strength of her construction, the excellence of her engines, and the unremitting attention of her commander to all the duties committed to your care. They likewise feel it due to the proprietors to express their sense of obligation for the arrangements and ample supply for

their comforts during the passage; and they conclude by an ardent prayer for the continuation of that prosperity which has hitherto attended this undertaking, as well as their sincere thanks to ... The committee, moreover, feel they are only doing justice to the sentiments of their fellow passengers, in requesting that every publicity may be given to the above declaration in England, France and the United States.

Such was the enthusiasm generated by the passengers for transatlantic steam. The letter was signed by eleven of the passengers, some of whom were very influential Americans. Among them was William Strickland, a highly regarded architect and engineer. He designed the Second Bank of the United States and the United States Mint and is credited with inspiring the Greek Revival architectural style in America, which led to many fine buildings. He also had a strong interest in railways, being appointed in 1826 as the engineer in charge of the Eastern division of the Pennsylvania Mixed System, which was a combination of railway and canal.[1] Another signatory was John Grattan Gamble, a merchant, planter and banker. He was the President of the Union Bank.[2] George Knight was a wealthy American merchant based in Havana and Samuel Swarthwout was possibly the most prominent of them all. He was the Collector of the Port of New York, the person in charge of the Custom House. This was a highly prestigious and a wealthy position with extensive patronage over a large number of jobs as it employed nearly 500 staff. He was very well connected at a high level in the United States government. Millions of dollars in duties went through his office, and its role was to ensure that all duties were paid. What his fellow passengers did not know was that the esteemed and very important Swarthwout was on the run. He had only been in office for one year but had managed to divert more than a million dollars to some of his private ventures. He was now rapidly putting a distance between himself and the authorities in New York by taking passage on the fastest transport across the Atlantic.[3]

Unaware of this and gratified by the endorsement of such eminent passengers, the directors of the steamship company instructed their New York agent to insert the following advertisement in the New York papers:

The Great Western Steam Ship Company –

  This enterprising company at Bristol, to whom we are indebted for the most complete demonstration of the practicality of steam navigation across the ocean, at an unprecedented reduction of time from the voyages made by the sail craft, through their agent here, Mr Irvin, No 98, Front-Street, invite the capitalists, bankers, merchants and ship-owners of our city to cooperate with them in the construction of four steam-ships, two at Bristol and two at New York.[4]

This was not a new idea. John Junius Smith had proposed a similar transatlantic partnership in New York with two American and two British ships in 1833.[5] He had failed to get financial support then, but now the Great Western Steamship Company were in the happy situation that they had proved the feasibility of such a scheme. Emboldened by the public praise, they had been encouraged to propose the same idea.

  After just a few passages the directors of the Great Western Steam Ship Company could well feel as self-satisfied as they appeared in the advertisement. Everything was going very well; the *Sirius* was no longer competing for passengers, having been returned to her Irish Sea duties after just two transatlantic crossings. With no cargo space and few passengers, the *Sirius* had cost her charterers, the British and American Steam Navigation Company, a loss of £3,500.[6] It had been an expensive exercise in publicity. Meanwhile their new ship, *British Queen*, was still having her engines fitted in Scotland, so the *Great Western* was the sole steamship on the Atlantic.

  Demand for berths on the *Great Western* was increasing, and all 130 berths were taken for her next outward voyage on 8 September. Such was the clamour for berths that 'premiums of twenty guineas have been offered, and would be given, for berths on the first refusal of vacancies from parties who by any accident might be prevented from going'. One group from Devon who had booked a double berth were asked if they could take another passenger if they did not require their four berths. Extra cabin space was built on deck and below to provide additional sleeping space.[7] The newspaper reports suggested healthy profits to be gained:

> Upon the 87 passengers home, and the 130 out, at 40 guineas passage money per head in the saloon, and 35 guineas cabin, each way, the directors of the *Great Western* will have received, therefore, upwards of £8,000, exclusive of the benefit derived from the conveyance of goods, of which the Great Western brought from New York to the extent of about 200 tons measurement.[8]

In New York the *Herald*, which had earlier been less than supportive of the ship after the newspaper debacle, when their rival had managed to get the very first British newspapers delivered by steamship, was now an enthusiastic supporter. The editor, Bennett, who had travelled over rather grumpily on the *Sirius*, was now sending reports back from London to his paper praising the financial success of the ship. Despite the 'vast outlay and expense incurred in fitting out the *Great Western* and the loss incurred by her voyage to New York', shares in the company, he reported, had risen by 10 per cent in one day and continued to rise with her successful return. He urged his countrymen to support the ship.[9] But unlike the demand for berths there was no great rush of enthusiasm from New York investors to finance transatlantic steamships. Apart from any other more parochial considerations, it was not a good time to be investing in schemes of this type. Many New Yorkers were trying to recover from the disastrous financial crash the year before. So, the Bristol-based company remained as it was.

The original proposal that saw the launch of the *Great Western* was the wish to see the railway line extended by the use of a steamship so that the Great Western Railway would reach from London to New York. A question that has not been examined is why there was a separate company since the idea originated in the railway's board meeting. The answer lies in the contemporary legislation governing railways. Brunel and Guppy would have been told that legally the Great Western Railway was barred from owning ships. A joint-stock company at this time could only be established by a special Act of Parliament, and the powers granted to the early railway companies authorised them to build lines and operate trains but provided 'no legal powers to handle traffic afloat'.[10] So a separate company had to be established and from the beginning it was a very local project.

The decision was taken not to go down the expensive joint-stock route. Their legal advisers were Osborne and Ward, who had steered the original railway bill through Parliament. Instead a partnership was established by a deed of settlement. A partnership meant that all partners were individually liable for the debts of the other partners. Actions taken by one of them had the possibility of bankrupting the rest as there was no limitation of liability. A deed of settlement vested the property in the hands of nominated trustees who divided it into transferable shares and established directors to manage the concern. The directors were normally – but not always – the same as the trustees.[11] Limited liability did not appear in English law until 1855, so trust in the directors to do the best for their fellow shareholders, who were partners in the eyes of the law, was crucial. The shareholders were known as proprietors and this is a better term since it indicates the very much closer relationship to the company than shareholding.

The local newspaper approved of the names of the gentlemen on the provisional committee. They included P. Maze, W. E. Acraman, R. Bright, H. Bush, J. Cookson, T. R. Guppy, John Harford, Thomas Kington, Robert Scott, John Irving, T. B. Were and Thomas Pycroft. These men, they wrote, 'offer guarantee, now that all doubts of the feasibility of the project have been removed, that it will be prosecuted to a successful issue.'[12]

The Bristol press approved of these fellows as they were all well-known and well-connected local businessmen. Robert Scott and barrister Thomas Pycroft were from Bath, and Bath investors held a quarter of the shares. The rest were Bristol-based and had overlapping connections in the key bodies that ran the city. Several were elected to membership of the exclusive Society of Merchant Venturers, had estates in, or connections with, the West Indies, were bankers, shipowners and/or members of the town council and Chamber of Commerce. For example, Henry Bush was a Merchant

Venturer and town councillor (as was Acraman), and Harford was a banker. Several were named as those who were compensated at the abolition of slavery in 1833. Research has shown that in the period 1835–97, fifteen families of merchants and industrialists provided fifty-six councillors. It was a tight-knit group, but not unusual for the times.[13]

Like many of the key personalities here, Robert Bright was an extremely busy man. He was active in a large number of organisations, mostly in Bristol but also in Liverpool. He was born in 1785, so he was in his early fifties at the establishment of the company. He came from an important Bristol family which had several interests in the West Indies. By 1838 he was a senior partner in the firm of Gibbs, Bright and Company of Liverpool and Bristol. He was a shareholder in the Great Western Cotton works at Barton Hill in Bristol and he was an early supporter of the Great Western Railway, with 259 shares, and became deputy chairman. His father had been a long-term member of the City Council and his brother was a Member of Parliament for ten years, although Robert did not go into politics. He was a strong advocate of municipal reform in Bristol and a member of a committee endeavouring to get free port status. He became High Sheriff of Bristol in 1852.[14]

One particular connection was cotton. With the changing fortunes of sugar in the West Indies, the Bristol merchants looked to other industries and cotton was a target. The Lancashire mills were working non-stop to handle the raw cotton coming in to Liverpool via New York. In 1831, cotton exports made up 50 per cent of all British merchandise exports and 69 per cent of the mills were in Lancashire. There were 1,500 in Lancashire and now one in Bristol. The Bristol venture, which the owners hoped would lead to many more local mills, employed fifteen men and fourteen women, all under twenty-one. The mills were powered by steam and the plan was to bring raw cotton from New York to Bristol on the *Great Western*.[15]

If the Great Western Steam Ship Company was set up as a separate organisation, it had the tacit support of the Great Western Railway Company. The railway offices in London provided the booking service and their man in charge, Thomas Ward, had a busy time managing the affairs of the Great Western Steamship Company in London. It indicates a close working relationship with benefits to both organisations from the projected flow of passengers traveling between London and New York. This cooperation was fully evident with the opening of the first part of the railway in 1838 when the steamship company's name was very evident in the celebrations. Plus, the railway company's brilliant and energetic young engineer, Brunel, was providing his services free to the steamship company, presumably with the knowledge and support of the railway board. Bright, Guppy, Scott and Pycroft were directors of both companies. In what was left of his spare time, Brunel put considerable energy into matters to do with the *Great Western* and then *Great Britain*. He had apparently been one of the original shareholders, but his name was among those who had not fully paid for their shares. He did not settle this debt until 1844.[16] This rather suggests that in the beginning his services were not quite as free as was suggested. In shipowning it had been common practice for shares under the shared ownership scheme to be given in lieu of payment to some suppliers. It is purely speculation, but it is possible that Brunel was rewarded in this way and that the financial problems that later afflicted the company meant he had to contribute.

At the first annual general meeting after the successful start of the service to New York, the chairman, Peter Maze, asked Christopher Claxton to read his report. Claxton took pleasure in pointing a finger at the doom-mongers and naysayers. 'Your first ship,' he announced, 'has disproved all unfavourable auguries, and has rewarded your enterprise with great repute, and an encouraging return upon your capital has firmly established your line, and laid the foundation of its increased prosperity.'[17]

It had not, however, been without its challenges; being the flagbearer of a wholly new service with an experimental ship carried with it costs and lessons to be learned. These challenges he described as grave, and they arose from 'the novelty of the undertaking itself, the before untried scale of Passenger accommodation involved in it, the variety of departments which the business of the Ship has to embrace and the very short periods to which her stay in Port has been limited'.[18] He expressed thanks to Guppy and Claxton, but the 'warmest acknowledgments are due to Mr IK Brunel for a continued and deep interest in your undertaking, by which the same eminent science is ensured in aid of its progress, which was the groundwork of its first success'.[19] The ship had proved itself beyond doubt and reflected well upon the building committee's thorough research, Brunel's engineering and Patterson's skills. Even after 35,000 nautical miles and heavy weather in the Atlantic, the ship was as sound as ever and had scarcely a wrinkle in her copper sheathing, showing that the hull had not been unduly worked or strained.

The biggest lesson learned involved the most important revenue stream: the passengers. As the passenger numbers had increased, so too had the limitations of the original design in the steward's department, where there was insufficient space for preparing food. The winter voyages had also shown up problems for passengers that were not enumerated, and in anticipation of demand, additional passenger cabins were added.[20]

The ship, with her Maudslay engines, had performed steadily and consistently, travelling out in just under sixteen days with an average time home of thirteen and a half days. Nearly 1,000 passengers had been carried in 1838 and around 100 tons of freight. Fuel was the great expense, and there was careful monitoring of different types of coal. American-sourced coal was less effective and they had proved what they already knew: that Welsh coal was the best. The implication was expensive, as the coal had to be shipped to New York, and 1,000 tons was sent over to their yard in New York. Additionally, the United States imposed a duty of two-pence per bushel for imported coal. The other big cost was at Bristol. Due to her size, she had to remain at the mouth of the Avon at Kingroad, where moorings were put down for her. This was some miles downriver from the Bristol docks, but the Bristol Dock Company still insisted on charging dues.

The original plan was to build an identical sister ship to provide continuity of service and resilience. The directors, however, had changed their minds – supposedly due to 'the unusual caution in the construction and an increased conviction that the nearest possible approach to perfection must be kept in view'. Despite already having purchased the necessary timber, progress had slowed and they announced that the second vessel would be made of iron. The company had acquired premises on the banks of the floating harbour, and workshops and machinery were now being built. This decision was to have consequences for the fate of the *Great Western*.

A dividend of £5 per cent was declared and the meeting finished in the normal way, with thanks to the board of directors, bankers and auditors. Brunel was particularly thanked for his important services, and Claxton was singled out for his 'zeal and ability and exertions on behalf of the company', but the final vote of thanks, described as the 'best thanks of the meeting', went to Thomas Richard Guppy Esquire, the 'original projector of this undertaking'. It was an upbeat report with much possibility for the future, but there were rather more clouds looming on the horizon then the directors were prepared to admit.[21]

The directors did not have it all their own way; a local newspaper published a highly critical letter from John Jacque of Clifton who opined, 'On a calm review of the whole case you will be inclined to ask what is to be done? Our receipts have been enormous, our profits nil. One thing is clear, the expenditure on the ship has been profuse.' Jacque was amazed at the expenditure on the furnishings and plate and seemed to have forgotten the principal aim had been to attract superior paying passengers and to outdo the sailing packets in luxury. 'Stewards stores, earthenware, hardware and plate £1,073,' he exclaimed, and words failed him over the 'Cabin furniture £3,478 !!!, Bed and table linen and upholstery £1,073 and Glass £435.'[22]

Keeping the shareholders happy was important, and as long as it was just the occasional grumble, this could be managed. There were some minor operational challenges, not least the continuing interest of the public in visiting the ship. Being moored at Kingroad required the hiring of steam packets to convey passengers and luggage from Bristol to the mouth of the Avon. The steam packets were the regular operators along the river, and other interested parties decided they would join to visit the ship. This caused problems in boarding the increasing number of passengers, who were probably unimpressed about being pushed aside by sightseers. The company then had to place an advertisement declaring that the steamers on these occasions were hired for the exclusive use of the *Great Western* and that 'no person unconnected with the ship's business will be allowed to intrude on the accommodation engaged for the passengers'.[23] The distance to and from the ship also had implications for servicing and provision of supplies, so disbursements more than doubled.

While many of the directors were on the town council and other influential bodies and could influence much that went on in Bristol, the Bristol Dock Company was a major obstacle. Other ports, notably Liverpool, were spending large sums of money improving facilities to attract trade, but not Bristol. A local poet summarised the situation in an ode dedicated to Captain Hosken:

Hull, Liverpool and other ports aloud
Cry 'Go a-head';
A certain place that I know seems to say
'Reverse,' instead.[24]

The reason for the apparent intransigence was that the Dock Company was a private company and was undercapitalized. Repairs to the floating harbour regularly took up the entire operating surplus. It was not attractive to investors. The Dock Company directors' policy was to extract every possible dock due to which they were legally entitled, and they took a very cautious approach since many shareholders were children or widows, so income rather than investment was the priority. High dues and limited facilities and a long and tortuous passage along the Avon was not a profitable scenario for shipowners. Claxton and others had been convinced that this could be changed and that the dock company would work with them to ensure the success of such a high-profile enterprise for Bristol. In this they would be very much mistaken.

The town council and its nominated directors on the Dock Company found themselves unable to persuade the owners to change their attitude or to understand the accumulating effects of neglect and penal tariffs. Finally, threats by the Great Western Steam Ship Company that without support it would move its headquarters elsewhere led in June 1839 to a conference to try to resolve the impasse. Massive borrowing was proposed, harbour rates were to be abolished and tonnage dues cut to attract trade and benefit the *Great Western*. Though some minor progress was made the Dock Company overall remained recalcitrant, seeing minimal returns in the short term, and it would not be until 1848, too late for the *Great Western* by then, that the Bristol Docks Transfer Act repealed all dock Acts and transferred the docks and associated assets to the council.[25]

Mooring the ship downriver at Kingroad was a logistical problem. Here all passengers, their luggage and freight had to be transported along the Avon to load and unload the ship, a task that would have been considerably easier had she been lined up against a wharf. Management of freight and luggage can be handled more easily and controlled better on a quayside. A particular problem occurred on the fifth voyage. With limited time, not all packages were properly stowed; in addition, some items were too large to be passed through the hatches. But Claxton ordered the ship to sail at its appointed time, even with its decks so cluttered. Normally this could have been managed, but they were unfortunate to meet a hurricane which damaged the goods on deck, resulting in claims of £1,500. This led to new rules limiting the amount of passenger baggage – restrictions on passenger luggage are not new – and requiring cargo for outward journeys to be at the quay at Bristol several days before sailing.[26] Henceforth the advertisements announced a limit of 15 cubic feet per person, and any extra had to be booked as cargo.

Servicing the ship was proving difficult. She could be inspected partly while at low tide, but a detailed and thorough inspection demanded dry docking. The ship, with its paddle wheels, could not go through the locks at the Cumberland Basin entry and into the floating harbour. Claxton had been confident that the Dock Company would widen the gates, but this did not happen and so the first dry-docking had to be done elsewhere. Fortunately, good relations with the Admiralty enabled the use of their dockyard at Pembroke in Wales. Although little repair work was needed, there were the other matters to be attended to: improvements to the amount of cabin accommodation, providing a promenade area, extending the space for cooking and stewarding. The following season, due to a shift of attitude by the Dock Company, they were able to get the ship into the Bristol docks. The Dock Company assisted by moving some bridges and, with part of the paddle wheels removed, access was achieved. While there, the company took the voluntary step of asking the local Lloyd's surveyor of shipping to examine the ship. At that time, there was no official classification for the *Great Western*. George Bayley, the surveyor, was most impressed. Even after 75,000 miles of service he found the ship, particularly in those areas where he would have expected some strain and some movement in a steamship, to be 'in the same state as when I examined them on receiving the machinery on board in London' – praise indeed as he congratulated them on 'the magnificent experiment'.[27]

Having the ship once more in the heart of the city, and easily accessible, attracted an increased stream of visitors. There were 5,000 visitors during the winter of 1839/40 and the company still charged an entrance fee so they could keep some control but, fully alert to the bad publicity previously generated, they donated all funds to the General Hospital and Bristol Infirmary, raising £53.

Meanwhile, in 1839 the ever creative and energetic Brunel had some suggestions to make for improving access. These he outlined in a report to the committee of the council of the councillors in Bristol; in other words, not to the dock organisation. He made many suggestions, including stripping and widening the course of the river, and constructing docks at Sea Mills about 2 miles below Bristol. He also came up a with a solution to the docking and mooring challenge by suggesting a large pier at Portishead. Due to the tidal conditions in the Bristol Channel, which were extreme, it could not be a conventional pier. It was also very muddy, which would cause considerable difficulties in building a structure. Brunel saw the best option as a floating pier.[28]

I propose two or three vessels of 300 or 200 feet in length, built of iron, as the material cheapest and best adapted to the purpose, of 16 feet or 20 feet draught of water, and a boat 38 beam, moored close stem and stern and so as to form one continuous floating body. Any steam vessel alongside would, of course be on the same level as the pier; the passengers on disembarking will at once be on a level platform or deck, on the shelter, with the luggage and goods can also be placed, and the communication with the shore will be affected without steps ... Such a pier would afford stowage of almost any quantity of coals, freshwater and general goods, which could be stored here for embarkation.

It would not be until 1847 that an Act of Parliament was passed for a railway from Bristol to Portishead with a pier at Portishead. Brunel's design then was the same described in this report of 1839, but the later project did not proceed either.[29]

The directors, as ever, were optimistic that local difficulties could be managed, and there was a big prize on the horizon that would alleviate financial challenges. In November 1838, the government placed an advertisement asking for companies to tender for the postal service between England and Halifax with an additional link between Halifax and New York. Steam vessels were to be of no less than 300 horsepower and would sail each month throughout the year. The departure port was to be one of five options: Liverpool, Bristol, Plymouth, Falmouth or Southampton. In view of the limited number of steamships then in operation or in build, it gave an impossibly tight schedule, requesting that the service would commence on 1 April 1839.[30] The subsidy available would resolve any operational cost for the successful bid, and by the closing date of 15 December 1838 the St George Steam Packet Company, owner of the *Sirius*, with strong links to the British and American Steam Company, put in a tender to the Admiralty; so did the Great Western Steam Ship Company.

Claxton, on behalf of the company, wrote a very confident letter to their lordships:

Sirs,

I am instructed by the directors of the Great Western Steam Ship Company to express to their lords of the Admiralty their willingness to enter into a contract for the conveyance of Her Majesty's mails to and from England and Halifax, Nova Scotia; but I am desired to state that the time specified in the form of tender is too short to allow them to make the necessary arrangements.

The experiments of the last voyage of the *Great Western* has established, in the opinion of the directors, that no vessel of less than 1,000 tons register if built of iron, or 1,200 tons register, if of timber, and with engines of not less than 350 horse power, will be adequate to the duties required, and three such vessels will be necessary.

The time required for the construction, equipment and trial of these vessels and engines will be not less than 18 to 24 months from the date of the contract.

From and after such a period, the directors will be willing to contract for monthly departures to and from England and Halifax, for the sum of £45,000 per annum; on condition that the contract remains in force for the seven years from its commencement, and subject to all other conditions being agreed upon between the board of Admiralty and the directors.[31]

The Great Western Steam Ship Company knew it was in a strong position. It was the only active steamship service then in operation across the Atlantic. The *British Queen* had been launched in June 1838 but was not yet in service.[32] In October, the Transatlantic Steamship Company in Liverpool had launched the *Liverpool* into service. They had tried out an existing steamship called *Royal William* (not the original Canadian ship), a 617-ton coastal vessel, rather like the experiment of the *Sirius*. The *Royal William* was withdrawn after just three crossings. Their new ship, the 1,050-ton *Liverpool*, had accommodation for ninety-eight passengers and 468 horsepower engines and two funnels. But she was no competition, being plagued with slow crossings and inefficient fuel consumption.[33] Claxton's confidence also came from the knowledge that work was progressing on their second highly innovative ship. In addition, they had good reason to think that their proposal would be warmly considered as they had already had several meetings with influential figures in Canada and at the Colonial Office.

The events that led to Claxton's confident letter went back to the highly publicised first crossing of the *Sirius* and *Great Western* and to growing Canadian determination for increased autonomy. The economy was expanding and investment was needed in infrastructure and communications. The Canadians – Joseph Howe, a journalist and politician, and Thomas Haliburton, a

Supreme Court judge – were close friends and were on board the packet ship *Tyrian* on route to Falmouth in May 1838. With them was Charles Fairbanks, a barrister and Master of the Rolls of Nova Scotia, who was hoping to raise money for the proposed Shubenacadie Canal. He was also a former director of the Halifax Steam Boat Company. Then there was Captain Robert Carmichael-Smyth, who was interested in building railroads in North America.[34] While becalmed they met the *Sirius* on her return passage. The *Tyrian* commander, concerned about the delay to the official mail he was carrying, asked his fellow naval officer, Roberts, to take them on board his steamer. The letter bags were transferred via a small boat and Howe and Haliburton took the chance to go with the mailbags to see the steamship for themselves. Returning to the *Tyrian*, it aroused a debate over the possibility of a steam mail service between England and Halifax. They were on the only Admiralty Service between Britain and North America, a direct monthly service to Halifax from Falmouth served by sailing packets, dependent on the wind or, as they were experiencing then, a lack of wind.[35] Fired with enthusiasm that a steam service could now be accomplished, they landed in May 1838 at Falmouth, then the major packet station in England with sailing ship connections to many different countries. Here, they were surprised to find that there were already rumours that the government was contemplating a steam line for mails to Halifax or New York. As Falmouth, had been the base for government mail packets since the seventeenth century, it is not surprising that the place was well informed. Howe, in a letter to his Canadian newspaper, warned Nova Scotians of the risk of such a service going to New York and that it would be sad to see 'instead of this natural nurture, the tide of importance and prosperity suicidally directed to strangers and rivals'.[36]

The two men headed for London, but instead of taking a direct route across the country they went via Bristol. Here Judge Haliburton managed to meet with Claxton and later met some of the other owners. Haliburton laid out his ideas and the steamship company naturally expressed an interest – dependent, however, on government subsidy.[37] Haliburton later wrote that he was grateful to Claxton and the board of directors at Bristol for their most 'courteous treatment', when 'personally suggesting the propriety and discussing the feasibility of establishing a steam communication with Nova Scotia'.[38]

His fellow passengers from the *Tyrian* had not been slow to canvass support either. Fairbanks was also pursuing the matter and he was talking to the owners of the *British Queen*. Howe and Haliburton eventually reached London, where Judge William Crane and Henry Bliss were also petitioning the government for a regular steam service. Crane had personal experience of the crossing, having just arrived on the first eastward passage of the *Great Western* in May that year.[39] Howe and Crane sent a letter to the colonial secretary, Lord Glenelg, on 24 August 1838 pressing the point about a steam service to Halifax and saying it was a 'measure of absolute necessity' and crucial if Great Britain was to 'maintain her footing on the North American continent', and highlighted the vital importance of the speedy transmission of government dispatches and commercial information through channels 'exclusively British'.[40] There was another Halifax man in London at this time who was fully alive to the possibilities and he certainly met at least with Howe and Fairbanks therefore he had first-hand information on the progress of both transatlantic ships. This was Samuel Cunard, a highly experienced businessman with investments in more than thirty ships, and it is estimated that he gained at least £2,000 a year from his East India Company tea agency.[41] He had been involved in the early steamship *Royal William*, albeit in management rather than investment.[42] His experience of that project was not one to encourage investment in transatlantic steamships at the time and Cunard was a man of caution. Now he had the direct evidence from Howe and Crane of the success of the two latest steamships.

A patriotic motive has been suggested for Cunard's interest. 'The New York packet lines, faster and more reliable, had taken most of the transatlantic mail away from the Admiralty's ships', and it is suggested that as a Canadian and British subject Cunard was keen to take it back to Canada.[43] This sounds noble, but far more likely is that, knowing it was now practically possible, Cunard's business nose told him that with government backing this would be a worthwhile investment. He promptly booked passage, not on a direct packet ship to Halifax but on a steamship to New York, the

Great Western, and sailed with her from Bristol on 18 June 1838.[44] He was going to experience it for himself.

Back in Bristol, the Great Western Steam Ship Company had not lingered since their meeting with Haliburton and they enlisted the assistance of their friendly local Member of Parliament. The always well-informed *Bristol Mercury* announced in September that a deputation from the company 'composed of Mr Hawes MP, Mr Claxton, and Mr Guppy, had an interview with Lord Glenelg on Monday at the Colonial Office'.[45] There was but one topic they wanted to discuss.

Judge Crane and his wife returned to New York on the *Great Western*, arriving on 15 November 1838. The advertisement for the mail contract came out while they were at sea, but a man with his good connections in government may already had some idea of what was being proposed. On returning to Canada, the various interested parties had the opportunity to share information and continue the push for a direct link to Halifax.

One historian suggests that 'holding all the cards, the Bristol company proceeded to overplay its hand' and that the superior tone of the letter annoyed the Admiralty. He also adds a second reason why the Admiralty might not support the bid, which is annoyance over Guppy's previous criticism of the design of the Royal Navy's steamships. Guppy had been reported as saying that their power and size were disproportionate, and made jokes at the Admiralty's expense, suggesting they were more suited as museum exhibits.[46] But Guppy was not alone in his criticism of the Admiralty ships; they were aging, and the pace of technological change was very fast. Then there is this new evidence of the meeting with both Haliburton and Lord Glenelg of the Colonial Office. Claxton, ever the optimist, must have felt that all was on their side. In this they were to be disappointed. The short, formal and quite standard reply from the Admiralty came on 10 January:

Having laid before my Lords Commissioners of the Admiralty, your letter of 13th ultimo, stating the conditions under which the Great Western Steam Ship Company would be disposed to enter into a contract for the conveyance of Her Majesty's mails from

England and Halifax by steam vessels, I am commanded by Their Lordships to acquaint you that they decline this offer.[47]

In Halifax the original Admiralty tender was advertised, although now somewhat out of date. Samuel Cunard took passage to England apparently unaware of what had occurred between the Great Western Steam Ship Company and the Admiralty, but well aware of the potential for a mail contract and what he might need to do to achieve it. Cunard later stated that he came to 'England in the winter of 1839 with a view expressly trying to persuade the government'. He was asked if he knew of the advertisement. He replied, 'No I was not. When I came here my views were perfectly irrespective of anybody else's plan and I knew nothing about anybody else's plan.' He also confirmed that he had not discussed his plans with anyone except his son. Cunard was a little careful in his language here as he had arrived well prepared with letters of introduction from Sir Colin Campbell, Lieutenant Governor of Nova Scotia, to Lord Glenelg and he had excellent personal connections with James Melvill, secretary of the Honourable East India Company, and Sir Edward Parry, who was the Controller of Steam at the Admiralty.[48]

Cunard's unofficial proposal was made on 11 February and offered a more regular service of forty-eight voyages per year for a subsidy of £55,000 a year compared to the Great Western Steam Ship Company's proposal of £45,000 for twenty-four trips. Meanwhile, Cunard's brother Joseph travelled back from England to Halifax via New York on the *Great Western* in the company of Judge Haliburton, taking with them the news of the contract and testing out the new service.[49] The Admiralty signalled its interest and Cunard headed to Scotland for discussions with the shipbuilders Robert Napier and John Wood of Glasgow. Cunard needed to raise money and brought in George Burns and David and Charles MacIver, all of whom were experienced coastal steamship operators. The contract signed with the government in June 1839 by Cunard, Burns and the MacIvers was for four steamships sailing monthly between Liverpool and Halifax, and then the mail would be sent onward by steam packet to Boston. The British Government would pay £60,000 a year for seven years.[50]

Cunard's service commenced on the 4 July 1840. It was not straightforward and after the first winter season a request was made to reduce the sailing to one per month in the winter to twenty rather than the contracted twenty-four voyages in the year. Seeing the risk that Cunard might abandon the contract, the Admiralty increased the contract price to £80,000, which included a small steamer to be operated on the Saint Lawrence River. Cunard began with three vessels built in Scotland in 1840, and the fourth, *Columbia*, began operating in 1841.[51]

For the Great Western Steam Ship Company the lack of a contract was major blow, not just financially but also to their prestige, and Claxton was to remain convinced that the government had acted wrongly and that the contract had been stolen from them. From his perspective he had a point, but from the government viewpoint the deal with Cunard was the right one. Cunard was an established and experienced owner of shipping; the Navy had, they said, examined his business accounts thoroughly. Cunard also had mail experience, handling government mail along the rivers and coasts of Canada. Since the early 1820s the Bermuda mail had been taken by a branch packet from Halifax. The contractor for this service was Samuel Cunard of Halifax. Newfoundland was also served from Halifax.[52] In contrast, the Bristol company was small, had been in operation a very short time and had yet to produce its second experimental ship. The other major consideration was that Cunard was well connected in the Canadian hierarchy. With recent tensions over the land border with the United States and internal disputes between upper and lower Canada, the British Government needed the support of the Canadian authorities and to satisfy what was clearly a strong Canadian lobby group.

The *Great Western* continued her steady passage back and forth across the Atlantic and the building of her sister ship began. For one more year she would be untroubled by direct competition. She continued to make excellent time and her fifteen days became a steady thirteen. In May Hosken was presented by the passengers with a telescope, inscribed with a record of the 'then unparalleled achievement'.[53] Cunard's service to Halifax began in 1840 with three vessels departing from Liverpool. He did not have it all his own way, and the New York destination and the *Great Western* remained very popular.[54]

While the Transatlantic Steamship Company sold their poorly performing ship *Liverpool* to P&O in July 1840, the ship which caused Claxton and the directors greater concern was John Junius Smith's *British Queen*. His company, the British and American Steamship Company, began its service to New York from London in July 1839 and it was an advantage to those passengers who did not wish to take the more complex journey to the *Great Western*. The railway was open only as far as Twyford, so they had to transfer to a coach and then transfer again to steamer for a three-to four-hour journey down the Avon. Claxton kept a close eye on the *British Queen*, seeing her as their biggest rival. Anxious to ensure the good reputation of the *Great Western*, he wrote a short but effective letter to the editor of *The Times* in October 1839 to correct a report. It had been claimed by a city merchant that despite repeated calls at the office in London he had been unable to get his goods from the ship as they were not yet landed. Claxton rushed into print to point out that they did not have offices in Billiter Street and that the *Great Western* was mid-ocean so it could not be them. For good measure, he wrote, 'I take leave to add, that we of the *Great Western* are too well aware of the importance of despatch to spare exertion in the speedy delivery of whatever is intrusted to our care.'[55] *The Times* corrected their report and the *British Queen* was named as the dilatory ship.

Mr Ward in the London office of the Great Western Railway kept Claxton well informed about the *British Queen*. He wrote in April 1840 with the news that the *British Queen* had arrived with fifty-seven passengers and a full cargo of flour and that they were boasting of beating the *Great Western* by nine hours. Ward obtained a copy of the log of the *British Queen* and sent it down to Bristol and continued to give occasional reports on her passenger numbers.[56] The rival company was well on its way with their second ship, *President*, which made its maiden voyage from Liverpool in August 1840. But Claxton need not have been so concerned as both ships belonging to the British and American Steamship Company had difficulties. Neither performed as well as the *Great Western*, and 1841 was a disastrous year. The *British Queen* had serious damage to her port paddle wheel and encountered a bad storm; she limped into Halifax as the nearest port. When she eventually arrived in New York she had taken twenty-four days. She returned in sixteen, another slow crossing. Her sister ship was lost in the same storm on the eastward passage. This tragedy claimed 136 passengers and crew including Captain Roberts, who had been master of the *Sirius* and later of the *British Queen*. Unable to recover from this, the company sold the *British Queen* to the Belgian government and later, after unsuccessful attempts to run her across the Atlantic, she was laid up in 1842 and subsequently scrapped.[57] The main competitor now was Cunard, but at least his ships were not in direct competition for New York.

The port problems in Bristol were not resolved, and so in 1842 it was decided to try Liverpool as a departure point and alternate it with Bristol. Liverpool had spent vast sums on its docks, which lined the Mersey River. Here, cargo and passengers could be boarded more easily and there were hopes of increased cargo to and from the industrial Midlands. Some Bristol shareholders were not happy to see their ship move away from the port, but there were other financial woes in Bristol.

A national recession was taking its toll on some Bristol businesses, and this affected some of the company's proprietors. Acraman was a leading shareholder in the *Great Western* and his firm were iron merchants, wholesale ironmongers and founders, with a foundry at Bathurst Basin. They had big expansion plans, and were moving into building locomotives and steam engines at St Philips and ships at a new yard at Clift House, Bedminster. But the recession forced them into bankruptcy, and the effects were felt widely in the local business community.[58] Other *Great Western* shareholders were also feeling the pinch and put pressure on the steamship company to cut costs as the new ship became increasingly expensive. The directors had decided, against Brunel's advice, to build the engines themselves and had purchased a dockyard and other premises in Bristol. In January 1842, with a need for more capital, these were put up for sale.[59]

At the company's annual general meeting in March 1842, the directors – Kington as chairman, with Bright, Bush, Guppy, Scott, Goodwin, Miles, Were and Claxton – reported falling income.

Initially it had been intended to run a full-year service, but the winter runs were stopped after three seasons. From six round voyages in 1840 they had income of £49,267 and expenses of £41,186. In 1841 there were five round voyages and income had fallen to £33,763 with expenses of £30,649. In addition, there were still those who had taken out shares but who had as yet not paid for them, giving a cash shortfall.[60]

The ship was still a considerable tourist sight and the local steamers provided day trips. The *Cambrian* advertised for passengers to travel from Hotwells, just outside the floating dock in Bristol, to see the ship at its moorings and to witness its departure. 'The *Cambrian* leaves the Hotwells at ten o'clock in the morning and returns in the evening.'[61] But despite such interest the financial pressure was on the directors, desperate as they were to keep their big new project, *Great Britain*, on track, with its innovative design and screw propeller. After the success of the *Great Western*, this new ship would be another world first and the directors were confident of success. The rest of the proprietors, who had seen their shares diminish in value, were less convinced and the decision was made to sell the *Great Western*. It was, however, a very odd auction.

The auction had been advertised for a while, and private bidders had been encouraged. As none were forthcoming, or not at the right price, it proceeded to the public auction on 17 October 1842. The conditions of sale included the clause that the purchaser must complete the voyage already arranged – it was due out on the 22nd – and indemnify the company against any loss. Strangely no directors, not even Claxton, were present at the auction. The only representative was Robert Osborne from their lawyers, Osborne, Ward & Co. The potential bidders requested more information from the auctioneer as it was not clear what was included. There was no inventory of the plate and furniture, which would be normal in any sale. The auctioneer, Mr Clark, could not say, and Osbourne was similarly unsure but eventually said it was included. The bidding opened at £16,000, went up by increments of £1,000 to £39,000 then slowed, bids only coming in £100 increments. Eventually, when the open bidding reached £40,000 it was announced as sold, but not to anyone in the room. When asked who was the buyer, Mr Clark said, 'Gentlemen I have to announce to you that the ship is bought in for the proprietors, but I shall be happy to treat with any gentleman by private contract.' There was uproar and confusion. A Mr Cunningham protested loudly and was supported by his fellow bidders: 'I beg as a proprietor to enter my protest against this solemn mockery of pretending to knock down the vessel at £40,000.'[62] Either the ship had not realised the sum of money wanted by the directors or they were simply trying to appease the shareholders by testing the market.

Newspapers were quick to report this, and the Liverpool newspaper *Albion* got wind of the difficulties and suggested that the ship would 'shortly be obliged to discontinue running between this country and America'. They thought it madness on the owners' behalf to continue to run the ship and make losses. Debt figures from the recent meeting were reported and it was also suggested that a minimum of £40,000 or more would be required to 'pay off their outstanding debts and complete the enormous ship now in the course of building'. The calls outstanding for arrears on the shares were given as £27,000.[63] If some shareholders were concerned, then such adverse reports made them even more uneasy, and it needs to be remembered that under the deed of settlement arrangement they were not just shareholders, liable for their shares' costs, they were all equal partners and liable for any further debts run up by the company. Things looked bleak.

The negative publicity continued. The *Albion*'s prediction was picked up by *The Times*, and the rumour found its way across to the United States via 'the Boston boat', as Cunard's steamship service was known. Additionally, the *Albion* suggested that the Boston boat made 'shorter passages than the *Great Western*'. This was too much for Claxton who leapt into the fray, writing to *The Times* with a statement to show that an injustice was done to the *Great Western*. *The Times* published the letter, adding that their original source for the story came from a proprietor of the *Great Western*. Being used to Claxton's letter writing, they then added, 'We may be permitted to say, that gentlemen in the situation of Captain Claxton are too prone to suspect the writers of paragraphs respecting the performances of rival steamers as actuated by sinister motives' and stood by their story.[64]

The Liverpool *Albion* could not resist a reply in its columns, again picked up by *The Times*, and gave their opinion that 'Captain Claxton was, and always is, too sensitive about the *Great Western*'.[65] The *Bristol Mirror* naturally came to the aid of Claxton, claiming the originator of the rumours to be a dissatisfied shareholder and wondering what that person had been paid for the article. They accused the Liverpool paper of bias, and urged Claxton not to take the debate further.

> We cannot conclude our remarks without stating that this is the third time that influences favourable to competing vessels, and at the expense of the Great Western, have been drawn through the London journals, that it is, in your opinion, the duty of Captain Claxton to be watchful. It is certainly extremely hard that the only Atlantic steamer (and that, too, the one whose success led the way to the establishment of the several lines now steaming) which up to this moment is ploughing the Atlantic unsupplied by public money in the form of government grants, should not meet with fair support from the public press.[66]

Despite the local newspaper attempting to calm matters, the rumours, the oddly run auction, poor financial returns and general nerves induced some proprietors to rebel. The unhappy proprietors appointed a separate committee of ten who wrote a report with several proposals to be put to the whole of the shareholding, and they requested it was widely circulated. Since the main thrust of their argument was that it 'may not be desirable to complete the *Great Britain*', unsurprisingly this circulation did not occur. The committee of ten proprietors requested a meeting of all shareholders to consider the situation of the company's affairs and asked that the directors reduce the expenditure at the yard until the meeting. The meeting was set up for an angry confrontation, and the next month there was an extraordinary general meeting. The press were refused entry, but fortunately for the newspapers they were subsequently well briefed by one of those attending the meeting.

George Jones, chairman of the proprietors' committee of ten, presented the report, which recommended the sale of all the company property and the winding up of the concern. A lengthy debate elicited further information. Again the costs were attacked, including salaries: Captain Hosken 'was paid a considerably higher salary than any captain in the service of West India Mail Company or Cunard's line'. (Claxton's salary was stated at £300 per annum; he was, as many people knew, still taking the salary as quay warden at £400 per annum.) Once again, the cost of the cabin furniture, plate, glass and linen of the *Great Western* was given as excessive.

Robert Bright, on behalf of the directors, disagreed with the committee and showed a different set of figures that gave a less bleak picture. The *Great Western*, he said, was yielding profit to the company at present, and he talked the meeting into a new deal. It was agreed by the proprietors that the ship could resume her station in the spring unless advantageously sold, and the *Great Britain* would be completed and fitted for sea; furthermore, a loan not exceeding £20,000 would be taken out to carry out the objects.[67] With a vote of thanks to the chairman, heartfelt in some cases, and to the committee of ten, the proprietors separated in a 'much better humour than they manifested at the commencement of proceedings'. Robert Bright had saved the day for the *Great Britain*, but the *Great Western* was still to be sacrificed.[68]

Meanwhile, the company had not given up on the mail contracts. Claxton was terrier-like on this issue, and a petition had been handed in to the Lords of the Treasury earlier in the year complaining about their treatment as, in their view, they deserved support as the pioneers of Atlantic steam navigation. It was generally agreed, at least in Bristol, that as the pioneers of such an advance in communications and commerce something more was due to them than the cool and discouraging reply 'that their tender had not been accepted' and their enterprise had been badly rewarded, with the mail contract being 'handed over to a rival, who had borrowed their discovery and benefitted by their experience'. But it did say that they would have been better to continue by building another *Great Western* rather than 'attempting to surpass their own original design by constructing that leviathan of the deep which is now on the stocks'.[69]

The 1843 season was difficult to plan, with the ship potentially up for sale. It was decided that Liverpool would become the sole terminal as the costs at Bristol were just too high, and in February the ship sailed for New York, but unusually it took a longer route and sailed via Madeira. Fifty passengers were booked for New York at forty one guineas each and a few more to Madeira at a fare of £24 10s. But why stop at Madeira? This was apparently done at the request of 'large mercantile houses, and other parties in the habit of travelling by her'.[70] At her launch the ship was bathed in Madeira; it was very popular fortified wine, and the Madeiran merchants had for some time been managing business on a global scale. 'By the early nineteenth century, a Madeira wine trader managed suppliers, shippers, customers and products over multiple years and vast distances.'[71] They had extensive contacts from the small Atlantic island across to North America and across Europe and were well connected in Bristol.[72]

The ship arrived at Funchal on 19 February and remained for thirty hours, taking on extra coal in very windy conditions. The merchants on the island hoped that the ship would also call there on the return journey, and so a poster was circulated by John Blandy and Sons advertising that, subject to demand, the ship would call back to the island on or about 28 March. The ship then took twenty days from Funchal to New York and on the way discovered the disadvantages of sailing south. All the ice in the icehouse melted and the thermometer measured 70°F. Fortunately, there were enough provisions on board.[73]

After a speedy four-day turnaround in New York, she headed back direct to Liverpool since there was insufficient demand for a return via Funchal. The *Great Western* was a ship that had suffered few mishaps and had an enviable reputation for safety. This time, however, on her way out of port she ran aground on a sand bank, the error being attributed to the pilot. She floated off and proceeded with care to Liverpool, but the insurers wanted a dry dock inspection. As none were available in Liverpool the ship had to use the Admiralty facilities in South Wales again. This caused a delay in sailing, and the next one was cancelled; passengers were refunded where required, and a reduced fare of 30 guineas was announced.[74] *Lloyd's List*, the weekly shipping newspaper, was sympathetic and full of praise.

Not the slightest blame attaches to Captain Hosken; the misfortune is entirely attributed to the pilot. We cannot but regret that any injury should have occurred to this celebrated vessel, seeing the great success that had before attended her. It is about five years this vessel has been running, and, with the exception of her last voyage which occupied 28 days on the outward and 15 days on the homeward passage, her performance has been very astonishing.[75]

It was a financial loss to the company, but she was holding up well against Cunard, who dropped some of their fares to Halifax and Boston to 30 guineas, notably only on those sailing on the same dates as the *Great Western*. Samuel Cunard later denied any personal knowledge of the fare cutting as he was in Halifax at the time. He added that he had 'been sorry for it since ... it was done without my concurrence', which was a remarkably similar answer to that given on previous occasions when Cunard distanced himself from unpopular management decisions. It is hard to believe that a businessman as experienced as Cunard did not have clear lines agreed about his agents' authority. The Cunard company had also cut their freight rates to compete directly with *Great Western*, again only on some sailings – and this, too, he denied. For the rest of 1843 the *Great Western* passenger numbers held up well, but there would be only five round voyages instead of the normally expected six.[76] In 1843, at the annual general meeting, Robert Bright retired 'in consequence of a domestic bereavement'. His loss to the company was much regretted. He had been there from the very beginning as 'a valued friend, a steady consistent and far seeing counsellor; one who far from being shaken by difficulties, brought fresh vigour to your counsels'.[77]

Meanwhile, in the autumn some maintenance was needed on the *Great Western*. Guppy recommended replacing the boilers as the old ones had reached the end of life and he strongly recommended a new type of tubular boiler that would take up less room, with the added advantage of providing more cargo space. It was done in the winter at their own yard. They consumed less fuel, the reduction saving was £275 in fuel per voyage, but the 'efficiency of operation was not matched by steaming capability'. Claxon was not happy about this reduction in efficiency and consulted Brunel for his advice. Brunel recommended different coal and a small auxiliary boiler to provide a boost, but his advice was not taken.[78]

Amid the general gloom there was a glimmer of success and hope for the future. The *Great Britain* was launched in July 1843 to great fanfare and the Prince Consort, Prince Albert himself, had attended the occasion. By the annual general meeting in 1844 the directors could report an improvement in profits. The receipts for 1843 were £33,406, expenditure £25,573, which was an improvement over 1842's receipts of £30,890 and expenditure of £28,615. Liverpool proved to be the better station for business.

A few months later there came news of a 'curious dispute' regarding the *Great Western*. The Peninsular and Orient Company (P&O) had the mail contract for India. They ran steamers through the Mediterranean, took passengers and mail overland across Egypt and then continued by steamer through the Red Sea. They made a bid for the *Great Western* for £32,000 and wished to use her between Southampton and Alexandria. Government mail contracts had strict conditions and any newly acquired vessel had to pass a survey. The Great Western Steam Ship Company undertook to do whatever the Admiralty surveyor might deem necessary to qualify the vessel for mail services and were wholly confident of a positive result. Every surveyor since the ship was launched had made glowing comments on the quality of the build of the ship. The original building committee had been proved right in the ability of the ship to sustained the pressures of Atlantic service. In fact, the ship had at one time been over-strengthened with additional trusses to the transverse bulkheads. This caused problems of rigidity as a vessel needs some flexibility in the water. Patterson later wrote about this: 'The vessel having complained severely forward and aft and at the bulkheads until these fastenings were cut away, since which time she complains no more.'[79]

There was a trial of the ship and the Admiralty surveyor found everything in good order except for the new boilers, which did not supply enough steam in his view – and so he declined to pass the survey. Some adjustments were made and a second survey requested but no surveyor arrived on behalf of P&O. Deciding that they had lost interest, and anxious not to lose further revenue, the company advertised her for a voyage to New York, 'thus virtually cancelling the contract'. However, P&O did still want the ship and applied to the Court of Chancery 'to prohibit the vessel being sent to sea', and this was granted. The Great Western Company appealed against the injunction and sent the ship up to Liverpool to get ready for departure. The injunction was lifted and the contract for sale cancelled.[80] Having failed to realise any capital from the sale, the company now made a strange move considering their opposition to Cunard. They offered to remove the *Great Western* from the Atlantic crossing in return for a grant of £3,000 or £4,000 from Cunard. Cunard was not interested in the offer.[81] So, the *Great Western*, still with the company, was now at Liverpool preparing for departure but with a new master. Captain Hosken had moved to the *Great Britain* to get her ready for her inaugural voyage, so his number two, Barnard Mathews, at last had command.

8

Changing Hands

The future of the *Great Western* was still in doubt. Following the abortive sale to P&O, the ship, with Barnard Mathews now in command, left Liverpool on its first passage of 1844 in June. The confusion over the sale had affected passenger numbers, and it sailed with just thirty-five passengers on board. Also on board was Captain Hosken, but as a passenger; Hosken was on his way to New York to arrange berthing facilities for his new command, *Great Britain*, which was rapidly approaching completion in her fitting out.[1]

For the next few years, Mathews took the ship across between Liverpool and New York. In August 1844 the ship left Liverpool with 138 passengers, and this was Barnard Mathews' first true voyage as captain of the ship. Among his passengers on this occasion were first-timer and lace merchant George Moore, several actors and actresses, and the impresario George Simpson. Passenger numbers from Liverpool were still good and remained steady, averaging 108. Passengers numbers from New York were averaging 65 and had always been lower as the sailing packets still provided stiff competition on the eastward passage. The highest number between 1844 and 1845 was in May when 141 passengers came from New York.

Moore described Mathews as a 'gentlemanly, courteous, obliging little fellow'.[2] It was a different story, however, in September 1845 when John Jay Smith was left unimpressed by Mathews. The ship was overcrowded, the staff and service slow, and he and others were generally very unhappy passengers, contrasting the ship unfavourably with American ships:

> At our outset, it was evident to all that we were in an overcrowded ship; the *Great Western* is calculated for comfortably conveying about 100 and a commended 120 passengers; we had on board 160, a number purposely decreased in the statement on arrival to 153. Everybody that wished to go was admitted, and sometimes receipts were given twice for the same berths.

There was much confusion, all the settees were allocated, officers were turned out of their berths and the 'overworked servants slept on the back deck'. Service was slow and there were insufficient seats for everyone at the dining tables. 'In short so great was the number ... that we had a most comfortless passage.'[3] Captain Mathews, it seems, did not have Hosken's social skills: 'The present captain does not give as much satisfaction as did Captain Hosken; indeed, very serious complaints were made both respecting him and the steward.'[4] But Mathews' main task was the safety of his ship and the people on board and in that respect he never failed.

Smith suggests there was double booking of some berths that added to the problems. Bookings were made through various offices and agencies – London, Glasgow, Paris, Liverpool and Bristol – and had been coordinated at Bristol, with certain numbered berths allocated to each office. The London office was managed by the highly efficient Mr Ward, who was in daily communication by letter with Bristol, checking berths, confirming numbers and dealing with a variety of passenger enquiries. Now he had to work through Gibbs, Bright and Co., who handled all the main bookings in their Liverpool office. Ward's careful checking suggests that the overcrowding was an accidental miscommunication between the offices resulting in duplication of sales for berths.[5]

The passengers were not the only complainers, as payments were slow to suppliers. Grayson was a shipbuilder in Birkenhead and had problems getting his payment for work on the ship from Gibbs, Bright & Company, the Liverpool agents. Long lines of credit were the usual practice, but the letter from Grayson hints that he was getting concerned about the financial stability of the Great Western Steam Ship Company – and no doubt others were too.

> Dear Sir
>
> We omitted to mention in ours of the 14th ult that Messrs. Gibbs Bright and Co did not pay our account against the *Great Western* for the voyage before last and beg therefore to enclose you a copy in case the original has been mislaid. We hope we may augur formally from your silence on the subject of our last, at least if the adage be true that 'the news is good' by the way of it is intended to put the *Great Western* into the Graving Docks as we heard rumoured before she went out, it would be advisable to have her entered soon, as you are probably aware there is only one Dock here large enough to admit her & that generally in great demand.
>
> We remain your very obedient servant
> Thos Grayson.[6]

The Great Western Steam Ship Company had another priority: the *Great Britain*. At long last the great ship was almost ready to commence service and to realise the hopes of her owners. In July 1845 the *Great Britain* arrived in Liverpool, from where she would sail, and from then the sailing of both ships was managed so they did not berth at the same time. The company at last had two ships providing a full service. Bookings for both ships were good, and the future looked rosy. Passengers were attracted to the new ship, but bookings for the *Great Western* remained strong, regularly attracting more passengers than the new ship – perhaps out of loyalty to a tried and tested vessel.[7]

That same month, on the 29th, Claxton had an important meeting in London. After much lobbying he had succeeded, with the help of William Miles MP, to get a parliamentary enquiry into the awarding of the contract for the Halifax and Boston mails. It was a short enquiry, lasting a few days, and it called just four witnesses, including Samuel Cunard and Claxton. Claxton confirmed in his testimony that they had repeatedly asked the government for 'some remuneration for carrying the mails and to be allowed to be part of a contract'. He also confirmed that before the very first tender 'we had a good deal of communication with the Treasury and Post Office long before the government had told of having a contract at all'. He reaffirmed the pioneering nature of the company and the *Great Western*, which to that date had made eighty-four passages across the Atlantic and had always been punctual and efficient. Now matters were urgent, as Cunard's contract had been extended without any re-tendering and there were strong rumours that Cunard would be providing a subsidised mail service direct to New York.[8]

The committee presented its findings one week later in three short paragraphs. It concluded that the arrangement was on terms 'advantageous to the public service' and that Mr Cunard had efficiently performed the service. The committee then found that it was unable to comment whether things might have been better had it been thrown open to a public competition. Finally, in a sop to the Great Western Steam Ship Company, it finished with:

> ... cannot but regret that the above arrangements in both consequences were injurious to the Great Western Steam Ship Company; and, considering the meritorious character of the services as rendered by the latter company, and its priority of establishment of the New York line, will be glad if, on any future extension of the Royal Mail service, it receives the favourable consideration of the government.[9]

It was of little consolation and of no practical use whatsoever to the company, which had strained itself financially to achieve great marine engineering feats.

The year 1846 continued to provide memorable occasions, and both ships featured in the newspapers. The *Great Western* sailed out of Liverpool on 12 September and encountered the terrific gale already described in an earlier chapter. The *Illustrated London News* had a dramatic drawing of the ship in enormous seas on its front page. 'The engraving upon our front page shows this well-tried vessel, during the awful gale, on her late passage to New York. The moment depicted by the artist is when the steamer was struck amidships by a tremendous sea.'[10] They then quoted directly from the logbook: 'Eleven o'clock a.m. – a heavy sea broke over the fore-part of the starboard wheel-house.' The icehouse and other structures were washed away off the deck, the sails blew out in tatters and boats were torn from their fixings.[11] Mathews and his crew steamed the battered and damaged ship into New York on 30 September, grateful to the sturdy ship and engines which had brought them through safely but unaware of events on the coast of Ireland that would bring yet more headlines of a very unwelcome sort.

On 22 September, the *Great Britain* left Liverpool with 180 passengers to take the northerly route south of the Isle of Man and head around the Irish coast. She never made it into the Atlantic due to a major navigational error, and that night the new ship, the pride of the company, was stranded in Dundrum Bay. All passengers and crew were safe, but the financial situation of the Great Western Steam Ship Company was now fated. With little money for salvage and the Atlantic crossing under severe threat from a potential new mail contract for Cunard that would see it go into New York as a direct competitor, the writing was on the wall. The *Great Western* made one further round voyage, unusually late in the year, arriving back in Liverpool on 12 December 1846. She then headed to Bristol to be laid up as the cash-strapped company urgently needed funds from her sale to salvage the *Great Britain*.[12]

While the *Great Britain* continued to attract a different type of publicity – there was much speculation about the cause of the accident and debates about her future – the future of the *Great Western* was sealed in 1847. There was a public auction in Bristol on 11 March, but the bidding did not meet the reserve price of £25,000. William Patterson, her original builder, together with others, offered £22,000, but this was turned down. In April the full asking price was offered by another party, which would lead to a new lease of life for the ship.[13]

Sale of the *Great Western* steamship
The *Great Western* steam ship was sold at Bristol, on Friday, to Captain Chappell, the secretary of the West India steam packet mail company, for £25,000 exclusive of her plate, and which was the reserve price put on her when she was offered for sale by auction a few weeks since. She will proceed in a few days to

Southampton, from which port it is intended that she shall sail for a five month voyage, and that the expiration of the period we are informed that it is the company's intention to lay her up and expand a large sum upon her (a report says £10,000) in repairs, refitting etc.[14]

The West India Company's correct name was the Royal Mail Steam Packet Company, and it had the official mail service to the West Indies. The Royal Mail was an altogether bigger company, with sound financial backing and close connections at the very heart of the British establishment. It was a royal charter company rather than a small local partnership, and the *Great Western* itself had been a major influence on the Royal Mail's fleet of ships.[15] It was a natural fit.

The leading figure in the establishment of the Royal Mail Company was James MacQueen, but he was not from a conventional shipping background. Born in 1778 in Lanarkshire, Scotland, by 1796 he was the manager of a sugar plantation in Grenada and travelled extensively through the other West Indian colonies, having a personal interest in geography. By 1821 MacQueen had returned to Scotland and turned to journalism, becoming the editor and part-owner of the *Glasgow Herald*, heavily promoting West Indian interests. He was 'one of the first to advocate the extension of legitimate commerce as the way to overcome the slave trade in Africa.'[16]

MacQueen used his newspaper to promote the idea of worldwide ocean steamship routes in the service of the British Empire. In 1837 he sent a paper to the government with a plan for a Pacific steamship route from Britain. He published it as a pamphlet in early 1838 with a letter to Francis Baring, then Secretary to the Treasury. When the *Great Western* and the *Sirius* had successfully demonstrated the crossing of the Atlantic, he wrote again to trumpet the advantages of steam communication with the West Indies. In his view, this was not just a matter of commercial importance but crucial to Britain's power and influence in the region. 'Great Britain, by thus possessing all the channels of communication with the western Archipelago, would thereby secure the principal political influence therein.' He feared that this influence would otherwise fall into the hands of the United States, which was seeking to extend its remit in that area.[17]

His ideas came to the attention of the West India committee, an association of London merchants and planters. John Irving, a Member of Parliament and a leading merchant banker, together with four City of London merchants, submitted MacQueen's plans to the government. A new company was set up in July 1839 with MacQueen as General Superintendent of Affairs on a salary of £1,000 per annum. It gained a royal charter in September. Irving was its first chairman and another director was Thomas Baring, brother of Francis Baring, the Chancellor of the Exchequer. Thomas was the head of Barings merchant bank, with considerable financial interests in the Americas. The other directors were equally part of the establishment, with close links to the government; these included the Earl of Auckland, who had recently been First Lord of the Admiralty. It is little surprise, with such connections and such a well-financed company (£1.5 million), that in March 1840 a mail contract was agreed. This required a bimonthly service, with the ships calling at Barbados, Grenada, Santa Cruz, St Thomas, Môle-Saint-Nicolas, Santiago de Cuba, Port Royal, Savanna-la-Mar and Havana. At each port they would connect with smaller steamers. The annual distance would exceed 684,000 miles and the government subsidy was £240,000 per year. The government mail subsidy would make up as much as 40 per cent of the company's overall receipts.[18] Fourteen steamships were needed to fulfil the contract, and these oceangoing vessels would spend a considerable amount of time steaming around the islands. The whole scheme was on a much grander scale than any other steamship company, including Cunard, General Steam Navigation Company, P&O and, of course, the relative minnow that was the Great Western Steam Ship Company.

With such a large fleet of ships to be built, the orders were spread around Britain: Cairds of Greenock (4), Pitcher of Northfleet (4), Scotts of Greenock (2) Acramans of Bristol (2), Whites of Cowes (1) and Menzies of Leith (1). In Bristol, Acraman subcontracted their two hulls to William Patterson, shipbuilder of the *Great Western*. In Scotland there was another change with the early death of Caird, which meant that John Scott Russell, an ambitious young engineer, was now in charge of that contract. Their key role was as mail ships, but in order to maximise revenue they planned accommodation to carry as many passengers as possible. In building their ships the Royal Mail Company was influenced by the successful *Great Western*, and they consulted Maudslay and Oliver Lang, master shipwright at Woolwich. Scott Russell had several meetings with Patterson, whose experience of the *Great Western* gave him considerable authority in his views. This advice influenced the hull and the machinery design. By January 1841 the sail plan was under debate, and this time Captain Hosken was consulted, together with two other transatlantic steamship captains. Instead of the four-masted sail plan of the *Great Western* they opted for simplicity with three masts, square sails on the foremast and fore and aft on the main and mizzen.[19]

The Royal Mail used Southampton as their base. There was a direct railway link to London, and they were well supported by the London & South Western Railway, which offered good rates, and also received favourable tariffs from the Southampton Dock Company.[20] Steamships were capital intensive, with repair and maintenance being major costs. In order to contain some of these costs the Royal Mail established its own repair facility at Southampton.[21] The service began in December 1841, and the first mail consignments went out in 1842. As Cunard had found, the practicalities of running the mail service, in this case across so many miles and so many islands, had the Royal Mail going back to the government to reduce the number of ports of call.[22]

Edward Chappell, who had purchased the ship for the company, was yet another half pay naval officer. He saw service during the Napoleonic Wars and had served in the West Indies, becoming a commander post-war in 1826. He was appointed by the Post Office to be in charge of the steam packet service at Milford. When the packet service transferred to the Admiralty, he was appointed to command their steam packet, *Redwing*, in 1837. In 1840 the Admiralty put him on board to report on the *Archimedes* steamer as it made its way around Britain. This ship was the screw-propelled vessel that had excited the Great Western Steam Ship Company to change their second ship. Chappell knew both Brunel and Guppy well. Being something of a steam expert, his views were sought; in 1839 he presented evidence to a parliamentary committee in relation to safety at sea. He became the Marine

Superintendent to the Royal Mail Company in December 1840 and then secretary in February 1842. James MacQueen resigned and left a few months later.[23]

Ship losses were high in the tropical waters of the West Indies. The *Medina* was lost in 1842, and in February 1847 the steamer *Tweed* was lost together with forty-one crew members and thirty-one passengers. This was the fifth ship lost by the company since the service began. A replacement was urgently needed to maintain the mail contract, and Chappell headed to Bristol, where fortuitously a familiar ship was available.[24] The *Great Western* was inspected on 14 April and negotiations began. The condition of the ship's hull was excellent and so was the accommodation. The concern was whether the tubular boilers would pass the required government inspection. The Great Western Steam Ship Company, with memories of the abortive P&O sale still in their mind, did not wish survey difficulties to get in the way and Chappell was in dire need of another steamship. So, knowing the potential limitations, the Royal Mail purchased the *Great Western* on Chappell's recommendation and took her round to their dry dock in Southampton. Here she was inspected by their senior shipwright and William Pitcher of Northfleet, their preferred shipbuilder. As predicted, the government's surveyor was not impressed with the boilers but permitted the ship to be used for one voyage to the West Indies and back. After the repair and trials, the latter being witnessed by a group of directors who came specially to see the ship, the *Great Western* headed off on her first voyage to the West Indies. She carried thirty-three passengers and a cargo that included 1,650 bottles of mercury for the silver mines, and because she was now an official mail ship she also carried a government agent on board. Admiralty agents were responsible for the mail and its safe delivery and had the power to direct the master of the ship in certain circumstances.[25]

On the way out the ship made a call at Madeira, her second visit to the island. When she returned to Southampton in September, Captain Abbott expressed considerable satisfaction with the ship and its performance, even with its much-criticised tubular boilers. The ship was now dry docked for replacement boilers and other work. This should have been done in Pitchers yard at Northfleet on the Thames, but there was no space there and so the work was carried out at Southampton. On completion of the work the Admiralty survey determined that she was fit for purpose and in February 1848 she began her regular service for the Royal Mail Company.

Unlike in her time as the sole ship with the Great Western Steam Ship Company, she was now part of a large fleet and this meant regular changes of personnel on board. Under Captain Chapman she remained in the West Indies for six months as a feeder ship for the transatlantic vessels. She was still a ship of interest to the newspapers, and the sudden death of Lieutenant Brand, the on-board Admiralty agent, at Tampico on 12 March was widely reported. No further information was given about the death, which may have been from natural causes as no tropical disease was mentioned.[26] In August she returned and went to Northfleet for a thorough inspection after so long in tropical waters. Yet again she proved the quality of her initial build, with only very minor defects to be corrected.

The *Great Western* arrived back in Southampton in January 1850, with the press reporting that it was the 'most rapid voyage from Bermuda ever achieved by any of the Royal Mail company's steamers'. She was still remarkably fast, and the newspapers continued to file reports of the news she carried.[27] There was a new communications invention: the telegraph, which sped information along the wire to London from Southampton.

Mexican mail by electric telegraph (from our correspondent) Southampton 18 September

The *Great Western* steamship, Captain Wolff, arrived here this morning from Mexico. That intelligence had he been anticipated via New York, there is nothing of importance to communicate. She brings $50,761 on account of the dividend, and $753,049 on merchants' account. But Tampico business was dull. At Vera Cruz the cholera was but slight; in Havana it had nearly disappeared; at Jalappa it was very severe. The *Great Western* left Vera Cruz on the 14th of August, and Havanna the 26th and Bermuda on the 3rd of September.[28]

The ship became a well-known sight in many ports in the West Indies, her four masts – in contrast to the three masts of the rest of the Royal Mail fleet – making her instantly recognisable. But she suffered a mishap in March 1851, largely due to poor navigation, when she went aground off Cape Aguiya near Santa Marta. The ship was able to return to Southampton, where there was an inquiry, and the master, Captain Wolfe, and chief officer, Rogers, were suspended from the company's service.[29] In May 1851 she was again in dry dock at Northfleet. In the dock beside her was the Royal Mail company's brand-new ship, *Orinoco*, ready to be launched. The launch was reported in the *Illustrated London News* with a sketch of Pitchers yard showing both vessels. The report happily noted that the *Great Western* was also flying colours, which 'added not a little to the liveliness of the scene'.[30]

In January 1852, another new vessel belonging to the Royal Mail suffered an appalling tragedy when the brand-new 2,000-ton steamer *Amazon* was destroyed by fire. It had only been launched a few months before and was heading out of Southampton with mails for the West Indies. The fire broke out around her funnel, and as it occurred during a gale the winds fanned the flames and the ship had to be abandoned in the English Channel. Of the 159 people on board, only twenty-one were rescued. The scale of the tragedy was such that there was a subsequent parliamentary enquiry, which found the number of lifeboats to be inadequate and more lives were lost as some boats failed to be released fully from the davits.[31]

The *Great Western* continued to maintain her good reputation, and as with the other ships of the fleet it was regularly maintained. Any reported incidents were more related to the difficult conditions of the West Indies, where yellow fever was epidemic during 1852. By 1853 the newspaper could report the safe return of the *Great Western* with eighty passengers and $808,855 and the good news that the 'yellow fever had almost disappeared in the West Indies'.[32] The master on this occasion was John Henry Jellicoe, who was also in overall charge of the whole fleet of Royal Mail ships. His son, also John, was born in Southampton, joined the Navy and would later be better known as Admiral Jellicoe.[33]

It was in July 1853 that the ship headed further south than she had ever gone before, and certainly much further than her originators had foreseen. Investment of British capital was increasing steadily in Latin America during the 1850s. MacQueen's original plan had been outlined as *A General Plan for Mail Communication by Steam between Great Britain and the Eastern and Western parts of the World*. He envisaged British mail ships linking the world across the Atlantic and Pacific oceans. The Royal Mail Company had provided a good service in the West Indies since 1841 and proposed to the government that their route should be extended. They had previously suggested a branch mail line from the West Indies to Brazil in 1844, but this had been declined. Four years later, however, the mail routes from Britain to Brazil and the River Plate were put out to tender and in 1849 the Royal Mail Steam Packet Company won the bid. Their new steamers were used to the West Indies and older ones were put on the new line. This extension became not just a mail carrier but a symbol of British influence in South America. In Britain, the Liverpool shipowners were not happy as they saw their port as the main link with South America. There was a concerted, but ultimately unsuccessful, attempt to put pressure on the government to switch the South American mail contract from Southampton to Liverpool. As with the Cunard contract, the government was not prepared to change its decision. For the new service the Royal Mail had to hire premises, build up coal stocks and appoint packet agents. The British government, keen for the success of this new service, helped in negotiations over facilities and port charges with the relevant foreign governments and even allowed two local consuls, one at Valparaiso and one at Callao, to act as packet agents.[34]

The *Great Western* was placed on the route in July 1853 and literally became a flag carrier for the British government in South America. She was now regularly calling at Lisbon and Madeira on the way to South America and so carried many Portuguese and Spanish passengers. During 1854 she made four round voyages.[35]

Last Monday the *Great Western* steamship left this port with the usual monthly mails for Lisbon, Madeira, Teneriffe, Saint Vincent's, Pernambuco, Bahia, Rio De Janeiro, Montevideo and Buenos Ayres, taking 35 passengers and a full general cargo of English and French merchandise, and jewellery valued at £10,560.[36]

The first half of the 1850s saw a recovery from the commercial crisis in 1848 and there was a surge in shipbuilding and freight rates.[37] The *Great Western* was now sixteen years old and had travelled vast distances. The Royal Mail company was now beginning to sell some of its older vessels and the ship together with others was put on the market.[38] Then in January 1854 the joint British and French fleet entered the Black Sea and there was an urgent requirement for transport shipping with the build-up to the invasion in September.[39] Managing a war in the Crimea posed logistical challenges for the military. Soldiers, horses and artillery had to be shipped out followed by the continuing supply of provisions, ammunition and other items for what was to be a prolonged campaign. While the Navy had some of its own transport ships they were insufficient in number and so the next call was to the mail companies, all of whom were bound to supply vessels in times of war as part of their contract.[40] The Royal Mail steamships *Orinoco*, *Medway* and *Trent* were the first to go into the transport service.[41]

The problem was that using mail ships inevitably disrupted the mail delivery and this meant that firms chartered other ships or used some of their slower vessels for carrying the mail. Around thirty mail ships were under government contract during the Crimean War, but the demand was great and this certainly impressive mobilisation was in fact less than 25 per cent of the total tonnage provided by commercial firms during the conflict. The steamships were effective for delivering large numbers of men but were not so effective for supplies. Military logistics required a mixture of fast steamers, slower large-capacity steamers and sailing ships. Steamships were extensively used as they were less vulnerable to the tricky Mediterranean wind conditions and could also tow the sailing ships.[42] So when transport contracts began in January 1854 they were initially mostly for sailing ships, but steam contracts took over by 1855.[43]

The *Great Western* continued her voyages to South America in 1855, but in September that year she returned to Southampton on her last Atlantic passage. In October it was announced in *The Times* that arrangements were being made between the government and the Royal Mail Company to engage the *Great Western* in the transport service. It added that the plan was for the ship to take 300 navvies and labourers, together with their working implements, to Sebastopol.[44] Shipowners were vocal in their complaints about the government demands for a transport service, but it was a lucrative employment for their ships.[45] On the other hand, it was suspected that owners were offering very old vessels that were reaching the end of their working lives anyway, in the hope of making considerable sums from ships that would probably otherwise have been sold for a much smaller figure.[46] The *Great Western* fell into this latter category, but the Royal Mail could argue for the importance of the mail routes and keep the newer vessels employed there.

The Crimean War was to set new standards in press reporting. Journalists such as William Howard Russell of *The Times*, and many others, provided grim and vivid descriptions of the appalling conditions in which the troops found themselves. The *Illustrated London News* gave this insight into the harbour of Balaclava, where so many of the transport ships were destined.

Compared with the dull marshy solitude of the Camp, Balaclava is quite a metropolis; in fact, there's not another village in the world which, for its size, but show the same amount of business and excitement as is perpetually going forward in that little collection of huts which all the world is talking of under the name of Balaclava. The harbour is now like the basin of the London Docks, so crowded is it with shipping of all kinds; and from every one of these vessels, at all times a day, supplies are being constantly landed. Along a flat dirty causeway rather beneath the level of the harbour, are boats and barges of all kinds laden with biscuit, barrels of beef, pork, rum, bales of winter clothing, siege guns, boxes of ammunition, piles of shell, trusses of hay, and sacks of barley and potatoes, which are all landed in the wet and stacked in the mud. The motley crowd that is perpetually wading about among these piles of uneatable eatables is something beyond description. But very ragged, gaunt, hungry-looking men, with matted beard and moustaches, features grimed with dirt, and torn great coats stiff with successive layers of mud – these men, whose whole appearance speaks toil and suffering, and who instantly remind you of the very lowest and most impoverished class of Irish peasantry – are the picked soldiers from our different foot regiments, strong men selected to carry up provisions for the rest of the camp.[47]

In these conditions disease was rife, and it didn't just affect the men on shore. The P&O ship *Himalaya*, on charter to the Admiralty, left Southampton in July 1855 and was in Balaclava in September. The chief engineer noted in his diary the death of three men on board from cholera.[48]

In the event the *Great Western* was not employed in September and remained moored in Southampton. Her time came the next year. Meanwhile, her interior was stripped back to the basics to provide large dormitories rather than separate cabins, and passenger dining gave way to mass catering. Deck space was cleared to build accommodation for horses. On 1 March 1856, with her name now Transport no. 6, she set sail with an officer, twenty men and forty-five horses from the Royal Artillery, thirteen officers and 300 sappers and miners from the Royal Engineers, plus other military men. She headed for the Black Sea and was due to stop at Gibraltar and Malta.[49]

She encountered severe gales in the Bay of Biscay, and the ship suffered structural damage and limped into Gibraltar with a split rudder. During the repair time, the government deducted two days of pay to the company. She then proceeded on her way to Malta for a five-day stop when some military men disembarked and the ship was refuelled. She then went on to Constantinople, arriving on 8 April 1856, and afterwards was probably in Balaclava or Scutari. She returned to Portsmouth via Malta, arriving back in England on 4 May. Her twenty-eight days (less the two-day repair) earned her owners nearly £3,000.[50] A few days later she was off on her next voyage to the Crimea, arriving there around 26 May. At the same time the *Great Britain* was in the same waters, also on transport duty. The great iron ship was now owned by Gibbs, Bright and Company and had been working on the Australia route before being called into the transport service. The two ships were not Brunel's only contribution to the war effort. He also designed an innovative pre-fabricated hospital at Renkioi which could be easily transported and erected for the many disease-ridden sufferers.[51]

Each hospital had all Brunel's trademark attention to detail, with a focus on heating, ventilation, drainage and sanitation. It was, writes his biographer, 'an outstanding example of Brunel's talents and methods of operation'.[52] His two great ships could also testify to that.

From Balaclava and Scutari, the *Great Western* returned to England, calling as before at Malta and Gibraltar. She carried twenty-three officers, 411 men, from the 3rd, 8th and 12th Battalions of the Royal Artillery, together with fifty-five horses and 15 tons of baggage. Also on board were assistant-surgeon Mitchell and two ladies, Mrs Stewart and Miss Marsh. The war had ended on 30 March and the evacuation of troops and civilians was now at last underway. The *Great Western* landed her last passengers and freight at Portsmouth, and then, with no further requirements from the government, she headed back to her home waters of Southampton.[53] No longer needed for transport duty, and with the Royal Mail far from eager to face the considerable cost of refitting an ageing paddle steamer for passenger use, the ship was now surplus to requirements.

9

Influence and Legacy

It was only when she passed to the Royal Mail Company that the *Great Western* achieved the status of an official mail ship. Throughout her time with the Great Western Company, Claxton and his colleagues fought hard to get the very real financial support of a mail contract. Such support could potentially cover all operating costs and meant that any income from passengers and additional freight was profit. But the fact that they did not have the government contract did not mean that she did not carry mail. The official mail ships carried government correspondence, despatches and mail that was sent via the Post Office, but many more letters never went through this system. Almost all merchant ships carried post, and the ship letter system was well developed and of long standing.

Regulations on ship letters dated from the seventeenth century, when Colonel Roger Whitley, the Post Master General, began the practice of giving captains a penny for every letter and packet delivered to the local postmaster at a port.[1] The Post Office tried to increase revenue in 1780 by charging an additional tax on incoming post, and attempted to supervise letters going out of the country on private ships. Such was the volume of post going across to so many colonies and foreign countries that a clerk in the Foreign Office, Frederick Bourne, suggested a separate office, and the Ship Letter Office was established by an Act of Parliament in 1799. Inducement rather than regulation was found to be more effective. The gratuity to ship captains bringing letters into the country and delivering them to a Post Office agent at the port was raised from 1*d* to 2*d*. 'Such mail was to be charged 4*d* per single letter, in addition to the inland charge from the port where the letter was landed.'[2] The Post Office endeavoured to get outgoing post to go via the Post Office but the coffee houses, which played a key part in getting letters overseas, did not wish to act as Post Office agents and customers could see no value in sending letters going out by private ships via the Post Office.[3]

The Penny Post was introduced in 1840 to regulate internal letters. Overseas post remained a challenge. Even lowering the charge from a half to a third of the packet rate for the outgoing letters if sent via the Post Office had little effect and brought in little revenue. Merchants felt that trade would be hindered if they had to always go via the Post Office. The Chancellor of the Exchequer between 1812 and 1823, Nicholas Vansittart, under pressure from mercantile interests, threw open 'the whole of the conveyance of letters outward'. Letters went out of England in any way the writer found convenient, and the official route was shunned as too time consuming. The official Post Office ship-letter bags at Liverpool, for instance, were so ignored that Francis Freeling, secretary of the Post Office, declared in frustration, 'We have not one letter in one year for America from Liverpool.'[4]

The American fast-sailing lines from New York ran scheduled services carrying passengers, mail and freight. The mail for these was from the Tontine Coffee House in New York, which hung a bag to receive letters for England and Europe.[5] They became the main means of letters between Liverpool and New York and vice versa as Admiralty brigs out of Falmouth ceased to call at New York from 1828.[6] By the time of the *Great Western* and the *Sirius*, letter bags were advertised as being at Hale's News Room and at the Exchange in New York and 'that no other charge will be made on letters or newspapers than has been customary in the packet ships'.[7] The mailbag system was long established in Britain and coffee houses hung up Black Ball, Red Star or Swallow Tail mail-bags to receive letters.[8] So, from its beginnings the *Great Western* carried ship letters.

The main coffee house in London for anyone with business of any type in the Americas was the North and South American Coffee

House and hotel in the heart of the city in Threadneedle Street, nicely situated near the Bank of England and the Royal Exchange. There were spacious and handsomely furnished bedrooms, and rooms for private meetings. It offered wines of the finest quality. But its importance rested on its position at the heart of the mercantile network. It advertised widely in newspapers in seaports in Canada, United States and elsewhere offering 'every personal comfort and convenience, a regular succession of authentic and commercial intelligence from every part of the world'. In its subscription room it had

… daily and provincial papers and commercial publications of the United Kingdom, British India, Canton, Singapore, New South Wales, Van Diemen's Land, Cape of Good Hope, British America, West India Islands, and every other British colony or possession: journals and commercial communications for more than one hundred places in the United States, from Brazil, Buenos Ayres, Mexico, and every other state of South America, and also from the principal ports, cities and commercial towns of France, Spain, Portugal, Belgium, Holland, Germany, Hamburg and other parts of continental Europe.

Captains of all the American packet ships reside at the above Hotel and are to be seen there daily. Also, the Bags are left open there for the reception of all letters, and newspapers leaving London for America which are regularly forwarded by those vessels.[9]

At this coffee house there was also a bag for the *Great Western*. James Gordon Bennett arrived in London and rushed off three letters via the *Great Western*: 'I write this from the North and South American coffee house, the great centre of all the monetary and commercial intelligence in London.'[10]

On the ships, passengers were often witnesses to the postage system. Mailbags were emptied on deck for the purpose of sorting out letters for delivery in New York. Harriet Martineau, who crossed on the *United States* in 1834, wrote, 'It is pleasant to sit on the rail and see the passengers gathered around the heap of letters, and to hear shouts of merriment at an exceedingly original superscription.'[11] John Jay Smith on his eastbound crossing in 1844 also helped to sort the 1,037 letters mostly for Ireland, where his ship was bound. He noted one optimistic address of 'Miss Smith, Ireland' and another addressed simply to 'Mrs Porter'.[12] Official government dispatches were sent in special bags, and often under the care of an official messenger. Post Office letters went in sealed bags and boxes, but ship letters were not handled with such care, 'given to the captain of the packet or to the passengers upon whom there is no check whatever'.[13] However, the lack of comment from any passenger diaries about ship-letter sorting on board the *Great Western* suggests that Captain Hosken, a naval officer, fully appreciated the importance of his role in safeguarding the letters – a duty underlined by the embarrassing accidental capture of the letters on the ship's very first visit into New York.

On the early years the *Great Western* brought large numbers of letters and newspapers on each crossing. In 1839 the *London Despatch* reported her arrival with 7,723 letters and 1,153 newspapers and declared it the largest number she has carried to date. 'The London letters were despatched by the post-office authorities of Bristol by the evening's mail.'[14] By the end of that year the directors could report a total of 96,587 letters and 19,571 newspapers conveyed in 1839, which earned good, steady additional income.[15]

Letters carried by the ship were both business and personal and now provided the receiving party with speedy and essential information. A letter in 1839 was from an agent in Liverpool anxious to get the latest cotton prices to his client, Bell & Co in New York but the important and urgent information was of the stoppage of the Phoenix Bank due to mismanagement. A letter in the opposite direction from a newly arrived emigrant to New York contained the news of his safe arrival, his health and his current prospects to his mother and sisters at home in London. Hemmings was single and a trained compositor in the printing trade. His long letter to his sister Anne was posted via the *Great Western* in 1845. Unlike the typical image of the poor, unskilled emigrant labourer, Hemmings was one of many skilled young men who travelled to New York in search of greater opportunities. He shared a room with four others and paid two and half dollars a week. He had found employment in the printing business but only on a trial basis so far.[16]

By 1840, however, the Post Office wished to get more letters going via them and sent peremptory letters demanding that agents in ports cease to take letters. The practice was so widespread that it was hard to stop. Receiving such a letter, the Bristol office asked Ward in London for his view. He replied that it was the 'practice of the Merchants & Brokers here to keep letter bags for all the packets by which almost any Parties are in the habit of sending out letters'. Additionally, they believed they had a right to do so – a claim which had been proved correct. He added, 'I am also told that they frequently have letters of a similar kind to that sent to you but that they always disregard them.' Although on further enquiry he found that the General Steam Navigation Company only took letters that came via the Post Office as their ships served the Continent. The Great Western Steamship Company publicly protested but changed postal arrangements.[17]

For business, it mattered little which route the letters took as long as it was dependable and speedy. Financial information was crucial to New York, which had overtaken Philadelphia as the nation's premier money market. The city was making money fast and was the great emporium of the western world.[18] A financial panic in 1837 and a banking crisis ushered in a recession that lasted until the 1840s. Such financial panics were not necessarily sudden events but were periods of uncertainty and in such times good, reliable and speedy information was highly prized. To maintain confidence, networks of correspondents, 'both merchants and newspaper editors, had to continually trade financial information. Communication was essential to growth.'[19] Business, banking and informal credit systems relied on good information and the newspapers had a crucial role to play.[20] As mentioned, as soon as he arrived in London in 1838 James Gordon Bennett sent three letters full of the latest news via the fastest route back to New York on the *Great Western* with what information he could glean about the London markets and the banking situation. He then reported on debates in Parliament, which since his arrival had been mainly on Irish affairs and West

Indian slavery.[21] Information flowed from London to New York and back again to anxious London investors like Barings, who were heavy investors in America, and also to those in Liverpool and elsewhere, where cotton was vital to British interests.[22] Mr Joshua Bates, the American representative of Baring in New York, was a regular passenger on the *Great Western* and they often sent other messengers over on the ship, together with correspondence and gold.[23]

The British government, too, had need of fast channels of communication. The disputed border between Maine and the British Canadian province of New Brunswick had been unclear since the end of the American Revolution in 1783. Matters came to a head in 1838 as New Englanders and Canadian lumberjacks disagreed over territory in the Aroostook area. Troops were mobilised on both sides and it looked possible that war might again break out between the United States and Britain. But by 21 March 1839 a truce was agreed between President Van Buren and the British negotiator, Sir John Harvey. The *Great Western* played its part in getting swift information back to Britain.

> At the time of the disputed Territory question, Mr Fox, British minister to Washington, requested to me to wait half an hour for despatches to Lord Aberdeen; this I did, and on arriving at Liverpool I went immediately to London and delivered them into Lord Aberdeen's hand at the very moment of debate going on in the House of Lords on the subject of the negotiations with the American government.[24]

1838 was a busy time for dispatches as there were armed uprisings in Canada itself in what was then Lower and Upper Canada. The *Great Western* arrived in Bristol in December 1838 with dispatches for the government from Sir John Colbourne. 'He seems to have fairly subdued the rebellion and the Government of the United States remains true to its good faith with Britain' was the report in the newspapers.[25] For some time afterwards there remained concerns about events in North America and the ship carried military men and diplomats backwards and forwards until Cunard's service began in 1841.

The Great Western Railway link was assisting the speed of communication, and even when only part opened the dramatically improved times were celebrated in London by national newspapers who saw the beginning of a new era:

Paddington October 5, 8 minutes past 3:00 AM
An Express has this moment been received from Bristol by the Great Western Railway, to state that the *Great Western* steam-ship has arrived from New York in 12 days and 13 hours, bringing 43 passengers, and £117,051 in specie. The *Great Western* left New York on the 22nd of September when the *British Queen* had arrived. This express reached the Paddington station in 48 minutes from Twyford.[26]

It was not just governments and the press that welcomed the speed of the *Great Western*. Swartwout, the Port Collector of New York, had made a quick exit from there to Europe and a few years later another government official also used the ship for a speedy departure in the opposite direction, which hit the headlines across Britain and Ireland. The elected City Treasurer of Dublin, Mr James Flinn, fled the city to Liverpool, taking with him corporate funds to the tune of £4,000 or £5,000. His reason for heading to Liverpool was clear to observers. 'This excellent and trustworthy public servant is now by this time on board the *Great Western* steamship bound to that land of refuge of gentlemen who, like Mr Flinn, have left their country for their country's good.' After him in hot pursuit was Sir Drury Jones Dickenson, the accountant of the corporation, but he failed to arrive before the ship sailed on 29 April at nine o'clock.[27] James Flinn, described on the passenger list as a thirty-three-year-old merchant from England, had carefully planned his moves – with him on the ship was his twenty-six-year-old wife.

In Dublin the police head office now acted and sent 'their intelligent Chief Clerk, Mr. Ross Cox, the experienced American traveller' in pursuit via a Cunard ship.

Mr Cox was to sail from Liverpool this morning by one of the liners; and it was arranged that he should land at the port named, from whence he will proceed by railroad, in the confident hope of arriving at a certain other port, twenty-four hours before the *Great Western* can, in the ordinary course of sailing, reach the same destination.[28]

The anxious citizens, among them the two men who had stood surety for the appointment of Flinn as Treasurer, awaited the news. When the *Great Western* returned to Liverpool she brought with her the New York papers up to 25 April. A quick scan confirmed there were no reports of any arrest of Mr Flinn who 'it appears has distanced Mr. Ross Cox'. The two guarantors had to pay up to refund the missing monies.[29]

From the beginning, there was much anticipation at the volume of trade to be achieved by the ship. The New York newspapers heartily welcomed the *Great Western* and were concerned in the first year of its service about questions over the financial viability of such a scheme. In an editorial, James Gordon Bennett had urged members of the community at large to 'impress upon the public mind the absolute necessity of patronising these steamships by every means in our power'. While acknowledging the value and importance of the American packet ships, the steamships had to be supported in every way.[30] It was the possibilities for cotton that caught the imagination of many.

A letter from Richard Cobden, published in the *Aberdeen Free Press* and dated Manchester 7 April 1838, referred to the Stockport cotton trade and said, 'Hoorah for the *Great Western* steamship that sails today from Bristol to bring the United States within 14 days of England!'[31] The Great Western Steam Ship Company had in mind cotton mills closer to home. The Bristol Chamber of Commerce applauded the prospects of commercial profit from the 'spirited exertions of the Bristol Cotton Company and of the Great Western Steam Ship Company' and urged every encouragement and support. Mr Clarke of the Great Western Cotton company, of which Robert Bright was a director, anticipated that in two years' time the consumption of cotton in the Bristol mill would be 300 bags a week.[32] Peter Maze, the chairman of the Great Western Steam Ship Company, was quoted as having received a letter from one house in New York to send out 100 tons of goods on every trip the *Great Western* makes, 'in consequence of their having established a trade to Bristol'.[33] At their meeting in 1839, the directors were happy to report a high demand for freight.

> On every outward voyage they have been compelled to resist very pressing entreaties from owners of goods, and not only does this afford a most satisfactory profit to the Company, but they have the pleasure of believing that the new facilities afforded to mercantile transactions by the rapid communication through your Vessel, have powerfully tended to increase the Shipments by the sailing lines.[34]

In New York one headline article described the 'Adventure of a Bale of Cotton'. A bale was shipped on board the *Great Western* at New York on 6 May and arrived at Bristol on the 22nd. It was sent to the new cotton factory and the resultant yarn was exhibited at a public meeting as a specimen of the first cotton ever manufactured in Bristol.[35] In Wiltshire there was also a *Great Western* effect, with the clothing trade in Trowbridge being reported as 'very brisk at present; business is much increased by American orders, received by the *Great Western* Steamer'.[36] By the shareholders meeting in 1840 the directors could announce that the ship had carried 1,214 tons of goods.[37]

Paton and Stewart were regular freighters; for example, in 20 June 1843 they were requesting 6 to 8 tons of freight space for the August voyage from Liverpool. But freight was never a big item since most freight was bulk carried by the regular sailing lines. Trade samples were often sent out. There was the shipment of a packet of samples addressed to Mr E. Phalon, Broadway, New York in May 1842. Phalon was a hairdresser and wigmaker and also the inventor of a 'hair invigorator', presumably a tonic for hair loss.[38]

Getting news, samples or illustrations of the latest fashion was essential and the *Great Western* helped to speed up the flow of information on styles from London and Paris. Every shop window of every tailor, milliner and dressmaker in New York displayed plates of the newest fashions.[39] Lydia Sigourney's European travel had the specific purpose of reporting back for *Godey's Lady's Book* on fashions in Paris and London. News of fashion changes, particularly with a young and fashionable court in London, were keenly read. Lydia noted Victoria's dress at the opening of Parliament in 1841: 'She wore a dress of white satin and lace, superbly decorated with diamonds; a robe, or mantle of crimson velvet, with a train; and on her head glittered the crown of the kingdom.'[40] Even Bennett, not a man known for his fashion knowledge, knew that the latest information on the spectacle in London was essential to sell newspapers: 'The coronation of Victoria will be a splendid affair – greater and more gorgeous than ever took place in England. I shall take particular care to give my fair readers in the United States such a full, animated and picturesque account as no other paper can give.'[41]

The ship had other commercial influences too, as its name was used to effect by companies such as Bucklins, an American firm who advertised their 'Great Western' cooking stove for ships, steamboats and hotels just a few months after the ship's first arrival in New York.[42] In England, a very British condiment, Lea & Perrins Worcestershire Sauce, had an advertisement running for many years up to 1847 with a string of testimonials from top hotels and royal chefs. Monsieur Malaret, chef de cuisine, wrote that it had long been an accompaniment to the royal table. The steward of the Wyndham Club said it was a favourite, and the steward of the Conservative Club said it had given universal satisfaction. The Union Club said it superseded several other sauces formerly used at the establishment. The Royal Western Hotel in Bristol provided a testimonial, and then there was one from Captain James Hosken:

Great Western steam ship June 6, 1843
The cabin of the *Great Western* has been regularly supplied with Lee and Perrins Worcestershire sauce, which is adapted for every variety of dish – from turtle to beef, from salmon to steaks, to all of which it gives a famous relish. I have great pleasure in recommending this excellent sauce to Captains and passengers for its capital flavour, and as the best accompaniment of its kind for any voyage.[43]

No wonder the ship became the toast of the Atlantic trade. At the Earthenware Trade convention held in Philadelphia around 1838, there were seven toasts during the convention dinner. The first was to the Earthenware Trade convention itself; established to give efficiency to judiciary regulations in trade and 'may its influence long be felt in smoothing down the asperity of rivalry and elevating friendship over self-interest'. Then to the 'Commerce of our country', followed by the Baltimore Earthenware trade, the Philadelphia Earthenware trade and the Earthenware Trade of Boston. Number six was to the *Great Western*: 'The bridge over the Atlantic, it is drawing more closely the bonds that unite us to our Fatherland, and bids fair to bring the hills of Staffordshire to the valleys of America.' The seventh was naturally to the 'Fair Sex' who were addressed in their absence as, 'the chief end of man's joys – if they break some of our hearts they break all our crockery. Let them eschew diamond cement and mend anything but china.'[44] In England by 1847, it was even helping to sell sermons on the topic of the perils at sea. The Reverend C. Herbert MA, the Vicar of Lechlade, a parish far distant from any seas, offered *The late Wonderful Escape of the Great Western Steamship, Compared with the ship wreck of St Paul; with practical reflections by the Vicar of Lechlade*. The price was a very reasonable sixpence.[45]

There were cultural influences apart from the considerable number of famous actors, artists, writers and musicians who crossed with the ship. Such was her fame that many pieces of music were written in honour of the ship. There was a broadside ballad printed in London 1838 which was, it claimed, 'sung by the passengers on board that unrivalled Atlantic steamer'. The first verse gives an indication of its style:

Merrily o'er the waves we go
Far far away from shore
No music half so sweet
As the noise of the ocean's roar
Merrily merrily o'er the wave
I speed on the gale's swift wing
The surges round me may rage
As their foam to the skies they fling.[46]

Since none of its verses seem to make even a passing reference to anything connected with engines or steam it may be concluded this was another opportunistic venture and was likely to be a set of established verses hastily re-dedicated. There was a more famous song dedicated to Captain Hosken and the directors of the Great Western Steam Ship Company called 'Farewell awhile my native isle'. It did not attract critical acclaim.

> *Farewell awhile my native isle*. Written by Mr. Wilson. Composed and dedicated to Miss Wilkes of Holloway by Edward Clare.
> Coventry and Hollier, Dean Street
> Mr Wilson having amused himself by writing some very silly and commonplace verses on board the *Great Western* steamship, two or three composers had eagerly set their wits to work in producing music for the same. All these by far the best we have seen is the present, by Mr. Edward Clare, who in our opinion has thrown away a charming ballad on a worthless subject. A running passage in 'The Lass', page three, is clever, and rather new for a ballad.[47]

At least *The Atlantic Steamer*, written, and inscribed to Captain Hosken by a passenger, William Nixon, and adapted to Mr T. Cooke's air, 'I was a Beauty then', did have some reference to a steamship. 'Now o'er the blue water we glide, my boys, o'er the water we glide. Our vessel is trim, and forward we skim, regardless of wind or tide my boys.'[48] No doubt Captain Hosken was forced to listen to many such offerings while on board unless important duties suddenly and, no doubt regretfully, called him away.

When in port the ship remained a great tourist attraction. When it moved to Liverpool there were still people who wished to visit the ship and yet again a fee was charged and the proceeds distributed to local hospitals. If the public could not see the real thing there were drawings, paintings, painted plates, models and, in New York, a moving diorama. At Hanningtons, opposite St Paul's among the automata of various kinds such as birds whistling and musicians playing, there was a novel attraction: 'The grand and vivid scene of the *Great Western* steamship proudly dashing around the steamer *Sirius* whilst lying at anchor, was received on each night of its performance to crowded audiences, with acclamations of continued applause.'[49]

BRISTOL HARBOUR

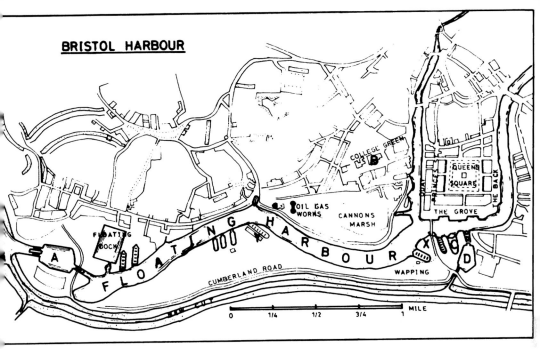

DRY DOCK.   **A** CUMBERLAND BASIN.   **B** CATHEDRAL.   **C** FLOATING DOCK.

D BATHURST BASIN.   **X** GREAT WESTERN BUILT HERE.   **Y** G.W. DOCK & YARD.

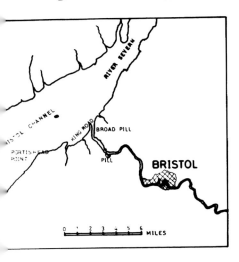

Top and above left: 1. Bristol Harbour showing site of Patterson's yard. (Denis Griffiths)

Above right: 2. Launch of the *Great Western*. (Denis Griffiths)

Right: 3. Saloon of the *Great Western*. (Brunel Institute, ss Great Britain Trust)

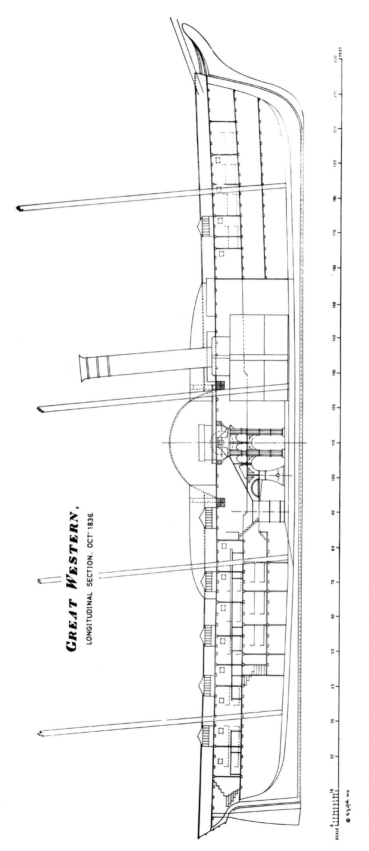

GREAT WESTERN,
LONGITUDINAL SECTION. OCT.ᵗ 1836.

4. *Great Western* longitude, 1836. (Denis Griffiths)

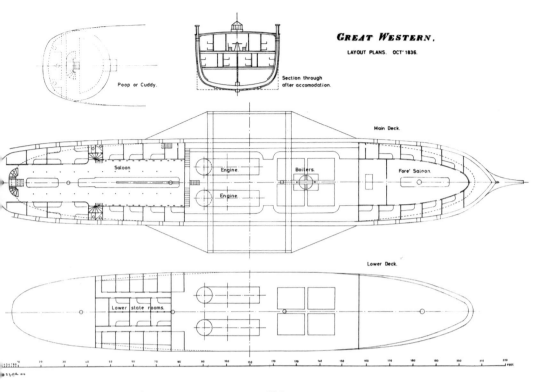

GREAT WESTERN,

LAYOUT PLANS. OCT.' 1836.

Poop or Cuddy.

Section through
after accomodation.

Main Deck.

Saloon

Engine.

Engine.

Boilers.

Fore' Saloon.

Lower Deck.

Lower state rooms.

FEET.

5. *Great Western* layout, 1836. (Denis Griffiths)

Above: 6. *Great Western* arriving in New York, April 1838. (New York Public Library)

7. Crowds greeting arrival of *Great Western* in New York. (New York Public Library)

8. *Sirius.* (New York Public Library)

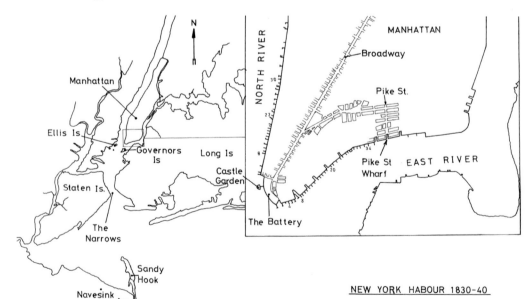

9. Drawing of New York showing Pike Street, where *Great Western* had mooring and coal yard. (Denis Griffiths)

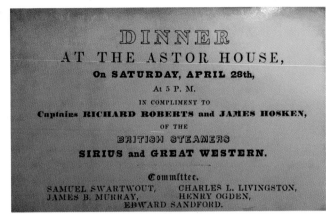

10. Astor House invitation.

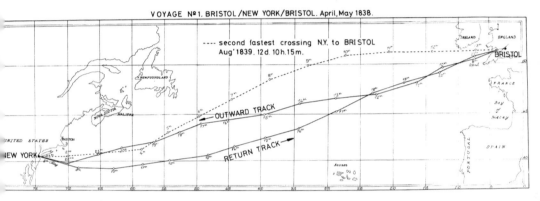

11. Voyage no. 1. (Denis Griffiths)

12. Engraving celebrating the *Great Western*, 1840. (New York Public Library)

Above left: 13. A portrait of Captain Hosken as a naval officer. (Michael Hosken)

Above right: 14. George Macready, surgeon on the *Great Western*. (Brunel Institute, ss Great Britain Trust)

Below: 15. *Great Western* sailing from River Avon. (Denis Griffiths)

Above left: 16. Guppy. (*A Short History of Great Western*, published 1938)

Above right: 17. Patterson. (*A Short History of Great Western*, published 1938)

Right: 18.
Great Western
in gale, 1846.
(*Illustrated
London News*)

Below: 19.
Great Western
longitude, 1846.
(Denis Griffiths)

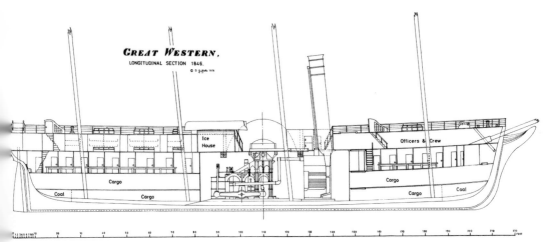

GREAT WESTERN,
LONGITUDINAL SECTION 1846.

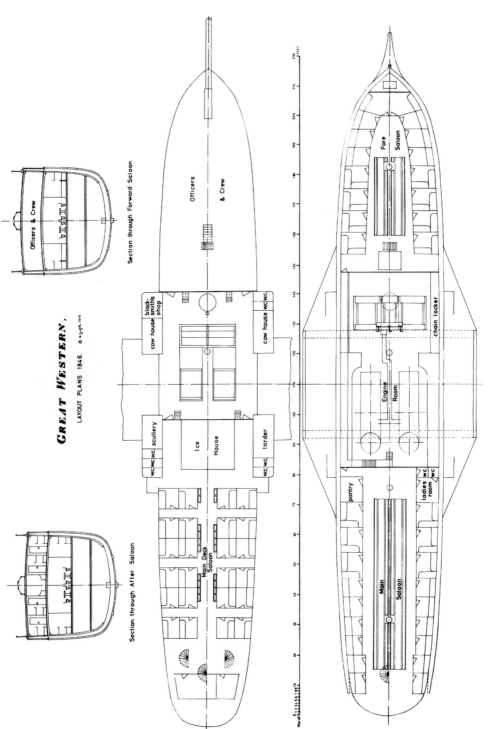

GREAT WESTERN,
LAYOUT PLANS 1846. © D. Griffiths 1979

Section through Forward Saloon

Officers & Crew

Officers & Crew

Section through After Saloon

blacksmiths shop

cow house

cow house

WC WC

scullery

Ice House

larder

WC WC WC

WC WC

Main Deck Saloon

Officers & Crew

Fore Saloon

chain locker

Engine Room

pantry

ladies room

WC WC WC

Main Saloon

FEET

20. *Great Western* layout, 1846. (Denis Griffiths)

Left: 21. *Great Western* ship's bell. (Brunel Institute, ss Great Britain Trust)

Right: 22. *Great Western* butter dish. (Brunel Institute, ss Great Britain Trust)

23. Barnard Mathews and his officers and cadets on ss *Great Britain*. Seated in front row, left to right: W. Martin, 2nd Officer; B. R. Mathews, Commander; H. T. Cox, 1st Officer. Standing, left to right: Edward State, Cadet; John Cleave, 3rd Officer; Archibald Alexander, Surgeon; George Christian, Cadet; Francis Pettit Smith, Patentee of the screw propeller; Robert C. Lambert, Cadet; John Anjer, Purser; George M. Miller, Cadet; Charles Peters, 4th Officer. (Brunel Institute, ss Great Britain Trust)

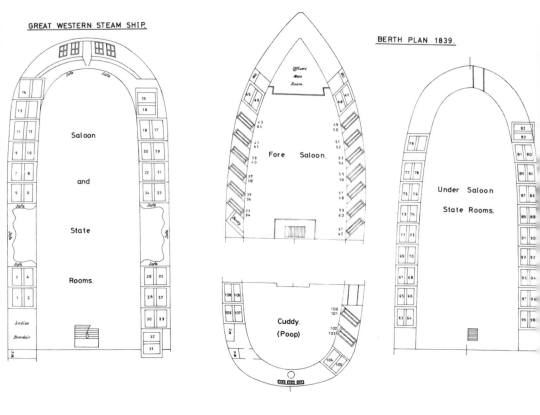

GREAT WESTERN STEAM SHIP.

BERTH PLAN 1839.

Saloon

and

State

Rooms.

Fore Saloon.

Cuddy.
(Poop)

Under Saloon

State Rooms.

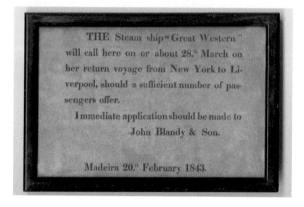

Above: 24. Cabin plans of 1839, used by booking office. (Denis Griffiths)

Left: 25. *Great Western* at her moorings. (*A Short History of Great Western* published 1938)

Below left: 26. Poster for voyage to Madeira, 1843. (Brunel Institute, ss Great Britain Trust)

THE Steam ship "Great Western" will call here on or about 28.ᵗʰ March on her return voyage from New York to Liverpool, should a sufficient number of passengers offer.

Immediate application should be made to

John Blandy & Son.

Madeira 20.ᵗʰ February 1843.

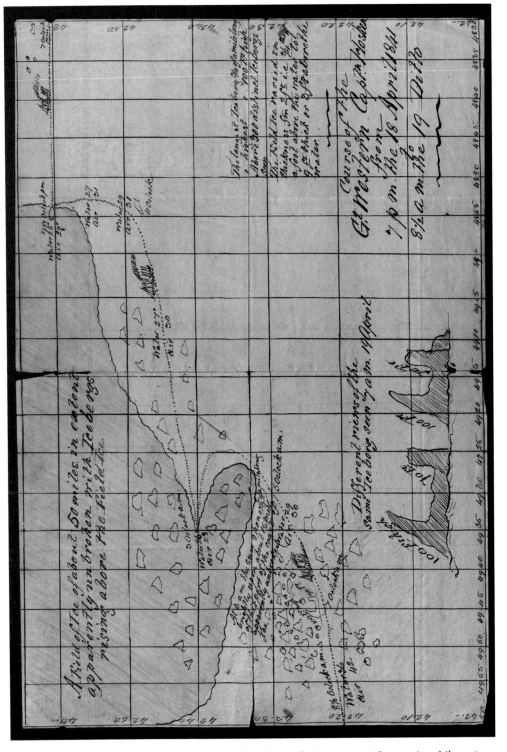

27. Drawing of the Ice Field Incident, 1840, by Lydia Sigourney. (Connecticut Library)

28. Astor House. (New York Public Library)

Above left: 29. Madame Celeste. (New York Public Library)

Above right: 30. Fanny Elssler in Park Theatre dressing room, 1845. (New York Public Library)

31. Cartoon of Aroostook War; Queen Victoria, Melbourne and President Van Buren. (New York Public Library)

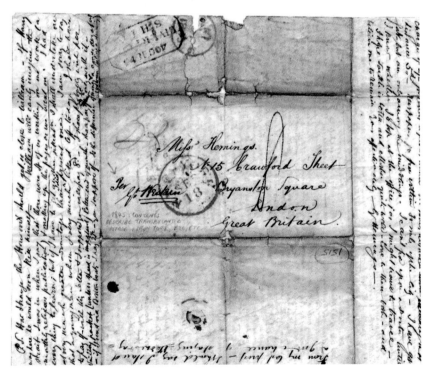

32. Letter carried on board *Great Western* to Miss Anne Hemmings, 1845. (Brunel Institute, ss Great Britain Trust)

33. Britannia Bridge engineers, 1850. Standing, left to right: Admiral Moorsom, Latimer Clark, Edwin Clark, Frank Forster, George P. Bidder, master mason Hemmingway, Captain Claxton, Alexander Ross. Seated, left to right: Robert Stephenson, Charles H. Wild, Joseph Locke, Isambard Kingdom Brunel. (Institution of Civil Engineers)

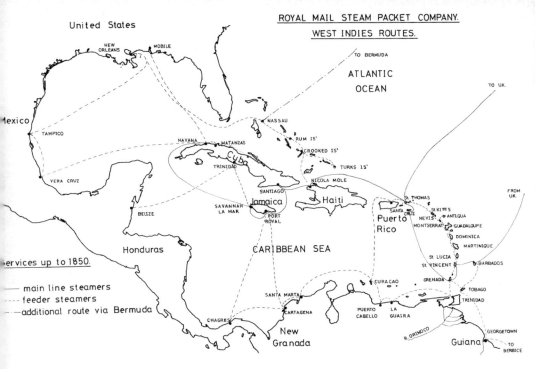

United States

ATLANTIC
OCEAN

TO BERMUDA

TO UK.

Mexico

TAMPICO

NEW
ORLEANS

MOBILE

NASSAU

RUM IS'

CROOKED IS'

HAVANA

MATANZAS

Cuba

TURKS IS'

TRINIDAD

FROM
U.K.

VERA CRUZ

SANTIAGO

NICOLA MOLE

ST. THOMAS

SANTA
CRUZ

FROM
UK.

BELIZE

SAVANNAH
LA MAR

Jamaica

Haiti

Puerto
Rico

ST KITTS
NEVIS ANTIGUA
MONTSERRAT GUADALOUPE
DOMINICA
MARTINIQUE

PORT
ROYAL

Honduras

CARIBBEAN SEA

St LUCIA
St VINCENT

BARBADOS

services up to 1850.

CURACAO

GRENADA

TOBAGO

—— main line steamers
---- feeder steamers
---additional route via Bermuda

SANTA MARTA

CHAGRES

CARTAGENA

PUERTO
CABELLO

LA
GUAIRA

TRINIDAD

New
Granada

R. ORINOCO

Guiana

GEORGETOWN
TO
BERBICE

34. The Royal Mail Steam Packet Company's West Indies routes, 1850. (Denis Griffiths)

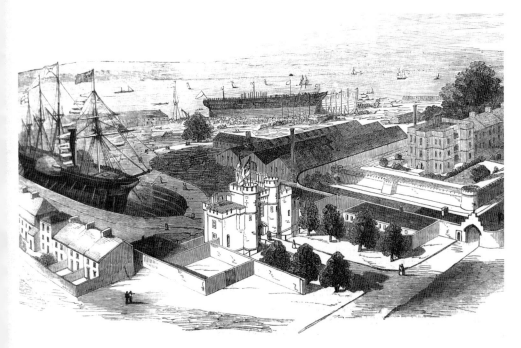

35. *Great Western* in drydock and *Orinoco* ready for launching at Northfleet on 17 May 1851. (*Illustrated London News*)

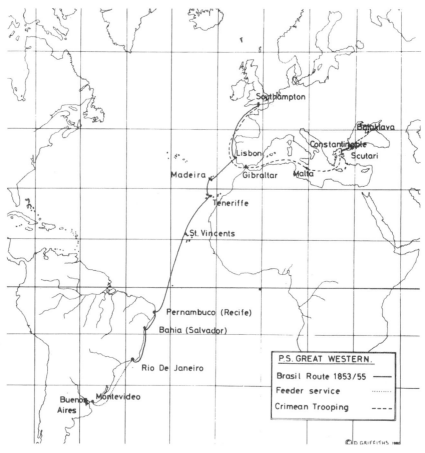

36. The Royal Mail Steam Packet Company's Brazil and Crimea routes. (Denis Griffiths)

37. Balaclava Harbour. (*Illustrated London News*)

The design influence of the *Great Western* has already been seen in the steamships that followed her, from the hull structure, the placement of the engines and the sail plan. The Royal Mail fleet was a tribute to the ship, and then of course there was the *Great Britain*. The extensive experiments, attention to every detail of the rolling and pitching, the fuel consumption and the engine performance all went into the calculations for the next generation of ships that pushed the steam, iron and propulsion technology yet further.[50] The *Great Eastern* also had its influence from the *Great Western* when Brunel consulted Claxton on the passenger accommodation, the layout and space plans from the *Great Western*.[51]

The Great Western Steam Ship Company, formed with such optimism in 1835, reported enormous financial losses in 1852 as a consequence of the grounding of the *Great Britain*. All the original holders of £100 shares, including Brunel and Guppy, saw their investment written off as a total loss. The loss on the *Great Britain* was reported as £107,896 and the shipyard and engineering works in Bristol as £47,277. What was left from the sale of the ship and works was received in dividends by the holders of the new or preference shares.[52] The originators of the company had seen the whole plan as part of a great rejuvenation of Bristol, when the city assisted by the new ship, the railway connection and the cotton mill would grow to rival the Midlands. But the city did not gain the benefits it had hoped.

The Royal Mail company, founded with imperial ambitions, well connected to the establishment and well financed, thrived as a shipping line. The Cunard line, bolstered by mail subsidies, was run as a highly efficient business and was now serving New York. When a fierce rate war was threatened by competition from the New York steamship line, Collins, they entered into a secret agreement in the 1850s to set minimum rates for the carriage of cargo and all classes of passenger.[53] The Great Western Company, perennially underfunded and somewhat parochial in its outlook, never really grasped the essential requirements or priorities of a successful business and engineering excellence was always its aim. This in itself was a worthy ambition and gave the world two justly famous results, but it was not one that rewarded or encouraged investors. It had, however, lasted longer them many rivals and outperformed them in speed, regularity and passenger numbers. In financial terms it had been more successful than its initial competitors, about whom it had once been so concerned. The Liverpool-based Transatlantic Steam Company sold out to P&O and the British and American Steam Navigation Company folded after the loss of the *President* in 1841. John Junius Smith, who had been so keen to compete across the Atlantic, returned to America and set up a tea plantation in South Carolina.[54]

James Hosken, who became so famous and feted on both sides of the Atlantic for his time as master of the *Great Western*, was forever haunted by the fate of the *Great Britain*. Things began so well – master of the largest ship in the world and presented to royalty – only for him to end his mercantile career on a sandy beach in Dundrum Bay, Ireland, on 22 September 1846. He went abroad and became harbour master, postmaster, and chief magistrate in Borneo. Then in 1851 he was reemployed in naval service as commander of a dispatch vessel, *Banshee*, in the Mediterranean. In the Crimean War, he was promoted and commanded the hospital ship *Belle-Isle*. By June 1857 he was promoted captain and retired in January 1868. He lived in Wood Lane, Falmouth, Cornwall, where he and his second wife lived in some style with five servants. By 1879 he was Vice-Admiral and living in Ilfracombe, Devon, where he died in January 1885. His second wife, Elizabeth Ann, privately published his memoirs in 1889, which were largely an attempt to re-establish his reputation.[55]

The second master of the *Great Western*, Barnard Mathews, followed Hosken's career by becoming master of the *Great Britain*, but with new owners. Gibbs, Bright and Company purchased the ship, and after considerable alterations to make her into an immigrant ship she was ready to sail in 1852. She was first sent across the Atlantic to New York as a shakedown trip, and on her return was put on her planned itinerary to Australia. As on the *Great Western*, Mathews was the subject of complaints. The provisions were poor, the ship was dirty and he became the focus of the passenger objections. His was not the temperament for a passenger ship. After his second voyage he left the company's employment and took up a post as a Lloyd's agent in Melbourne, Australia where his family joined him. He died there in 1869, aged sixty-six, a highly respected member of the community.[56]

Dr Lardner, whose confident predictions about the impossibility of an Atlantic crossing by steam caused so much publicity and anxiety, was proved wrong, although his early opposition continued to rankle with Brunel for many years. Brunel could not resist a dig at Lardner in 1851 when giving evidence before a parliamentary commission on Irish packet stations.[57] A colourful figure in his private life, Lardner was separated from his wife and had a relationship with a married woman with whom he had a son in 1820. In 1840 he eloped to France with the wife of a captain of the Guards, who pursued them. The resultant case made headlines. The couple escaped to America, where he had another successful career in public lecturing.[58] His scientific reputation still attracted crowds. This was where George Moore, who came over on the *Great Western*, went to hear him. 'He was the most complete elocutionist I ever heard, and impressed a crowded audience. What a melancholy loss to England by his one false step that degraded him to moral society!'[59]

So what of those who had such an important role on the shipbuilding committee? Patterson continued as a well-respected shipbuilder in Bristol, building a wide range of ships for both private companies and the Navy. The shipbuilding business was subject to considerable fluctuations in fortunes, and Patterson was not exempt. In the shipbuilding slump after the Crimean War he had to sell his yard where the *Great Western* was built. He reappeared working with his son in the old Great Western Company's dock, from where the *Great Britain* was launched (and where it is today). Patterson retired in 1865, moving to Liverpool, where he died in 1869.[60]

Guppy became directing engineer for the *Great Britain* and took out various patents connected with iron ships. In 1844 for a time he was the manager of the Cwm Avon copper mine in South Wales. Guppy moved to Naples, Italy in 1849 for health reasons and established a large engineering workshop, employing several hundred people, and lived there until he died in 1882.[61] Maudslay, Sons and Field continued successfully making marine engines for many years. Joshua Field, a modest, unassuming, courteous and kind man, was a founder of the Institution of Civil Engineers in 1816 and became its president from 1848 to 1849.[62]

Captain Christopher Claxton, the energetic, pugnacious, indefatigable fixer, continued to work with Brunel. He features in a famous painting of engineers, including Brunel, who assisted Stephenson with the Britannia Bridge across the Menai Strait in Wales. The bridge was completed in 1850. In 1847 Claxton was working with the South Wales Railway to look at the best way of crossing the Irish Channel. A steamship was chartered with Claxton in command to sound the channel and make surveys. 'A better officer sent to serve the undertaking could not be found. We may rest assured that under his guidance the best and shortest route will be secured.'[63] He was involved in trials of the *Great Britain* after her refurbishment in 14 July 1853. Described as an 'eminent naval engineer' who had worked with Mr Brunel for twenty-five years, Claxton gave a lecture in Whitehall in 1860 on the principles of a floating harbour.[64] In July 1864, while living in Brompton, London, he filed patents for improvements in railway carriages. He was the secretary of the Clifton Bridge Company, the titular project of which was completed in 1864. On 7 March 1868, after seeing the successful opening of the Clifton Bridge in memory of his great friend Brunel, Claxton died aged seventy-eight in Chelsea.[65]

Then there is the great engineer himself, Brunel, who continued his exhausting career doing numerous projects at once. He owed much to his first ship, the *Great Western*; together with the opening of the Great Western Railway, it had established his engineering reputation.[66] His last great ship, the *Great Eastern*, was built not in Bristol but on the banks of the Thames, and his partner was John Scott Russell. It should have been a successful partnership but was plagued by personality clashes and problems both financial and technical, all of which were fought out in the glare of publicity. It was while the great ship, the latest leviathan, was being built that Brunel's first ship came to the end of its days.

Too costly to bring back into the mail service and now surplus to requirements, the *Great Western*, together with the *Severn*, was put up for sale by the Royal Mail Company. Mr Marks, an iron founder of Greenwich, purchased them both for £11,550. The *Great Western* was towed from Southampton to the Thames in August 1856 to be stripped of her engines and metalwork, and then in 1857 she headed for Castle's yard at Vauxhall, where the ship was to be broken up.[67]

Henry Castle began his business in 1838 in Rotherhithe and moved to Baltic Wharf near Vauxhall Bridge in 1843. He had a steady trade breaking up the large numbers of wooden ships that were no longer required. The wood from the ships was sold as logs for fuel in London. Customers of Castle's yard included the House of Commons, Buckingham Palace, St James's Palace and the Bank of England. 'The celebrated old oak and ships timber logs were distinguished by their beautifully coloured flames created by the sheathing left from the copper bolts utilised in the construction of the wooden sailing ships.'[68] The *Great Western* was thus consumed in a swirl of coloured flames on endless open fires.

The *Great Western* steamship is the overlooked Brunel ship. Somehow since the 1980s she has dropped out of sight to posterity, overshadowed by his later ships. The *Great Western* was the first and the most commercially successful of Brunel's three ships. Like the other two she was technologically advanced and pushed several boundaries for speed and style. Highly influential in her time, she carried the rich and the famous across the Atlantic and established the first successful transatlantic steam liner route. Unlike the *Great Britain* and *Great Eastern*, she did what she was designed to do in her career, as she travelled the Atlantic for seventeen years and was in many ways a financial success, although limited detailed records make that hard to judge fully. The lack of any mail contract, the lack of an early partner across the Atlantic and the troubles of her sister ship were the factors that eventually finished her. But her second career maintained her excellent reputation, which never faltered – proof, if needed, of the outstanding work that went into her design and build. Her influence was wide and she deserves to be fully celebrated on both sides of the Atlantic.

She was, it seems, a special ship to Brunel. Brunel died in 1859, aged fifty-three, and it was his eldest son, another Isambard, who wrote his biography. Isambard junior was born in 1837 and was, therefore, the same age as his father's first ship, being twenty when she was broken up. In the biography, Isambard junior is understandably a little sentimental about his father's connection with the *Great Western*, but sees the ship off in style. He notes that his father took time out from the many challenges of the *Great Eastern* to go to Vauxhall. 'Among those who went there to take a farewell look before she finally disappeared was Mr. Brunel; thus he saw the last of his famous ship.'[69]

APPENDIX 1

Timeline

1833		Brunel appointed engineer to Great Western Railway
1835	Oct.	GWR board meeting proposes steamship to New York
1835	Dec.	Dr Dionysius Lardner at Liverpool
1836	Jan.	Great Western Steam Ship Company issues prospectus
1836	Jun.	*Great Western* keel laid
1836	Jul.	Brunel gets married
1836	Jul.	Stern post ceremony
1836	Aug.	Dionysius Lardner at BAAS Bristol meeting
1836	Aug.	Foundation stone of Clifton Suspension Bridge laid
1837	Jun.	Accession of Queen Victoria
1837	Jul.	Launch of *Great Western*
1837	Aug.	Ship leaves for London
1838	Mar.	Trials in London
1838	Mar.	Leaves for Bristol; fire on board
1838	Apr.	Maiden voyage to New York
1838	May	Triumphant return to Bristol
1838	Jun.	Coronation of Queen Victoria
1838	Jun.	Cunard travels on *Great Western*
1838	Oct.	*Liverpool* commences service
1839	Oct.	Mail contract advertised by government
1839	Jun.	Cunard signs mail contract
1839	Jul.	*British Queen* commences service from London
1839	Dec.	End of *Liverpool* on Atlantic service
1840	Feb.	Marriage of Victoria and Albert

1840	Jul.	Cunard service to Halifax begins with 3 ships
1840	Aug.	*President* commences service
1841	Feb.	Loss of *President*
1841		*British Queen* sold
1841	Jun.	London to Bristol railway opens
1842		*Great Western* ends three voyages in Liverpool
1842	Jul.	Great Western dockyard for sale
1842	Oct.	1st auction at Bristol
1843	Feb.	1st voyage via Madeira
1843		Now permanently sailing from Liverpool
1843	Mar.	Thames Tunnel opened
1843	Jul.	*Great Britain* launched
1844	Jul.	Abortive sale of *Great Western* to P&O
1845	Jul.	*Great Britain* makes maiden voyage from Liverpool
1846	Aug.	Parliamentary committee on mail contracts
1846	Sep.	*Great Western* survives severe storms
1846	Sep.	*Great Britain* stranded in Dundrum Bay
1846	Nov.	*Great Western* on final passage to New York
1847	Mar.	Unsuccessful auction of *Great Western*
1847	Apr.	*Great Western* sold to Royal Mail Steam Packet Company
1847	Jun.	Sails from Southampton to West Indies
1851		Great Exhibition
1853	Jul.	*Great Western* sails to Brazil
1854	Feb.	Start of build of *Great Eastern*
1854	Sep.	Start of Crimean War
1854		Royal Albert Bridge over Tamar begun
1855	Sep.	*Great Western*'s final Atlantic voyage
1856	Mar.	*Great Western* on Crimea transport duty
1856	Mar.	Crimean War ends
1856	May	2nd Crimea journey
1856	Aug.	*Great Western* sold for scrap
1857		*Great Western* broken up at Vauxhall
1858	Jan.	*Great Eastern* launched
1859	Sep.	Maiden voyage of the *Great Eastern*
1859	Sep.	Brunel dies

APPENDIX 2

Atlantic Voyages of the *Great Western*

Voyage	Sailed	Year	Arrived	Year	from	to	Master
a	18-Aug	1837	22-Aug	1837	Bristol	London	Hosken
b	31-Mar	1838	2-Apr	1838	London	Bristol	
1	8-Apr	1838	23-Apr	1838	Bristol	New York	
	7-May	1838	22-May	1838	New York	Bristol	
2	2-Jun	1838	17-Jun	1838	Bristol	New York	
	25-Jun	1838	2-Jul	1838	New York	Bristol	
3	21-Jul	1838	5-Aug	1838	Bristol	New York	
	16-Aug	1838	30-Aug	1838	New York	Bristol	
4	8-Sep	1838	24-Sep	1838	Bristol	New York	
	4-Oct	1838	16-Oct	1838	New York	Bristol	
5	27-Oct	1838	15-Nov	1838	Bristol	New York	
	23-Nov	1838	7-Dec	1838	New York	Bristol	
c	20-Dec	1838	20-Dec	1838	Bristol	Milford Haven	
d	17-Jan	1839	17-Jan	1839	Milford Haven	Bristol	
6	28-Jan	1839	16-Feb	1839	Bristol	New York	
	25-Feb	1839	12-Mar	1839	New York	Bristol	
7	23-Mar	1839	14-Apr	1839	Bristol	New York	
	22-Apr	1839	7-May	1839	New York	Bristol	
8	18-May	1839	31-May	1839	Bristol	New York	
	13-Jun	1839	26-Jun	1839	New York	Bristol	
9	6-Jul	1839	22-Jul	1839	Bristol	New York	
	1-Aug	1839	13-Aug	1839	New York	Bristol	

10	24-Aug	1839	10-Sep	1839	Bristol	New York
	21-Sep	1839	4-Oct	1839	New York	Bristol
11	19-Oct	1839	2-Nov	1839	Bristol	New York
	16-Nov	1839	30-Nov	1839	New York	Bristol
12	20-Feb	1840	7-Mar	1840	Bristol	New York
	19-Mar	1840	2-Apr	1840	New York	Bristol
13	15-Apr		3-May	1840	Bristol	New York
	9-May	1840	23-May	1840	New York	Bristol
14	4-Jun	1840	18-Jun	1840	Bristol	New York
	1-Jul	1840	14-Jul	1840	New York	Bristol
15	25-Jul	1840	9-Aug	1840	Bristol	New York
	18-Aug	1840	31-Aug	1840	New York	Bristol
16	12-Sep		27-Sep	1840	Bristol	New York
16	10-Oct	1840	23-Oct	1840	New York	Bristol
17	7-Nov	1840	24-Nov	1840	Bristol	New York
	9-Dec	1840	23-Dec	1840	New York	Bristol
18	8-Apr	1841	23-Apr	1841	Bristol	New York
	1-May	1841	14-May	1841	New York	Bristol
19	27-May	1841	10-Jun	1841	Bristol	New York
19	19-Jun	1841	3-Jul	1841	New York	Bristol
20	14-Jul	1841	29-Jul	1841	Bristol	New York
20	7-Aug	1841	20-Aug	1841	New York	Bristol
21	1-Sep	1841	16-Sep	1841	Bristol	New York
	23-Sep	1841	8-Oct	1841	New York	Bristol
22	23-Oct	1841	8-Nov	1841	Bristol	New York
	23-Nov	1841	6-Dec	1841	New York	Bristol
23	2-Apr	1842	17-Apr	1842	Bristol	New York
	28-Apr	1842	11-May	1842	New York	Liverpool
24	21-May	1842	4-Jun	1842	Liverpool	New York
	16-Jun	1842	29-Jun	1842	New York	Bristol
25	16-Jul	1842	30-Jul	1842	Bristol	New York
	11-Aug	1842	24-Aug	1842	New York	Liverpool
26	3-Sep	1842	17-Sep	1842	Liverpool	New York
	29-Sep	1842	12-Oct	1842	New York	Bristol
27	22-Oct	1842	6-Nov	1842	Bristol	New York
	17-Nov	1842	30-Nov	1842	New York	Bristol
e			4-Dec	1842	Liverpool	Bristol

28	11-Feb	1843	12-Mar	1843	Bristol	New York	
	16-Mar	1843	1-Apr	1843	New York	Liverpool	
f	4-Apr	1843	6-Apr	1843	Liverpool	Milford Haven	
g	17-Apr	1843	18-Apr	1843	Milford Haven	Liverpool	
29	29-Apr	1843	11-May	1843	Bristol	New York	
29	25-May	1843	8-Jun	1843	New York	Liverpool	
30	17-Jun	1843	1-Jul	1843	Liverpool	New York	
	13-Jul	1843	26-Jul	1843	Bristol	New York	
31	5-Aug	1843	21-Aug	1843	Liverpool	New York	
31	31-Aug	1843	14-Sep	1843	New York	Liverpool	
32	23-Sep	1843	7-Oct	1843	Liverpool	New York	
32	19-Oct	1843	1-Nov	1843	New York	Liverpool	
h	3-Nov	1843	5-Nov	1843	Liverpool	Bristol	Mathews
j	12-Jun	1844	14-Jun	1844	Bristol	Liverpool	
33	22-Jun	1844	6-Jul	1844	Liverpool	New York	
	20-Jul	1844	4-Aug	1844	New York	Liverpool	
34	17-Aug	1844	31-Aug	1844	Liverpool	New York	
	14-Sep	1844	29-Sep	1844	New York	Liverpool	
35	12-Oct	1844	26-Oct	1844	Liverpool	New York	
	9-Nov	1844	23-Nov	1844	New York	Liverpool	
k					Liverpool	Bristol	
l	28-Mar	1845			Bristol	Liverpool	
36	29-Mar	1845	16-Apr	1845	Liverpool	New York	
	24-Apr	1845	8-May	1845	New York	Liverpool	
37	17-May	1845	1-Jun	1845	Liverpool	New York	
	12-Jun	1845	27-Jun	1845	New York	Liverpool	
38	5-Jul	1845	21-Jul	1845	Liverpool	New York	
	31-Jul	1845	18-Aug	1845	New York	Liverpool	
39	23-Aug	1845	9-Sep	1845	Liverpool	New York	
	18-Sep	1845	3-Oct	1845	New York	Liverpool	
40	11-Oct	1845	27-Oct	1845	Liverpool	New York	
	6-Nov	1845	21-Nov	1845	New York	Liverpool	
m	23-Nov	1845	24-Nov	1845	Liverpool	Bristol	
n			10-Apr	1846	Bristol	Liverpool	
41	11-Apr	1846	28-Apr	1846	Liverpool	New York	
	7-May	1846	21-May	1846	New York	Liverpool	

42	30-May	1846	15-Jun	1846	Liverpool	New York	
	25-Jun	1846	10-Jul	1846	New York	Liverpool	
43	25-Jul	1846	10-Aug	1846	Liverpool	New York	
	20-Aug	1846	3-Sep	1846	New York	Liverpool	
44	12-Sep	1846	30-Sep	1846	Liverpool	New York	
	8-Oct	1846	24-Oct	1846	New York	Liverpool	
45	31-Oct	1846	16-Nov	1846	Liverpool	New York	
	26-Nov	1846	12-Dec	1846	New York	Liverpool	
p	Dec–16	1846			Liverpool	Bristol	
r	29-Apr	1847	1-May	1847	Bristol	Southampton	Vincent
46	2-Jun	1847			Southampton	West Indies	
	15-Aug	1847	5-Sep	1847	West Indies	Southampton	
47	2-Feb	1848			Southampton	West Indies	Chapman
			19-Aug	1848	West Indies	Southampton	
s	26-Aug	1848	27-Aug	1848	Southampton	London	Moss
t	16-Sep	1848	17-Sep	1848	London	Southampton	
48	2-Oct	1848			Southampton	West Indies	
		1848	22-Dec	1848	West Indies	Southampton	Chapman
49	17-Jan	1849			Southampton	West Indies	Clark
			24-Apr	1849	West Indies	Southampton	Wolffe
u	5-May	1849	6-May	1849	Southampton	London	
v	23-May	1849	24-May	1849	London	Southampton	
50	2-Jun	1849			Southampton	West Indies	
	1-Jan	1850	20-Jan	1850	West Indies	Southampton	
51	18-Feb	1850			Southampton	West Indies	
	15-May	1850	2-Jun	1850	West Indies	Southampton	
52	2-Jul				Southampton	West Indies	
			18-Sep	1850	West Indies	Southampton	
53	1-Oct	1850			Southampton	West Indies	
	19-Apr	1851	8-May	1851	London	Southampton	
w	10-May	1851	11-May	1851	Southampton	London	
x	20-May	1851	21-May	1851	London	Southampton	
54	2-Jun	1851	21-Jun	1851	Southampton	West Indies	Brown
	19-Oct	1851	10-Nov	1851	West Indies	Southampton	Wooley
55	2-Dec	1851	22-Dec	1851	Southampton	West Indies	
	23-Feb	1852	18-Mar	1852	West Indies	Southampton	
56	2-Apr	1852	23-Apr	1852	Southampton	West Indies	
	2-Apr	1853	22-Apr	1853	West Indies	Southampton	Jellicoe

57	9-Jul	1853			Southampton	Rio	Onslow
	15-Aug	1853	14-Sep	1853	Rio	Southampton	
58	10-Oct	1853			Southampton	Rio	Hast
	15-Nov	1853	17-Dec	1853	Rio	Southampton	
59	9-Jan	1854	7-Feb	1854	Southampton	Rio	Bevis
	14-Feb	1854	16-Mar	1854	Rio	Southampton	
60	10-Apr	1854			Southampton	Rio	
	16-May	1854	14-Jun	1854	Rio	Southampton	
61	10-Jul	1854			Southampton	Rio	
	15-Aug	1854	12-Sep	1854	Rio	Southampton	
62	9-Oct	1854			Southampton	Rio	
	14-Nov	1854	16-Dec	1854	Rio	Southampton	
63	9-Jan	1855			Southampton	Rio	
	14-Feb	1855	19-Mar	1855	Rio	Southampton	
64	9-Apr	1855			Southampton	Rio	
	15-May	1855	15-Jun	1855	Rio	Southampton	
65	9-Jul	1855			Southampton	Rio	
	14-Aug	1855	13-Sep	1855	Rio	Southampton	

Note: The numbers indicate complete voyages, the letters relate to movements between ports for repair etc.
Source: Denis Griffiths, *Brunel's Great Western* (Wellingborough: Patrick Stephens, 1985), pp. 141–145

APPENDIX 3

Transatlantic Steamer Comparisons

Details supplied by Mr Shaw, with additions by Messrs Curling and Young and Messrs Maudslay & Field

	British Queen	Liverpool	Great Western
Length extreme	265 ft	223 ft	236 ft
Ditto under deck	245 ft	216 ft	212 ft
Do keel	223 ft	209 ft 5 in	205 ft
Breadth within paddle boxes	37 ft 6 in	30 ft 10 ins	35 ft 4 in
Do incl. do	64 ft	56 ft 3 in	59 ft 4 in
Depth at midships	29 ft 6 in	19 ft 8 in	23 ft 2 in
Tonnage	1863	1149	1340
Tons of space	1053	559	679
Tonnage of engine room	963	581	641
Horse power	500	468	450
Diameter of cylinder	71½ in	75 in	73 ½
Length of stroke	7 ft	7 ft	7 ft
Diameter of paddle wheels	30 ft	28 ft 5 in	28 ft 9 ins
Extr.wt.; engines, boilers, water	500 tons	420 tons	480 tons
Do coals	600 tons	600 tons	600 tons
Do cargo	500 tons	250 tons	250 tons
Draught of water with above wt and stores	16 ft	16 ft 6 in	16 ft 8 in

Source: 'British Parliamentary Papers: Report on Steam Vessel Accidents to Committee of Privy Council for Trade' (1839), p. 23

Lydia Sigourney's Poem

The King of the Icebergs
by Lydia Sigourney

Serene, the Sabbath evening fell
Upon the Northern deep,
And lonely there, a noble bark,
Across the waves did sweep;
She rode them like a living thing,
That heeds nor blast nor storm,
When lo! The King of Icebergs rose
A strange and awful form

Upon the horizon's verge he frowned,
A mountain 'mid the main,
As erst Philistia's giant tower'd
O'er Israel's tented plain.
And hoarsely over the dark, blue sea,
Was a threat'ning challenge tost,
'Who is this that dares with feet of fire
To tread in my realm of frost?'

Yet on the gallant steamship went,
Her heart of flame beat high,
And the stream of her fervent breath flow'd out
In volumes o'er the sky;
So the Ice King seized his deadly lance
To pierce the stranger foe,
And down to his deed of vengeance rushed
Troubling the depths below.

The watchful stars looked calmly on
Girt with their silver zones,
When a flash of bursting glory trac'd
An arch around their thrones.
For Aurora Borealis bent
From her palace above the skies,
And the wandering billows opened wide
Their phosphorescent eyes.

Firm at his post the Captain stood,
Clear-soul'd, and undismay'd,
And the King of Icebergs power defied,
While night drew on its shade;
On, through the interdicted realm
With fearless prow he sped,
Though round him gathering dangers pressed
And nameless forms of dread;

And longer had he borne the strife
But the thought of those who gave
Their life and welfare to his hand
Upon the tossing wave;
The noble, and the true of heart,
The helpless and the fair,
The child upon the mother's knee,
That knew no fear nor care;

And felt in the far distant homes,
How deep the grief and sure,
If the lips of love for them should ask,
And they return no more.
And so, his gallant ship he steer'd
From the disastrous fray,
And fell in the teeth of the southern blast
Led on her venturous way.

'Not thus shall ye scape my stormy ire'
The King of Icebergs spake,
And bade unloose his vassal train,
In arctic stream and lake;
And swift, a countless monster-train,
Rode over the waters blue,
With their dazzling helms and stony eyes
A pitiless, ruffian crew.

An icy ambush around the keel
With breathless speed they laid,

And the vengeful monarch laugh'd to see
How strong the mesh was made;
And, clustering close, that squadron dire
Spread over the startled flood,
While the straws of frost flew thick and chill'd
The hardiest seaman's blood.

But there fell a gleam of that light above,
That with Mercy's angel dwells,
And aided the labouring bark to foil
The King of Iceberg's spells;
For this by many a hearth-stone bright
A strain of praise shall be,
To Him who guides the wandered home
And rules the faithless sea

Published in *Godey's Lady's Book* (1841), p. 43

Claxton Letter to *The Times* (1843)

A classic example of Claxton's defence of the reputation of the *Great Western*.

The Times, 24 May 1843

(Advertisement)
To the Right Hon. Lord Brougham

My Lord:- From a report of the proceedings at a Judicial Committee of the Privy Council, held a few days ago on a claim for an extension of time in the matter of Morgan's Patent the following speech is attributed to your lordship:-

'I know a very great sailor, one of the greatest seaman, perhaps, of the present time, who said to me that he would not cross the Atlantic in the Great Western if they were to give her to him, so dangerous did he think steamers were as sea-boats at sea, certainly not on a lee shore.' I apprehend, my Lord, that something must have passed which is not published, and which drew from your Lordship the remark of 'certainly not on a lee shore' to which I shall presently refer.

In the execution of the duties of managing director of the Great Western Steam Ship Company, I have frequently been called upon to appear before the public, to refute statements of parties who have had reasons of their own for instituting comparisons or running down the *Great Western*, and to guard the interests of the Company by explanations to those who have dropped observations without the least intention of checking the progress of the science of steam navigation, if I may so express myself, on the one hand, or of injuring the prospects of the Company on the other. I class your Lordship with the latter number.

As it is not likely any observation of mine will attract your attention, much less call forth a reply, I shall, in the remarks I am about to make, and which I should not have made at all had not 'one of the greatest seamen, perhaps, of the present time' been brought forward as authority, assume that the observations of a hazard in the infancy of our undertaking, at the time when most naval officers of my acquaintance predicted that the *Great Western* must either break her back, be swallowed up in the trough of the sea, or dive under the powerful swells of the Atlantic, if we attempted to force her against them. It is probable, my Lord, but the 'great sailor' you allude to made the observation either at or about this period, or when the President, a weak and under-powered ship, became missing. If, my Lord, such should be the opinion of the 'great sailor' at the present day, your Lordship will, although only a landsman, upon the strength of the information, and armed with the facts I am about to produce, be able to refute a host of nautical arguments by one homely observation, to wit, 'the proof of the pudding is in the eating.'

I could furnish many instances of steamers surviving gales in which the best found sailing ships must have gone on shore, but for brevity shall content myself with the two which are mentioned in the very same report of the proceedings before the Privy Council, and an extraordinary recent case out of the very many from which the *Great Western* has been able to extricate herself, and all the valuable lives of passengers and crew, with comparative ease.

The case of the *Spitfire* was simply this – she steamed from off a lee shore in the height of a hurricane, when most, if not all, the ships in Carlisle Bay, Barbadoes were forced high and dry from their anchors or moorings. The case of the *Hydra*, if I mistake not, was one of steaming to sea when one of Her Majesty's men-of-war cut away all her masts with three anchors ahead. If not the *Hydra*, some other steamer at or near Bayrout, and the *Hydra* is only another instance.

The *Great Western*, on her last homeward voyage, was caught in the very bight of the bay formed by Long Island and the Jersey Coast, within an hour and half's sail of the bar at Sandy Hook, with the wind at S.E., or dead on shore. It blew a furious hurricane for 12 hours (so hard that one of her boats rather slighter built than the rest, unstruck by a sea, was shivered to stems in the slings), the whole time in only 15 fathoms of water, and according to the captain's report when no canvas could have stood a minute, and yet, my Lord, instead of nearing the shore she increased her distance from it. The American papers teemed with losses in this really terrific gale, and great fears were openly expressed for the safety of our gallant ship.

Great Western, and all the noble ships of the Halifax line, have experienced quite as bad weather as in 6 years, with constant passages at stated periods, the Atlantic is or, probably, ever before has been subject to, and the former ship alone has travelled considerably over 100,000 miles with no other accident than the loss of a bowsprit in coming up like a whale to blew, after rather a deeper plunge than usual with fair head way, on her right course, my Lord, and against a head wind and sea,

The late Sir Thomas Hardy, my esteemed and lamented friend, had none of the prejudices against steam ships which for a time obtained so generally in the navy, and he approved of almost every step that was taken in the progress of the *Great Western*. Had it pleased God to lengthen his life, he would have been the champion of our cause in the present day. A seamen of the very first calibre, he would have been a noble champion to break a lance with your Lordships 'great sailor'; lacking such an one, if you would enter the lists with Captain Hosken, or even my humble self, I think we should be able to prove that the steam-engine with its appurtenances (to say nothing of other advantages) render a ship safer in bad weather, whether scudding before the wind or crawling off a lea shore, than a craft only propellable when the wind please this to blow, and whose safety depends upon canvass, which the steam ship, like herself, has also at command and in sufficient quantity for violent weather; and your Lordship may rely upon it that the steam ship, which can for 12 hours make head against a hurricane, when there would not have been two hours drift for any sailing ship in the world, would not do very badly in an ocean tempest of whatever strength or duration.

With great respect your Lordships humble servant

Christopher Claxton RN Managing director
Great Western Steam Ship offices
35 Princes Street Bristol
May 22nd 1843

Claxton Sea Chest Recommendations

Claxton made these recommendations for midshipmen and it is more than probable that he gave similar recommendations to the *Great Western* cadets. It shows his attention to detail.

He recommends sea chests should contain:

Four dozen shirts
8 pairs of duck trowsers
4 ditto jean
4 white waistcoats
2 suits of blue superfine
2 round second cloth superfine
2 white kerseymere waistcoats
24 pairs of cotton stockings
12 ditto worsted
4 tablecloths
24 pocket handkerchiefs.
24 towels
4 pairs of sheets
4 pillow-cases
4 pairs of shoes
Bed and blankets
Paper, pens and ink
Quadrant
Desk
Dirk and belt
Prayer book, bible and Hamilton Moore*
Washing materials, and chest
Two hats

Total £125

He also recommended if possible a sextant which was about £18 and other things if the parent could afford it such as a glass, drawing box, sword, books etc.

As a minimum annual allowance he recommends it should be £40 per annum and £60 pounds was not too much; more than that he felt would do more harm than good.

*Hamilton Moore, author of *Moore's Navigation*, *Seaman's Daily Assistant*, the *Monitor*, &c.

Source: Christopher Claxton, *The Naval Monitor* (London: 2nd edn, 1833).

Hosken Letter to Lord Goulburn (1846)

Captain Hosken was then at the height of his reputation and this letter was written a few weeks before the fateful passage that left his new ship stranded in Dundrum Bay.

Evening Mail
Tuesday August 25, 1846

To the Right Honourable H Gouldburn

From *Great Britain* steamship Liverpool August 20

Sir – I have read a statement made by you in the House of Commons, when a committee on the North American mail contracts was moved for by Mr. Miles, and as that portion of your speech relating to the *Great Western* steamship was not founded on fact (although there can be no doubt you, Sir, believed it true, and that you are induced to believe that by false information from interested parties), I feel called upon, in justice to myself, who commanded that still good ship, to call your attention to the following days of her departure and arrival during the years 1838, 1839 and 1840, which will clearly show you that the Great Western Steamship Company, with their ship the *Great Western*, under my command, have a right to the credit of *proving* to this country and to the world, the possibility of crossing the Atlantic by steam to and from America, at all seasons of the year; and this was done against the expressed opinions of high scientific authority, and also (of what I deem more important in this case), the strongly expressed opinions of good practical seamen.

You will see by the dates I shall give, that the Halifax and Boston contracts were not made until the *Great Western* had *proved* by making winter passages (being at sea in November and December 1838, and January and February and March 1839), the possibility of the voyage being accomplished at ALL times of year.

The following is copied from your speech, as reported in the times of the 25th of July:-

'Mr. Cunard has thus *proved* to all what no other company ever yet proved, that it was possible to maintain the communication regularly through the winter.'

'But the Great Western Company has never attempted to cross the Atlantic during the winter months. *The latest period they ever sailed from any port was November 6 and the earliest voyage was in April.* That company had made no attempt to face the difficulties of navigation through the ice. These were never faced by anyone but Mr Cunard and *therefore having overcome these he was entitled to a preference.*'

Now, Sir, for dates (*being every month you are told the Great Western never sailed from any port!*)

Left Bristol	Arr. at New York	Left Bristol	Arr. at New York
Oct 27, 1838	Nov 15	Nov 23 1838	Dec 7
Jan 28, 1839	Feb 16	Feb 25 1839	March 12
Oct 19, 1839	Nov 2	Nov 16, 1839	Nov 30
Feb 20, 1840	March 7	March 19, 1840	April 2
Nov 7, 1840	Nov 24	Dec 9, 1840	Dec 23

During this time the Great Western Company found that the winter passages were not profitable from a small number of the passengers, length of voyage, and consequent extra wear and tear of their ship; and could not compete with the company having government patronage, they have wisely decided on making passages in the finer months of the year only.

I do not blame men for using every exertion to obtain such patronage, but I do complain of false statements to obtain it, and as the statements affect my credit as one of those who first solved the problem of Atlantic steam navigation, I make no apology for thus placing myself before you and the public on this occasion in which I feel peculiarly called on to do so; and I trust all sense of justice to acknowledge that the statement made by you to the House of Commons (now referred to) was made on incorrect information.

I have the owner to be Sir
Your obedient servant
James Hosken

NB. Since writing the above, I find the name of Cunard on the *Great Western*'s passenger list several times, and more than once during the dates I have given you, three are Mr Cunard or his brothers.

Hosken Letter to Lord Goulburn (1846)

Evening Mail, Monday 14 September 1846

The *Great Western* Steam-ship
Captain Hosken has received the following answer from the late Chancellor of the Exchequer, to a letter which appeared in this journal some weeks ago.

North Aston, August 28
Sir
I have received, this place, your letter of the 20th of August

I can have no hesitation in assuring you that nothing was further from my intention than to make any statement in the House of Commons which could by possibility be construed as derogatory to the credit due to you for naval enterprise or skill.

I have not here any means of referring to what fell from me in debate with reference to the contract entered into by Messrs Cunard. Of this I am certain, at the truest from which I quoted the voyages of the *Great Western* were no further back than the year 1843; and, so far as I recollect, it was with reference to this period which has since elapsed that my observations as to the voyages of that ship were made

I have the honour to be, sir
Your most obedient humble servant
Henry Goulburn

APPENDIX 8

An English Businessman in New York

Extract from *Journal of a Voyage across the Atlantic: With Notes on Canada & the United States; and Return to Great Britain, in 1844*
By George Moore, Esq.

London:
Printed for Private Circulation.
1845.

From July 1844

Monday morning, the 2nd.—After breakfast dispatched three-quarters of a hundred newspapers to my old and valued friends in England. They keep no stock on hand for promiscuous sale: they printed them on purpose for me. After which I visited the business parts. All the streets filled with empty cases, which they had just cleared for the Fall trade: auctioneers hammering away in all corners, knocking goods about as if they cost nothing. In the stores there appears no system—all is confusion. The heat was awful till seven P.M., when the rain came down in torrents: at the same time the atmosphere was brilliantly lighted by flashes of electric fire. Took Mr. and Mrs. Green to the Park Theatre, to patronize Anderson as Othello, Miss Clara Ellis as Desdemona, and a Mr. Dowsett as Iago, all of whom crossed with us. A poor set out. Theatrical property in the States, I understand, is at a greater discount than in England. Poor Mr. Simpson, whom I sat next to in my passage, is the proprietor—a worthy man, and much esteemed. To bed at eleven.

Tuesday. —A long day of business. Observed with regret their loose mode. All busy; and they appear to think good times will last for ever. Nearly all have failed at one time or the other. Bankers discounting liberally at present; and all appear to be trying who can sell cheapest. Retired to rest at eleven, lost in amazement, and the reflection that this state of things cannot last long.

Wednesday. —Ascertained the geography of the town pretty well; and so I ought, for I walked till I was nearly red in the face, and my shirt wet through. Engaged at the present moment, ten P.M., writing this, with all my bedroom windows open, and in my shirt. Hot! Hot!! VERY HOT!!!

Thursday. —Called upon Mr. J. J. Echalaz, at Goodhue and Co.'s, where I received marked attention from both Mr. E. and his employers. When I introduced my letters from E. B. Webb, at Baring's, got some valuable information, and letters of introduction to Philadelphia, Boston, Baltimore, Washington, and Canada. Afterwards took a turn amongst the retail-shops, to see their system. Mr. Stewart, Broadway, and a few others, axe done upon the London style, but the lower class take any price they can get. a higher object than his pay. God grant that he may long be spared!—We then saw the avenues; and, as "variety is charming," we then visited Niblo's Theatre—something like what Vauxhall was: lots of handsome girls performing nonsense; and two or three men, more particularly one named Mitchell, kept us in roars of laughter. Bussed it home: no conductor: the driver has a strap with which he shuts and opens the door, and you pay him through a hole in the roof. To bed at eleven. Began to like my companion very much: found him a sober, religious, industrious man, who studies to make himself agreeable.

Friday morning.—Bought a lot of books, new publications, at desperately low prices: bought also a capital map of the United States and Canada for 10 dollars to send to Bow Churchyard, to show my journey when I return to Europe. Afterwards had a long consultation with my old friend and fellow-apprentice, Joseph Blane, who is in prosperity, esteemed by all who know him, and in possession of the best information about the standing of the different parties in the dry-goods trade. Spent the remainder of the day with George Pearce, and was rather favourably impressed with the object I had in view in taking this voyage. It is now ten, and I smoke my solitary cigar, having confined myself to one since my arrival.

Saturday morning.—Full of business all day. Had interviews with Brown Brothers, (the Rothschilds of America,) from whom I received marked kindness and attention, and most liberal offers to transact our money operations. Also spent an hour with Pickersgill and partners, who had been doing our business, and was much pleased with their straightforward manner. Also saw Mr. Ebbets, at the Union Bank, whom I found a business man. Heard all their propositions, and reflected upon them. Dined with Mr. Pearce, and stuck to my writing till seven o'clock. Then called upon Mr. Green; and he came and had an oyster supper with me. And I may here observe, they beat us altogether in cooking oysters: they fry, stew, roast, boil, and have every imaginable way of cooking them. Took a warm-bath to finish the week, and not before I required it, as I have been wet through every day with perspiration since I came here. To bed at ten.

Sunday morning.—Rose fresh. Had my head shampooed and cleaned in a most extraordinary manner. Breakfasted, and to St. John's Episcopal Church, and heard a very good sermon by Dr. Milliner: I forget the text, although I was much impressed with the discourse. Returned to the Astor, where my old friend, Joseph Blane, was waiting to take me to his house to dine. He has the best house I had been in yet - 774, Broadway; not living, like most of the New York merchants, at hotels, lodgings, or boardinghouses. Introduced to his wife, whom I found a delightful woman—of French extraction, but Yankee-born. Was introduced to Mr. Deseze, Mrs. B.'s brother-in-law, a Frenchman, who fought under Napoleon at Waterloo, and was offered to retain his commission by Louis XVIII., but he declined it. This was one of the pleasantest days I had spent since I left my own fireside. It brought old recollections to my memory that had long been buried —scenes of my boyhood, when Blane and I were serving our apprenticeship in Wigton. In the evening we went to Palmo's Opera-house, to hear Dr. Lardner, of Heaviside notoriety. It was his second lecture on the "Evidences of Religion afforded by the Phenomena of Nature, and the Consistency of Science with Divine Revelation." We were much pleased. He is the most complete elocutionist I ever heard, and impressed a crowded audience with his sublime subject. What a melancholy loss to England by his one false step, that degraded him in moral society! Walked to the Astor, and took one cigar each, when Mr. B. told me he was collecting charity for the poor widow of H. W—s, who had left her without a shilling to support four helpless children. He had 6000 dollars a year, and Mr. F. discharged him for intemperance. He took to his bed, and died of a broken heart. I envied this man, when I lived with him at 19 F.'s, for his position. Gave his widow 50 dollars; and to bed.

Monday morning.—Had a long interview with Prime, Ward, and King, the first house here whom I had letters to from Barings and Overend, and Gurney. They gave me all the information in their power, and introduced me to Mr. Halford's agent, a bill-broker, 46, Wall-Street. Was occupied till dinner writing to Bow Churchyard, and had Mr. Pearce to dine with me. Dr. Keene called in the evening, and we took steam-boat (as large as six of the Margate boats) to Hoboken. Had a delightful walk by the Hudson River, and saw some Indians, real Natives, with whom I was much struck. Returned by a steam-boat, still larger and more crammed: I should think there must have been 2000 souls, with lots of trotting-horses, and gigs from 70 lbs. to 120 lbs. weight each, returning from a trotting match. Heard some extraordinary grasshoppers, which repeated "Kate she did!" and "Kate she didn't!" quite distinctly. Thence, for the first time, to a mobocracy meeting, where they expressed awfully Liberal opinions— "Polk and Dallas for ever!" The room, a very large one, was crammed to suffocation: I should think there were 5000 wedged in, and I should say the thermometer stood at 106°. Liberal as I am, I went no length to them. Beat all the speeches I ever heard. Dan. O'Connell, Tom Duncombe, and the late Hunt and Cobbett were fools to them. Home again with a wet shirt, and to bed.

Tuesday morning.—Received letters of introduction from Goodhue and Co. to Philadelphia, Boston, Baltimore, Canada, and Washington. Had a long talk with Mr. M., 60, Cedar-Street. Introduced by Pearce, about my intended trip: found him very useful. Received an order from a good house, without soliciting them. Wrote and finished my letters home per *Great Western*. Mr. Blane, and my old friend Brough, the performer, dined with me. Was introduced to Capt. M'Lean, of the *Swallow* , running to Albany; and then walked with Mr. R., of Manchester, down to the Battery: a beautiful walk, To the Castle Garden, where there was another Polk meeting, which I should think 10,000 people attended. Lots of Liberality again. The Fort close to this is a splendid affair. Came by White Hall back to the Astor, and wrote a long letter to my wife; and, as it is just now ten o'clock, good night!

Wednesday morning.—Bought three splendid racoon skins—one each for Mr. Groucock, Mr. J. of Liverpool, and self, for our carriage driving-boxes (Mr J. having put upon my finger a magnificent diamond ring very unexpectedly when I was leaving my native shore, as a mark of gratitude for a disinterested act on my part towards him long, long ago, which he considered had been the groundwork of his fortune:) also some tobacco to pack in them, to prevent them spoiling. Then saw over the Custom-house, which is a very fine building; and the Exchange. Business is not done here as it is in London. Mr. Vyse, Mr. Palin, and I then visited the Tombs. Prisoners do not remain here long. If the sentence is long, they are sent to Blackwood's Island. The prisoners here are kept clean, have well aired cells, and are allowed to walk about at their pleasure. They get only two meals a day: a quart of coffee or more, and as much bread as they can eat. Dinner at three, with plenty of beef and bread. For very long sentences they are sent to Singsing, up the North River, and Auburn state-prisons. We then visited the Sessions-house, where there is no distinction between judges, counsel, or prisoners—all are in plain dress, spitting about in all corners. Heard an eloquent counsel defending a prisoner. Saw the lock-up, the warder's and grand jury rooms. Altogether the Tombs is a very fine building. Saw where the memorable J. C. Colt destroyed himself immediately after he was married, and two hours before he would have been hanged. We passed Washington Hall, where many a fine fellow has been ruined by gaming and drinking; and dined at Astor House, where I was told it for a positive fact they take 500 dollars a day ready money for drinks of brandy by people standing. They pay 40,000 dollars a year rent. We then took a drive, saw Mr. Vyse's fine horse and sulky, and spent an hour at his apartments, which are first-rate: then to Trenton Hall to see a Mr. Green, a reformed gambler, who exposed the rascality of gaming of all sorts, and taught me how to know the cards by their backs. I was much interested, and bought his "Life," with its scandalous exposures. Saw

221

Captain M'Arthey, who shot his brother in a duel, and has been distracted ever since. To bed at eleven o'clock.

Thursday morning.—Called upon Prime, Ward, and King, for letters of introduction for my future route. Read P. and S.'s articles of partnership, Wrote another long letter to my wife. Put Mr. Dowden's commission into Mr. Pearce's hands, and Mr. Carrick's into Mr. Brough's, who has friends at Vicksburgh. Bought my wife a handsome rocking-chair. Then walked down to see the *Queen of the West*, the finest packet-ship I ever saw. Visited the different markets: saw lots of fruit, but do not think they touch us in anything but apples; tasted a large pumpkin, but did not like it. Dined at the Astor; paid my bill, and packed up. To bed at ten.

Note: The original is in the Library of Congress, Washington

APPENDIX 9

Great Western Menu Comparison

The *Great Western*'s food compares well to the best hotels. Here are three different examples: a menu from the ship, the menu for the Astor House in New York and accounts from a hotel in London.

Great Western Bill of Fare 4 July 1846

Breakfast
Beef steak dishes 4
Mutton chops
Pork chops
Ham and eggs 6
Fried bacon 4
Fricassee chicken
Veal cutlets 4
Stews 4
Omeletes 4
Boiled eggs 24
Harmony 4
Hash
Mush
Fried fish 6
Broiled chicken
Broiled Mackerel 4
Cold meats 12

Dinner
Turtle soups 6
Boiled fish salmon 4
Baked fish lobster sauce 2
Roast beef 2
Roast mutton saddles 2

Roast lamb 1
Roast turkey larded 2
Roast veal 1
Roast pork 1
Duck and tomato 2
Roast fowls
Roast geese
Boiled Mutton 1
Gallentine Turkies 4
Fowles oyster sauce 2
Corned beef 1
Corned pork
Ham 2
Tongues 2
Fricandeau
Mutton cutlets 6
Macaroni 2
Curry
Irish stew
Calves Head Feet 6
Oyster Patties 8
Lobster salad 8
Chicken salad
Woodcocks 12
Cold Slaw 8

Pastry

Plum Pudding 4
Apple dumpling
Raspberry rollers 2
Baked apple pudding 2
Apple pies 6
Cranberry pies 4
Raspberry pies puff 8
Plum pies
Mince pies 2

Damson pies 4
Cherry pies
Rice pudding 8
Macaroni pudding
Custard in cups 4
Gooseberry pies 4
Jellies and blancmange 12
Pine apples 8
Brandy fruit 8
Beignet

Note: the numbers relate to the number of dishes placed on the table for diners to help themselves.

Source: Brunel Institute, ss *Great Britain* Trust

Astor House Menu (1844)

Gentlemen's Ordinary

Soup
Mock Turtle Soup

Fish
Baked Black Fish, Claret sauce
Clam Chowder

Boiled
Corned Beef
Ham
Tongue
Chickens and Pork
Smoked Corned Beef
Leg of Mutton
Cold Pressed Corned Beef
Cold Roast Beef
Cold Corned Leg of Pork
Cold Roast Lamb

Side Dishes
Lobster Salad
Mutton Chops, breaded,
Rib of Beef, Champagne sauce
Pigeons with fine Herbs
Broiled Chickens, Steward's sauce
Calf's Head, Brain sauce
Small Birds, Port Wine sauce
Small Oyster Pies

Ducks, Spanish sauce
Veal, Tomato sauce
Macaroni
Eels, Cold Sauce
Beans and Pork

Vegetables
Boiled Potatoes
Corn
Onions
Turnips
Tomatoes
Fried Egg Plants
Boiled Rice
Beets
Cabbage
Shelled Beans

Roast
Beef
Pig
Chicken
Geese
Lamb and Mint sauce

Pastry
Peach Pie
Kisses

Custard Pie	**Dessert**
Lemon Pudding	Filberts, Almonds, Raisins, Oranges,
Fruit Jelly	Figs, Plums, Apples, Pears, Melons,
	Peaches, &c.
	Ice Cream

Source: Moore, George. *Journal of a voyage across the Atlantic: with notes on Canada & the United States, and return to Great Britain in 1844* (London: s.n, 1845)

Two Accounts from a London Hotel in 1839

Mr Harris, Room No. 2

			£	s	d
Sept	30	Dinner		7	4
		Brandy			6
Oct	1	Laundress		6	7
Oct	2	Dinner & Brandy		9	
		Breakfast & beefsteak		9	2
		Brandy			6
		Stout			6
Oct	3	Breakfast & beefsteak		2	2
		Brandy & port		2	6
		Stout & ale		1	2
		Ale			5
		Paper			6
	4	Seidletz Powder			6
		Breakfast			4
		Soupe et pain		1	6
		Sherry		3	5
		Dinner			6
		Stout & biscuits		2	6
		Postage		1	8
	5	Dejeuner		3	
		Ham		1	
		Brandy			6
		Breakfast		1	3
		Beef		1	
		Brandy			6
		Ale & Stout		1	2

		£	s	d
	Paper		·	6
	Breakfast & beefsteak		2	2
	stout			6
	Hair oil		3	6
	Shoe strings			4
8	Soda			6
	Breakfast & beefsteak		2	2
	Brandy			6
	Seidletz powder			4
9	Breakfast		3	9
10	Ditto		3	4
	postman			2
	Medicine		1	

Note: Seidlitz powders, a common laxative and digestion remedy containing tartaric acid, sodium tartrate and sodium bicarbonate

Mr Buisson du Maurier, room No. 17

		£	s	d
10	soupe et pain			9
	ale			8
11	Breakfast & cutlets		1	11
	Dinner		2	
12	Dejeuner		1	3
	Dinner		1	9
	Soupe et pain			9
13	Dejeuner		1	3
	Dinner		3	
	Soupe & bread			9
14	breakfast		1	3
	Dinner		16	5
	postman			1
15	Breakfast		1	3
	postman			8
16	breakfast		1	3
	dinner		4	7
	postage		1	3
	soupe & bread			9
17	Breakfast		1	3
	Soda & whisky			8

Great Western *Menu Comparison*

	Postage	1	8
	Supper	1	7
18	breakfast	1	3
	Dinner	3	2
	ale & whisky	1	2
19	postage		8
	Breakfast	1	3
	Dinner	5	1
	Whisky		4
20	Breakfast	1	3
	Dinner	3	11
21	Breakfast & bacon	1	8
	Dinner	3	4
	Soupe & bread		9
22	Breakfast & bacon	1	8
	Laundress	5	9

Source: National Archives C 114/128: Chancery Exhibits Re Fricour, a bankrupt: Hotel inventory and account books (London, 1839)

Mock Turtle Soup

A New System of Domestic Cookery
By a lady

(John Murray: London, 1811)

Mock Turtle Soup
Put into a pan a knuckle of veal, two fine cow heels, two onions, a few cloves, peppers, berries of allspice, mace, and sweet herbs: Cover them with water, then tie a thick paper over the pan and set it in an oven for three hours. When cold take off the fat very nicely; cut the meat and feet into bits an inch and a half square; remove the bones and coarse parts; and then put to rest on to warm with a large spoonful of walnut and one of mushroom-ketchup, half the pint of sherry or Madeira wine, a little mushroom-powder and the jelly of the meat. When hot, if it wants any more seasoning add some; and serve with hard eggs, forcemeat balls, a squeeze of lemon and a spoonful of soy.

Another recipe
This is a very easy way and the dish is excellent

Stew a pound and a half of scrag of mutton with from three pints of water to a quart; Then set the broth on, with a calf's foot and a cow heel, cover the stew-pan tight, and simmer till you can get of the meat from the bones in proper bits. Set it on again with the broth, a quarter of a pint of Madeira wine or sherry, a large onion, half a teaspoonful of Cayenne pepper, a bit of lemon peel, two anchovies, some sweet herbs, eighteen oysters cut into pieces and then chopped fine, a tea spoonful of salt, a little nutmeg, and the liquor of the oysters; cover it tight, and simmer three quarters of an hour. Serve with forcemeat balls and hard eggs in the tureen.

Forcemeat as for turtle, at the *Bush*, Bristol
A pound of fine fresh suet, one ounce of ready dressed veal or chicken, chopped fine, crumbs of bread, a little shallot or onion, salt, white pepper, nutmeg, mace,

penny royal, parsley, and lemon thyme finely shred: be as many fresh eggs yolks and whites separately, as will make the above ingredients into a moist paste: roll into small balls, and boil them in fresh lard, putting them in just as it boils up. When of a light brown, take them out, and drain them before the fire. If the suet be moist or stale, a great many more eggs will be necessary.

Balls made this way are remarkably light; but being greasy some people prefer them with less suet and eggs.

APPENDIX 11

Roches Point and the Speed of Communications

Brunel had a pioneering interest in the electric telegraph. In 1862 a telegraph station was erected at Roches Point at the entrance to Cork Harbour, Ireland. This article in 1864 in a Bristol newspaper contrasts the transmission of news from America via the new telegraph system and the *Great Western*. Brunel's last ship the *Great Eastern* would go on to lay the first cable across the Atlantic in 1865.

Bristol Times and Mirror 25 June 1864
Roches Point

To what newspaper reader is Roches Point not a familiar name? It is now at least in Great Britain and Ireland a renowned spot: But before the breaking out of the American war who knew anything about it or had any idea where it was save some few yachting citizens of Cork? Roche's [sic] Point is a geographical fact not a mere geographical idea – Or a myth (as many for a while thought it) of Mr Reuter's and the *Times*' correspondent. A little – say about 500 yards or so-outside the Cove, and facing the seaboard, this bare projecting eminence stands. On it is a round white telegraph tower and telegraph post, but not a shrub, or tree, or a blade of grass. Lying inland and about half a mile or so from the clifted shore, is a great gaunt Irish mansion with its two great wings, built like itself of gloomy limestone, and filled with countless square windows. This I presume to be the house of Roche, after which the point is called. The owner has secured immortality for himself by the accident of a rock on his estate being suitable for Mr Reuter's purpose.

A week or two ago I was made acquainted for the first time by name with the renowned point. I had seen it before but did not know what it was. I was on my way from Bristol to Cork by the *Apollo*, and it might be three or four miles from the entrance to the latter Harbour, when Captain Poole, who had been sweeping the sea westward, handed me a powerful binocular telescope, saying 'Here is one of the great American liners coming in.' On the horizon was a long streak of smoke and as I looked, there loomed above

230

the waterline first the masts and chimney, and then the hull of a huge vessel. Rapidly it became more and more into sight, and then I could distinguish the passengers walking the deck to and fro, not a few of them, perhaps, seeing the outlines of a part of the Old World for the first time; for I noticed – or perhaps only fancied I noticed – the excitement and bustle of curiosity on board.

But Roche's Point, so still and lone a few minutes ago, is now all alive. The man on the lookout there had probably noticed from his white watch-tower the liner before we had; so up the signal ran to the summit of his flagstaff, and was promptly answered by the great ship still steering inwards. That answer was read in 10 or 15 minutes afterwards in all the telegraph of boards of all our Commercial Rooms and all the Commercial Rooms and Clubs in the kingdom. It is but a few words but it sets people of all classes in a fever of expectancy:-

'Roche's Point Wednesday 2:30 PM – SS *City of Edinburgh* coming in.'

By this very mail, all the world was expecting to hear more of Grant's advance on Richmond. The last accounts left him pounding his way onward: Shall we now hear he is beating or being beaten? You must wait an hour or so, or it may be, an hour and half before you know more; for that little steamer, which has been all the morning lying in wait just off Lighthouse Point will take 15 or 20 minutes before it reaches the *Edinburgh*, and when it reaches her, it's chimney hardly touches the top of the great ship, which delivers her mail bags, newspapers, and a passenger or two; and then once more her paddles revolve, and she is steaming, with this very trifling delay for Liverpool.

And now Roche's Point is again at work, flashing along upon the wires that travel inland from that lone white tower, the intelligence that has been stale news for the last 10 days to the passengers on board the *Edinburgh;* who have long since thrown aside, as flat and uninteresting, the latest additions of the New York papers which they purchased before going on board.

A friend of mine happened to be the guest of some Cork acquaintances at a picnic on this very point a couple of months ago, When movement of the flag staff called their attention away from the cold lamb and salad (keen as their appetite from the sea breezes was) to the telegraph tower. He then saw the manipulation of the intelligence take place – The rapid glancing through the newspapers just landed from the little steamer, The condemnation of the contents and a quick rattling off of the heads of the same by the quick telegraph operator. There went battle, murder and sudden death along the wire at every half dozen movements of his hands! Such was the terrible story the New World had to tell the Old. The newspapers had it cried around the streets in a couple of hours. 'Another great battle and fearful slaughter – several thousands killed!' That huge ship, which I saw enlarging as it neared me from the horizon, flinging back a long black pennon of smoke, might as well have been freighted with blood – might as well have been a plague ship. It came out of the far ocean from the far hemisphere to us, bearing such awful intelligence. It seemed to say to us, 'We left your Cousins fighting away harder than ever – Cutting one another's throats on a more multitudinous scale than ever. The carrion crows were gorging themselves on another foughten field when we sailed.'

Well I remember when not Roches Point but Portishead Point that used to be the first ground up on which American news alighted in this kingdom. When the *Great Western* was the only steamship between the two hemispheres. *The Times* and the *Morning Herald* were then the great competing channels for early intelligence, but there was no electric telegraph, and the short strip of the Great Western Railway from Paddington to Maidenhead was the only bit of railway between London and Bristol. The rival metropolitan journals were each locally represented; *The Times* correspondent is dead and the other gentleman though still flourishing in the flesh is no longer a citizen of Bristol. Wishing to see how they managed the work – how the earliest intelligence was made – I went down with the latter to Portishead one day before the great steam ship was expected in. We all stopped at the hotel, and the same evening Captain Christopher Claxton, as the acting director of the company, arrived, to be on the spot when the vessel cast anchor. We made ourselves comfortable to midnight, every now and then going to the bay window of the hotel, to look at in the dark up the channel, to see if the lights of the great incoming vessel were yet discernible. Then we went to bed, 'Our Special Correspondents' first going out to see that the boatmen, whom they kept in readiness to warn and launch off with them as soon as the signals of the steamship were shown, were at their posts. Each special had a boat of his own and that was rivalry between them- no accord or co-operation. When we had been a couple of hours in bed a detonating ball, and then a great bustle, were heard outside. The ship was coming in and our correspondents were up in no time, the oarsmen pulling towards the huge dark object – dark but for the lights on board at which the streaks of foam slashed out by the paddles reflected and refracted. Up went a blue light from ours (the *Herald*) boat; the *Times* tugging along behind us. The use of a blue light I could not tell you unless it were for a little bit of brag and display: for the great ship had not reached her station in Kingroad and dropped her mighty anchors. Most of the passengers were yet in their berths, but a few had come on board, and the sailors were bustling about, while weather beaten faces looked on us over the bulwarks on us, as we got under the tall black hulk. We were quickly up the ladder; 'our correspondents' had their bundles of papers and letters promptly given them, and exchanging a word or two with the captain, or some muffled passenger, so as to get a birds eye idea of the news they were presently to extract from these packages of papers, down the ship's side they went once more into their boats trying to read the contents of the whitey- brown pages of American intelligence while they pulled for Portishead Point. But there were no battles then to tell off – no awful slaughters: the price of corn, or at most a Presidential message, was all they had to chronicle, or that of bunkum or a Georgian duel. Nevertheless on to Bristol with their treasured dispatches rattled our correspondents, and then they had post-chaises and ran races along the road to Maidenhead, to see who would be in town first with their news: endeavouring to compiled the contents as they went, and writing on a flat board supported on their knees, which the jerking vehicle rendered anything but an easy task. Money no object in those days, let us see who'll win the race. Well, 'Tempora mutantur'. The *Times* (as well as the *Herald* and all other Papers) are changed – are now differently served, or rather served all alike, by Mr Reuter; as silently and invisibly in as many seconds as it took hours, the news is flashed from Roche's Point to London without the cracking of postillion's whips or the running of post-chaise races along turnpike roads.

Passengers to New York in 1838

Source: These are derived from *Passenger Lists of Vessels Arriving at New York, New York, 1820–1897*. Microfilm Publication M237, 675 rolls. NAI: 6256867. Records of the U.S. Customs Service, Record Group 36. National Archives at Washington, D.C.

Notes: 1. Names are as given in the on-line transcripts and have not been checked against the originals

2. Married women were frequently referred to as 'Lady of' and did not signify aristocracy, this has been changed to Mrs unless a title is obvious.

3. Occasionally the transcripts miss pages from originals e.g. Judge Haliburton does not appear in the index on-line but a further search shows him and others on board in April 1839.

Voyage no.	Passenger	Arr. port	Arr. Date	Dep. Port	DOB
1	C Bagster	New York	24 Apr 1838	Bristol, England	abt 1813
1	Eliza Cross	New York	24 Apr 1838	Bristol, England	abt 1818
1	W A Foster	New York	24 Apr 1838	Bristol, England	abt 1807
1	Jno Gordon	New York	24 Apr 1838	Bristol, England	abt 1813
1	W Graham	New York	24 Apr 1838	Bristol, England	abt 1783
1	Chas Tait	New York	24 Apr 1838	Bristol, England	abt 1813
1	James Welmer	New York	24 Apr 1838	Bristol, England	abt 1807
2	Dampier	New York	18 Jun 1838	Bristol, England	abt 1836
2	E Abeirn	New York	18 Jun 1838	Bristol, England	abt 1812
2	Mary Allheisen	New York	18 Jun 1838	Bristol, England	abt 1805
2	Peter Bennett	New York	18 Jun 1838	Bristol, England	abt 1778
2	Geg?? Bennett	New York	18 Jun 1838	Bristol, England	abt 1816
2	Mary Bertt	New York	18 Jun 1838	Bristol, England	abt 1810

2	Wha Bottomley	New York	18 Jun 1838	Bristol, England	abt 1811
2	John Bradberry	New York	18 Jun 1838	Bristol, England	abt 1811
2	E H Bradberry	New York	18 Jun 1838	Bristol, England	abt 1816
2	Jones Bridges	New York	18 Jun 1838	Bristol, England	abt 1807
2	Ludartt Butt	New York	18 Jun 1838	Bristol, England	abt 1818
2	E W Carpender	New York	18 Jun 1838	Bristol, England	abt 1798
2	Samuel Cunard	New York	18 Jun 1838	Bristol, England	abt 1788
2	William Dampier	New York	18 Jun 1838	Bristol, England	abt 1782
2	Mary Dampier	New York	18 Jun 1838	Bristol, England	abt 1788
2	Wm Dampier	New York	18 Jun 1838	Bristol, England	abt 1818
2	John Dampier	New York	18 Jun 1838	Bristol, England	abt 1819
2	Peter Dampier	New York	18 Jun 1838	Bristol, England	abt 1820
2	Elizabeth Dampier	New York	18 Jun 1838	Bristol, England	abt 1821
2	George Dampier	New York	18 Jun 1838	Bristol, England	abt 1822
2	Mary Dampier	New York	18 Jun 1838	Bristol, England	abt 1824
2	Henry Dampier	New York	18 Jun 1838	Bristol, England	abt 1825
2	Edward Dampier	New York	18 Jun 1838	Bristol, England	abt 1828
2	Thos Dampier	New York	18 Jun 1838	Bristol, England	abt 1829
2	Alexr Dampier	New York	18 Jun 1838	Bristol, England	abt 1834
2	Lionel Davidson	New York	18 Jun 1838	Bristol, England	abt 1816
2	Madame Didelot	New York	18 Jun 1838	Bristol, England	abt 1818
2	John Ersett	New York	18 Jun 1838	Bristol, England	abt 1800
2	John Forsyth	New York	18 Jun 1838	Bristol, England	abt 1788
2	C F Freidlin	New York	18 Jun 1838	Bristol, England	abt 1806
2	Nathan Harst	New York	18 Jun 1838	Bristol, England	abt 1800
2	M Harst	New York	18 Jun 1838	Bristol, England	abt 1808
2	H J Hippe	New York	18 Jun 1838	Bristol, England	abt 1811
2	Harvey Bachanan Hott	New York	18 Jun 1838	Bristol, England	abt 1820
2	W H Hoffe	New York	18 Jun 1838	Bristol, England	abt 1813
2	Eliz Jones	New York	18 Jun 1838	Bristol, England	abt 1813
2	Isaac Landenburg	New York	18 Jun 1838	Bristol, England	abt 1810
2	Luntt Lynch	New York	18 Jun 1838	Bristol, England	abt 1801
2	Virgil Maxey	New York	18 Jun 1838	Bristol, England	abt 1793
2	Edmund Morewood	New York	18 Jun 1838	Bristol, England	abt 1816
2	Rebecca Myers	New York	18 Jun 1838	Bristol, England	abt 1809
2	Thomas Oliver	New York	18 Jun 1838	Bristol, England	abt 1803
2	Mary Oliver	New York	18 Jun 1838	Bristol, England	abt 1810
2	Mary Oliver	New York	18 Jun 1838	Bristol, England	abt 1825
2	John Oliver	New York	18 Jun 1838	Bristol, England	abt 1831
2	Thomas Oliver	New York	18 Jun 1838	Bristol, England	abt 1833
2	Jane Oliver	New York	18 Jun 1838	Bristol, England	abt 1835

2	J R Prestly	New York	18 Jun 1838	Bristol, England	abt 1795
2	Sarah Prestly	New York	18 Jun 1838	Bristol, England	
2	Wm Berry Riddle	New York	18 Jun 1838	Bristol, England	abt 1810
2	Hugh Rocket	New York	18 Jun 1838	Bristol, England	abt 1808
2	W H Russell	New York	18 Jun 1838	Bristol, England	abt 1793
2	George Sampson	New York	18 Jun 1838	Bristol, England	abt 1810
2	E?? Smith	New York	18 Jun 1838	Bristol, England	
2	Daniel Sparks	New York	18 Jun 1838	Bristol, England	abt 1776
2	Thos Jones Spence	New York	18 Jun 1838	Bristol, England	abt 1808
2	Theodore H Ternanft	New York	18 Jun 1838	Bristol, England	abt 1810
2	W H Tilstone	New York	18 Jun 1838	Bristol, England	abt 1798
2	H Tobius	New York	18 Jun 1838	Bristol, England	abt 1805
2	James Watt	New York	18 Jun 1838	Bristol, England	abt 1788
2	Mary Williamson	New York	18 Jun 1838	Bristol, England	abt 1832
2	E J Woolsey	New York	18 Jun 1838	Bristol, England	abt 1803
3	Jas Barclay	New York	6 Aug 1838	Bristol, England	abt 1810
3	Wm R Beecher	New York	6 Aug 1838	Bristol, England	abt 1810
3	J Bentley	New York	6 Aug 1838	Bristol, England	abt 1808
3	Louis Bonoille	New York	6 Aug 1838	Bristol, England	abt 1824
3	James Broadbent	New York	6 Aug 1838	Bristol, England	abt 1798
3	E Caylus	New York	6 Aug 1838	Bristol, England	abt 1819
3	Louis M Canneaux	New York	6 Aug 1838	Bristol, England	abt 1798
3	Rev. I A Clark	New York	6 Aug 1838	Bristol, England	abt 1801
3	Pearce Clifton	New York	6 Aug 1838	Bristol, England	abt 1814
3	W E Evans	New York	6 Aug 1838	Bristol, England	abt 1800
3	Chas Farrand	New York	6 Aug 1838	Bristol, England	abt 1808
3	E D Fisher	New York	6 Aug 1838	Bristol, England	abt 1819
3	J G Flagg	New York	6 Aug 1838	Bristol, England	abt 1798
3	E W Fryon	New York	6 Aug 1838	Bristol, England	abt 1798
3	Mrs. J Fraser	New York	6 Aug 1838	Bristol, England	abt 1808
3	Mrs. Gannett	New York	6 Aug 1838	Bristol, England	abt 1803
3	Rev. E S Garnett	New York	6 Aug 1838	Bristol, England	abt 1789
3	Alex Grover	New York	6 Aug 1838	Bristol, England	abt 1800
3	Jane Herring	New York	6 Aug 1838	Bristol, England	abt 1818
3	Thos Hinton	New York	6 Aug 1838	Bristol, England	abt 1808
3	Mary Kench	New York	6 Aug 1838	Bristol, England	abt 1808
3	R S Kennedy	New York	6 Aug 1838	Bristol, England	abt 1818
3	Chas Lawford	New York	6 Aug 1838	Bristol, England	abt 1820
3	John Lord	New York	6 Aug 1838	Bristol, England	abt 1810
3	Saml Lord	New York	6 Aug 1838	Bristol, England	abt 1810
3	R C Maywood	New York	6 Aug 1838	Bristol, England	abt 1821

3	Thos Palmer	New York	6 Aug 1838	Bristol, England	abt 1813
3	Peter Patterson	New York	6 Aug 1838	Bristol, England	abt 1808
3	Joseph Pegg	New York	6 Aug 1838	Bristol, England	abt 1795
3	E Pleasant	New York	6 Aug 1838	Bristol, England	abt 1808
3	Reed R Quarrell	New York	6 Aug 1838	Bristol, England	abt 1799
3	Mrs. Quarrell	New York	6 Aug 1838	Bristol, England	abt 1808
3	Chas Seidlitz	New York	6 Aug 1838	Bristol, England	abt 1813
3	E Sharp	New York	6 Aug 1838	Bristol, England	abt 1808
3	H P Simmons	New York	6 Aug 1838	Bristol, England	abt 1788
3	Miss Alice Taylor	New York	6 Aug 1838	Bristol, England	abt 1818
3	Thos J Thompson	New York	6 Aug 1838	Bristol, England	abt 1808
3	H H Whitney	New York	6 Aug 1838	Bristol, England	abt 1807
3	Wm Wilson	New York	6 Aug 1838	Bristol, England	abt 1810
3	Mrs. Wright	New York	6 Aug 1838	Bristol, England	abt 1807
3	Miss Mary Anderson	New York	6 Aug 1838	Bristol, England	abt 1813
3	E Baker Sr.	New York	6 Aug 1838	Bristol, England	abt 1800
3	Jean Battiste	New York	6 Aug 1838	Bristol, England	abt 1809
3	Mr. Burnham	New York	6 Aug 1838	Bristol, England	abt 1799
3	R Butterfield	New York	6 Aug 1838	Bristol, England	abt 1811
3	Wm Draper	New York	6 Aug 1838	Bristol, England	abt 1820
3	James Ferrier	New York	6 Aug 1838	Bristol, England	abt 1815
3	Mr. Garby	New York	6 Aug 1838	Bristol, England	abt 1800
3	Infant Garret	New York	6 Aug 1838	Bristol, England	abt 1838
3	Capt Haggerty	New York	6 Aug 1838	Bristol, England	abt 1799
3	Philip Hazard	New York	6 Aug 1838	Bristol, England	abt 1798
3	Mr. Holbrook	New York	6 Aug 1838	Bristol, England	abt 1798
3	J Johnston	New York	6 Aug 1838	Bristol, England	abt 1804
3	Dr L Saynisch	New York	6 Aug 1838	Bristol, England	abt 1798
3	John Stephen	New York	6 Aug 1838	Bristol, England	abt 1811
3	MS. Stephen	New York	6 Aug 1838	Bristol, England	abt 1820
3	J R Walker	New York	6 Aug 1838	Bristol, England	abt 1798
3	Mr. Whittingham	New York	6 Aug 1838	Bristol, England	abt 1811
3	James Willes	New York	6 Aug 1838	Bristol, England	abt 1813
3	James R Wilson	New York	6 Aug 1838	Bristol, England	abt 1800
3	James Barber	New York	6 Aug 1838	Bristol, England	abt 1808
3	Henry Babad	New York	6 Aug 1838	Bristol, England	abt 1808
3	John Biddle	New York	6 Aug 1838	Bristol, England	abt 1815
3	John Broane	New York	6 Aug 1838	Bristol, England	abt 1798
3	Augtus Cleverland	New York	6 Aug 1838	Bristol, England	abt 1807
3	Fredk Coolidge	New York	6 Aug 1838	Bristol, England	abt 1798
3	James Cove	New York	6 Aug 1838	Bristol, England	abt 1798
3	Chas W Dayton	New York	6 Aug 1838	Bristol, England	abt 1798

3	B H Downing	New York	6 Aug 1838	Bristol, England	abt 1798
3	Geo B English	New York	6 Aug 1838	Bristol, England	abt 1800
3	Josh Goodland	New York	6 Aug 1838	Bristol, England	abt 1801
3	Aug Vanfour Hand	New York	6 Aug 1838	Bristol, England	abt 1800
3	John Harkey	New York	6 Aug 1838	Bristol, England	abt 1803
3	Lewis Hoffman	New York	6 Aug 1838	Bristol, England	abt 1798
3	E Hughes	New York	6 Aug 1838	Bristol, England	abt 1801
3	G Hughes	New York	6 Aug 1838	Bristol, England	abt 1824
3	Archibald Kerr	New York	6 Aug 1838	Bristol, England	abt 1798
3	Henry Lee	New York	6 Aug 1838	Bristol, England	abt 1821
3	J C Mcfarlane	New York	6 Aug 1838	Bristol, England	abt 1808
3	James McGinnar	New York	6 Aug 1838	Bristol, England	abt 1800
3	Francis Montoya	New York	6 Aug 1838	Bristol, England	abt 1788
3	Mrs. H Parsons	New York	6 Aug 1838	Bristol, England	abt 1808
3	Louisa Parsons	New York	6 Aug 1838	Bristol, England	abt 1836
3	Henry Parsons	New York	6 Aug 1838	Bristol, England	abt 1837
3	Hyron Power	New York	6 Aug 1838	Bristol, England	abt 1800
3	Wm Roberts	New York	6 Aug 1838	Bristol, England	abt 1798
3	M A Rosewell	New York	6 Aug 1838	Bristol, England	abt 1808
3	Wm Spragg	New York	6 Aug 1838	Bristol, England	abt 1800
3	Mrs. J Stewart	New York	6 Aug 1838	Bristol, England	abt 1770
3	George Stewart	New York	6 Aug 1838	Bristol, England	abt 1808
3	H Augustus Taylor	New York	6 Aug 1838	Bristol, England	abt 1813
3	Joseph S Taylor	New York	6 Aug 1838	Bristol, England	abt 1820
3	Mrs. Thornton	New York	6 Aug 1838	Bristol, England	abt 1800
3	A Thornton	New York	6 Aug 1838	Bristol, England	abt 1801
3	Henry Thornton	New York	6 Aug 1838	Bristol, England	abt 1824
3	Mr. Vouillemont	New York	6 Aug 1838	Bristol, England	abt 1818
3	B Warburton	New York	6 Aug 1838	Bristol, England	abt 1800
3	Washten Williams	New York	6 Aug 1838	Bristol, England	abt 1800
3	Henry Williams	New York	6 Aug 1838	Bristol, England	abt 1811
3	John Wymbs	New York	6 Aug 1838	Bristol, England	abt 1798
3	Mrs. Wymbs	New York	6 Aug 1838	Bristol, England	abt 1803
3	John Asborne	New York	6 Aug 1838	Bristol, England	abt 1808
3	Wm Baker	New York	6 Aug 1838	Bristol, England	abt 1806
3	W A Barnister	New York	6 Aug 1838	Bristol, England	abt 1811
3	Lt A Bigalow	New York	6 Aug 1838	Bristol, England	abt 1801
3	Prudent Casamayor	New York	6 Aug 1838	Bristol, England	abt 1799
3	MS. E Christmas	New York	6 Aug 1838	Bristol, England	abt 1820
3	John P Crosly	New York	6 Aug 1838	Bristol, England	abt 1808
3	Wm Davidson	New York	6 Aug 1838	Bristol, England	abt 1798

3	F Dorr	New York	6 Aug 1838	Bristol, England	abt 1808
3	Dr. Lewis Gegnoux	New York	6 Aug 1838	Bristol, England	abt 1798
3	Claudius Gignous	New York	6 Aug 1838	Bristol, England	abt 1808
3	Mrs. C Gigusux	New York	6 Aug 1838	Bristol, England	abt 1813
3	Chas Godd	New York	6 Aug 1838	Bristol, England	abt 1819
3	Helary Graffstedt	New York	6 Aug 1838	Bristol, England	abt 1793
3	J P Hamilton	New York	6 Aug 1838	Bristol, England	abt 1803
3	MS. Hamilton	New York	6 Aug 1838	Bristol, England	abt 1816
3	N Hayden	New York	6 Aug 1838	Bristol, England	abt 1800
3	James Little	New York	6 Aug 1838	Bristol, England	abt 1801
3	Mr Marx	New York	6 Aug 1838	Bristol, England	abt 1808
3	Eugene Martineau	New York	6 Aug 1838	Bristol, England	abt 1811
3	Mrs. C Mathews	New York	6 Aug 1838	Bristol, England	abt 1779
3	Chas Mathews	New York	6 Aug 1838	Bristol, England	abt 1803
3	John Nicholson	New York	6 Aug 1838	Bristol, England	abt 1807
3	A F Petrie	New York	6 Aug 1838	Bristol, England	abt 1809
3	Mrs. Sebby	New York	6 Aug 1838	Bristol, England	abt 1808
3	A Ware	New York	6 Aug 1838	Bristol, England	abt 1803
3	Col Webb	New York	6 Aug 1838	Bristol, England	abt 1798
3	J R White	New York	6 Aug 1838	Bristol, England	abt 1820
4	M Campbell	New York	24 Sep 1838	Bristol, England	abt 1809
4	John Cockery	New York	24 Sep 1838	Bristol, England	abt 1812
4	Wm Fisher	New York	24 Sep 1838	Bristol, England	abt 1813
4	Chs Jackson	New York	24 Sep 1838	Bristol, England	abt 1813
4	Thos Kinucar	New York	24 Sep 1838	Bristol, England	abt 1802
4	Mrs. J Langan	New York	24 Sep 1838	Bristol, England	abt 1808
4	Mr. J S Newstadt	New York	24 Sep 1838	Bristol, England	abt 1817
4	Lewis H Samuels	New York	24 Sep 1838	Bristol, England	abt 1812
4	Julius Sichel	New York	24 Sep 1838	Bristol, England	abt 1803
4	Pice D E Weylen	New York	24 Sep 1838	Bristol, England	abt 1811
4	MS. Weylen	New York	24 Sep 1838	Bristol, England	abt 1814
4	J S White	New York	24 Sep 1838	Bristol, England	abt 1812
4	Mary Wilson	New York	24 Sep 1838	Bristol, England	abt 1801
4	John Wilson	New York	24 Sep 1838	Bristol, England	abt 1835
4	Mary Wilson	New York	24 Sep 1838	Bristol, England	abt 1836
4	Mr. Bell	New York	24 Sep 1838	Bristol, England	abt 1810
4	Mr. Boule	New York	24 Sep 1838	Bristol, England	abt 1812
4	Carson Brenost	New York	24 Sep 1838	Bristol, England	abt 1817
4	James Comrie	New York	24 Sep 1838	Bristol, England	abt 1803
4	Fred Honold	New York	24 Sep 1838	Bristol, England	abt 1813
4	Washington Jackson	New York	24 Sep 1838	Bristol, England	abt 1773

4	Edgar Larne	New York	24 Sep 1838	Bristol, England	abt 1812
4	A S Lawrence	New York	24 Sep 1838	Bristol, England	abt 1808
4	Chs McEuar	New York	24 Sep 1838	Bristol, England	abt 1805
4	Mrs. Scholey	New York	24 Sep 1838	Bristol, England	abt 1803
4	Mrs. Steele	New York	24 Sep 1838	Bristol, England	abt 1798
4	R D Wilmot	New York	24 Sep 1838	Bristol, England	abt 1810
4	S Wilmot	New York	24 Sep 1838	Bristol, England	abt 1811
4	John Wilmot	New York	24 Sep 1838	Bristol, England	abt 1835
4	R Wilmot	New York	24 Sep 1838	Bristol, England	abt 1837
4	W G C Allen	New York	24 Sep 1838	Bristol, England	abt 1798
4	Mrs. Allen	New York	24 Sep 1838	Bristol, England	abt 1806
4	Mrs. Bolton	New York	24 Sep 1838	Bristol, England	abt 1798
4	Ws A Brown	New York	24 Sep 1838	Bristol, England	abt 1802
4	J Buckanan	New York	24 Sep 1838	Bristol, England	abt 1790
4	John Cannen	New York	24 Sep 1838	Bristol, England	abt 1810
4	James Fox	New York	24 Sep 1838	Bristol, England	abt 1812
4	Genl. G J Hamilton	New York	24 Sep 1838	Bristol, England	abt 1794
4	John Harris	New York	24 Sep 1838	Bristol, England	abt 1804
4	Mrs. Ws Jaques	New York	24 Sep 1838	Bristol, England	abt 1808
4	Henry Jessop	New York	24 Sep 1838	Bristol, England	abt 1810
4	Chust Loeser	New York	24 Sep 1838	Bristol, England	abt 1808
4	Mr. Mcclead	New York	24 Sep 1838	Bristol, England	abt 1810
4	E De Martinez	New York	24 Sep 1838	Bristol, England	abt 1808
4	Fran Migliore	New York	24 Sep 1838	Bristol, England	abt 1812
4	Mrs. Neilson	New York	24 Sep 1838	Bristol, England	abt 1813
4	Joseph Ogden	New York	24 Sep 1838	Bristol, England	abt 1799
4	John Parker	New York	24 Sep 1838	Bristol, England	abt 1805
4	Rufus Preine	New York	24 Sep 1838	Bristol, England	abt 1798
4	Mrs. R Preine	New York	24 Sep 1838	Bristol, England	abt 1806
4	Temple Prime	New York	24 Sep 1838	Bristol, England	abt 1832
4	Fred Steinhal	New York	24 Sep 1838	Bristol, England	abt 1810
4	S B Taylor	New York	24 Sep 1838	Bristol, England	abt 1808
4	Mrs. Cole Taylor	New York	24 Sep 1838	Bristol, England	abt 1808
4	A Taylor	New York	24 Sep 1838	Bristol, England	abt 1834
4	M Taylor	New York	24 Sep 1838	Bristol, England	abt 1835
4	Alex Von Benselan	New York	24 Sep 1838	Bristol, England	abt 1810
4	Vr Aazie	New York	24 Sep 1838	Bristol, England	abt 1802
4	Mr. Batler	New York	24 Sep 1838	Bristol, England	abt 1808
4	Dr. Beales	New York	24 Sep 1838	Bristol, England	abt 1798
4	Ws Bier	New York	24 Sep 1838	Bristol, England	abt 1792
4	MS. Sophia Bennet	New York	24 Sep 1838	Bristol, England	abt 1821
4	John Bennet	New York	24 Sep 1838	Bristol, England	abt 1823

4	Tha Brown	New York	24 Sep 1838	Bristol, England	abt 1838
4	M Cox	New York	24 Sep 1838	Bristol, England	abt 1808
4	M Davidson	New York	24 Sep 1838	Bristol, England	abt 1808
4	Mauroe Edwards	New York	24 Sep 1838	Bristol, England	abt 1814
4	Lorell Follett	New York	24 Sep 1838	Bristol, England	abt 1789
4	M Francoumir	New York	24 Sep 1838	Bristol, England	abt 1808
4	Edwd Hatchins	New York	24 Sep 1838	Bristol, England	abt 1813
4	MS. Harrison	New York	24 Sep 1838	Bristol, England	abt 1813
4	Prad W Hill	New York	24 Sep 1838	Bristol, England	abt 1810
4	A James	New York	24 Sep 1838	Bristol, England	abt 1798
4	D James	New York	24 Sep 1838	Bristol, England	abt 1802
4	Alex Mcray	New York	24 Sep 1838	Bristol, England	abt 1814
4	Mrs. Murphy	New York	24 Sep 1838	Bristol, England	abt 1803
4	Thos Murphy	New York	24 Sep 1838	Bristol, England	abt 1813
4	G Neilson	New York	24 Sep 1838	Bristol, England	abt 1801
4	Emma Pead	New York	24 Sep 1838	Bristol, England	abt 1814
4	Ellen Pine	New York	24 Sep 1838	Bristol, England	abt 1822
4	Mr. Pearson	New York	24 Sep 1838	Bristol, England	abt 1813
4	Mrs. Jane Taylor	New York	24 Sep 1838	Bristol, England	abt 1805
4	Wm Wetstein	New York	24 Sep 1838	Bristol, England	abt 1808
4	George Wostenholm	New York	24 Sep 1838	Bristol, England	abt 1799
4	Profe D N Bache	New York	24 Sep 1838	Bristol, England	abt 1798
4	Mrs. Bache	New York	24 Sep 1838	Bristol, England	abt 1803
4	MS. Bache	New York	24 Sep 1838	Bristol, England	abt 1812
4	Mr Birkle	New York	24 Sep 1838	Bristol, England	abt 1808
4	Elenezer Chadwick	New York	24 Sep 1838	Bristol, England	abt 1793
4	George Coombe	New York	24 Sep 1838	Bristol, England	abt 1788
4	Mrs. G Coombe	New York	24 Sep 1838	Bristol, England	abt 1803
4	Mr. Dalrymple	New York	24 Sep 1838	Bristol, England	abt 1803
4	Mrs. M Dalrymple	New York	24 Sep 1838	Bristol, England	abt 1808
4	Thos L Hamilton	New York	24 Sep 1838	Bristol, England	abt 1817
4	G Hodgdon	New York	24 Sep 1838	Bristol, England	abt 1803
4	Mr. Maitland	New York	24 Sep 1838	Bristol, England	abt 1808
4	G Sweeney	New York	24 Sep 1838	Bristol, England	abt 1806
4	M E Bacera	New York	24 Sep 1838	Bristol, England	abt 1811
4	S Berard	New York	24 Sep 1838	Bristol, England	abt 1812
4	MS. M Blundell	New York	24 Sep 1838	Bristol, England	abt 1808
4	Wm Bowar	New York	24 Sep 1838	Bristol, England	abt 1823
4	Ezra Bowar	New York	24 Sep 1838	Bristol, England	abt 1831
4	George Bowar	New York	24 Sep 1838	Bristol, England	abt 1835
4	Mary E Bowar	New York	24 Sep 1838	Bristol, England	abt 1838
4	Mrs. Bowser	New York	24 Sep 1838	Bristol, England	abt 1797

4	Ws Butcher	New York	24 Sep 1838	Bristol, England	abt 1792
4	Samuel Butcher	New York	24 Sep 1838	Bristol, England	abt 1802
4	Fred Chevennont	New York	24 Sep 1838	Bristol, England	abt 1806
4	Wm H Coffin	New York	24 Sep 1838	Bristol, England	abt 1798
4	E Coffin	New York	24 Sep 1838	Bristol, England	abt 1803
4	P Lee Dawson	New York	24 Sep 1838	Bristol, England	abt 1798
4	Mrs. Gans	New York	24 Sep 1838	Bristol, England	abt 1817
4	B Gans	New York	24 Sep 1838	Bristol, England	abt 1837
4	A Gaus	New York	24 Sep 1838	Bristol, England	abt 1798
4	B Gaus	New York	24 Sep 1838	Bristol, England	abt 1838
4	D A Johnston	New York	24 Sep 1838	Bristol, England	abt 1800
4	M Ludlow	New York	24 Sep 1838	Bristol, England	abt 1804
4	James Macbeth	New York	24 Sep 1838	Bristol, England	abt 1807
4	P Mcmullan	New York	24 Sep 1838	Bristol, England	abt 1808
4	Mary Marples	New York	24 Sep 1838	Bristol, England	abt 1813
4	Eliza Marples	New York	24 Sep 1838	Bristol, England	abt 1815
4	Thos May	New York	24 Sep 1838	Bristol, England	abt 1812
4	E P Melliken	New York	24 Sep 1838	Bristol, England	abt 1809
4	M Muhle	New York	24 Sep 1838	Bristol, England	abt 1803
4	Edwd Ovens	New York	24 Sep 1838	Bristol, England	abt 1817
4	B Parkinson	New York	24 Sep 1838	Bristol, England	abt 1803
4	Profe G Patteson	New York	24 Sep 1838	Bristol, England	abt 1783
4	Mrs. Patteson	New York	24 Sep 1838	Bristol, England	abt 1802
4	Ws Pyse	New York	24 Sep 1838	Bristol, England	abt 1811
4	Mrs. S Shariff	New York	24 Sep 1838	Bristol, England	abt 1768
4	Joseph Sile	New York	24 Sep 1838	Bristol, England	abt 1806
4	Mrs. Sile	New York	24 Sep 1838	Bristol, England	abt 1808
4	M P Sile	New York	24 Sep 1838	Bristol, England	abt 1835
4	John Sile	New York	24 Sep 1838	Bristol, England	abt 1836
4	MS. Sheriff	New York	24 Sep 1838	Bristol, England	abt 1812
4	Wm Strickland	New York	24 Sep 1838	Bristol, England	abt 1776
4	Thos W Sudlow	New York	24 Sep 1838	Bristol, England	abt 1798
4	Joseph Thomson	New York	24 Sep 1838	Bristol, England	abt 1800
4	T Tuicende	New York	24 Sep 1838	Bristol, England	abt 1812
4	H M Walker	New York	24 Sep 1838	Bristol, England	abt 1803
4	John Wilson	New York	24 Sep 1838	Bristol, England	abt 1801
4	Dadge Woodward	New York	24 Sep 1838	Bristol, England	abt 1782
5	Servant	New York	15 Nov 1838	Bristol, England	abt 1818
5	Andrw L Addison Esqr.	New York	15 Nov 1838	Bristol, England	abt 1798
5	W H Aspinwall Esqr.	New York	15 Nov 1838	Bristol, England	abt 1808
5	Mrs Aspinwall	New York	15 Nov 1838	Bristol, England	abt 1813

5	Servant of Aspinwall	New York	15 Nov 1838	Bristol, England	abt 1818
5	John Bentley Esqr.	New York	15 Nov 1838	Bristol, England	abt 1798
5	Clement C Biddle Esqr.	New York	15 Nov 1838	Bristol, England	abt 1818
5	Andw Brand Esqr.	New York	15 Nov 1838	Bristol, England	abt 1813
5	James Campbell Junr.	New York	15 Nov 1838	Bristol, England	abt 1813
5	Honble Judge Crane	New York	15 Nov 1838	Bristol, England	abt 1788
5	Mrs Crane	New York	15 Nov 1838	Bristol, England	abt 1808
5	G G Dakin Esqr.	New York	15 Nov 1838	Bristol, England	abt 1798
5	William Davison Esqr.	New York	15 Nov 1838	Bristol, England	abt 1808
5	James A Dickson Junr.	New York	15 Nov 1838	Bristol, England	abt 1808
5	Rev. Ed Duroche	New York	15 Nov 1838	Bristol, England	abt 1798
5	S Gerghogan Esqr.	New York	15 Nov 1838	Bristol, England	abt 1808
5	David Gibson Esqr.	New York	15 Nov 1838	Bristol, England	abt 1808
5	Henry Goardon Junr.	New York	15 Nov 1838	Bristol, England	abt 1813
5	James Grimshaw Junr.	New York	15 Nov 1838	Bristol, England	abt 1808
5	S N Helie Junr.	New York	15 Nov 1838	Bristol, England	abt 1808
5	Children Helie	New York	15 Nov 1838	Bristol, England	abt 1830
5	Children Helie	New York	15 Nov 1838	Bristol, England	abt 1833
5	Mrs Helie Junr.	New York	15 Nov 1838	Bristol, England	abt 1813
5	two children of S N Helie age 5 & 8	New York	15 Nov 1838	Bristol, England	
5	servant of Helie	New York	15 Nov 1838		
5	Joseph Harvey Esqr.	New York	15 Nov 1838	Bristol, England	abt 1810
5	Wm Heyward Esq	New York	15 Nov 1838	Bristol, England	abt 1808
5	Mrs Heyward	New York	15 Nov 1838	Bristol, England	abt 1813
5	Daughter of Heyward	New York	15 Nov 1838	Bristol, England	abt 1835
5	John Tronbat Jene Esqr.	New York	15 Nov 1838	Bristol, England	abt 1798
5	James Johnson Junr.	New York	15 Nov 1838	Bristol, England	abt 1813

5	Aba Kintzing Esqr.	New York	15 Nov 1838	Bristol, England	abt 1813
5	William Land Junr.	New York	15 Nov 1838	Bristol, England	abt 1820
5	Geo B Lightfoot Esqr.	New York	15 Nov 1838	Bristol, England	abt 1808
5	George L Lowden Esqr.	New York	15 Nov 1838	Bristol, England	abt 1808
5	Dr. Macaulay	New York	15 Nov 1838	Bristol, England	abt 1798
5	Servant to Dr Macaulay	New York	15 Nov 1838	Bristol, England	abt 1813
5	T A Napier Esq	New York	15 Nov 1838	Bristol, England	abt 1798
5	V Nolte Esqr.	New York	15 Nov 1838	Bristol, England	abt 1809
5	Jas Owen Esqr.	New York	15 Nov 1838	Bristol, England	abt 1810
5	A G Ralston Esqr.	New York	15 Nov 1838	Bristol, England	abt 1788
5	Mrs Ralston	New York	15 Nov 1838	Bristol, England	abt 1798
5	Servant of Ralston	New York	15 Nov 1838	Bristol, England	abt 1818
5	H Wreaks Esqr.	New York	15 Nov 1838	Bristol, England	abt 1798
5	Manning Roster Esqr.	New York	15 Nov 1838	Bristol, England	abt 1798
5	Walter Rutherford Esqr.	New York	15 Nov 1838	Bristol, England	abt 1798
5	John Siter Esqr.	New York	15 Nov 1838	Bristol, England	abt 1788
5	Rev. Dr. Schroeder	New York	15 Nov 1838	Bristol, England	abt 1798
5	Mrs Schroeder	New York	15 Nov 1838	Bristol, England	abt 1808
5	Son of Schroeder	New York	15 Nov 1838	Bristol, England	abt 1828
5	James Sobin Esqr.	New York	15 Nov 1838	Bristol, England	abt 1808
5	James Stewart Esqr.	New York	15 Nov 1838	Bristol, England	abt 1808
5	I S Spencer Junr.	New York	15 Nov 1838	Bristol, England	abt 1808
5	C W Taber Esqr.	New York	15 Nov 1838	Bristol, England	abt 1798
5	Mrs Taber	New York	15 Nov 1838	Bristol, England	abt 1808
5	A Tudor Esqr.	New York	15 Nov 1838	Bristol, England	abt 1808
5	Edward Unhart Esqr.	New York	15 Nov 1838	Bristol, England	abt 1798
5	Mrs Unhart	New York	15 Nov 1838	Bristol, England	abt 1808
5	J W Ware Junr.	New York	15 Nov 1838	Bristol, England	abt 1821
5	Geo Waterman Junr.	New York	15 Nov 1838	Bristol, England	abt 1813
5	John Watson Junr.	New York	15 Nov 1838	Bristol, England	abt 1813

5	M L Webb Esqr.	New York	15 Nov 1838	Bristol, England	abt 1808
5	Joseph Wheeler Junr.	New York	15 Nov 1838	Bristol, England	abt 1818
5	W H Ash Esqr.	New York	15 Nov 1838	Bristol, England	abt 1813
5	J Battenley Esqr.	New York	15 Nov 1838	Bristol, England	abt 1808
5	B Bounethean	New York	15 Nov 1838	Bristol, England	abt 1808
5	H Brasnel Esqr.	New York	15 Nov 1838	Bristol, England	abt 1813
5	Alfred Burton Esqr.	New York	15 Nov 1838	Bristol, England	abt 1814
5	F Collomb Esqr.	New York	15 Nov 1838	Bristol, England	abt 1798
5	H A Vandamme Esqr.	New York	15 Nov 1838	Bristol, England	abt 1808
5	E Daron Esqr.	New York	15 Nov 1838	Bristol, England	abt 1814
5	Jno G Flagg Esqr.	New York	15 Nov 1838	Bristol, England	abt 1798
5	T Frey Esqr.	New York	15 Nov 1838	Bristol, England	abt 1811
5	Joseph Gautur Esqr.	New York	15 Nov 1838	Bristol, England	abt 1808
5	Chevalier De Gerstner	New York	15 Nov 1838	Bristol, England	abt 1798
5	Lady of Gerstner	New York	15 Nov 1838	Bristol, England	abt 1808
5	Wm Gibbons Esqr.	New York	15 Nov 1838	Bristol, England	abt 1808
5	A Gordon Esqr.	New York	15 Nov 1838	Bristol, England	abt 1814
5	Mrs Gordon & son	New York	15 Nov 1838	Bristol, England	abt 1818
5	Morie De Grieff Esqr.	New York	15 Nov 1838	Bristol, England	abt 1818
5	H Green Esqr.	New York	15 Nov 1838	Bristol, England	abt 1818
5	John Hamilton Esqr.	New York	15 Nov 1838	Bristol, England	abt 1813
5	W A Hayden Esqr.	New York	15 Nov 1838	Bristol, England	abt 1808
5	Louis Hoffman Esqr.	New York	15 Nov 1838	Bristol, England	
5	H R Johntz Esqr.	New York	15 Nov 1838	Bristol, England	abt 1798
5	Servant To Johntz Esqr.	New York	15 Nov 1838	Bristol, England	abt 1813
5	David Jones Esqr.	New York	15 Nov 1838	Bristol, England	abt 1813
5	D Kimpe Esqr.	New York	15 Nov 1838	Bristol, England	abt 1820
5	Charles Kororre Esqr.	New York	15 Nov 1838	Bristol, England	abt 1811
5	Alexr Mcalpin Esq	New York	15 Nov 1838	Bristol, England	abt 1808
5	James MacKar Esqr.	New York	15 Nov 1838	Bristol, England	abt 1818

5	Milton Mcindoe	New York	15 Nov 1838	Bristol, England	abt 1798
5	C D Mcindoe Esqr.	New York	15 Nov 1838	Bristol, England	abt 1814
5	Rev. Edmund Neville	New York	15 Nov 1838	Bristol, England	abt 1808
5	J W H Pattison Esqr.	New York	15 Nov 1838	Bristol, England	abt 1813
5	Mrs. Ransom & children	New York	15 Nov 1838	Bristol, England	abt 1798
5	Servant To Ransom	New York	15 Nov 1838	Bristol, England	abt 1818
5	Rauser Esqr.	New York	15 Nov 1838	Bristol, England	abt 1813
5	E A Rautenberg Esqr.	New York	15 Nov 1838	Bristol, England	abt 1813
5	P A Rost Esqr.	New York	15 Nov 1838	Bristol, England	abt 1813
5	Mille Rion Esqr.	New York	15 Nov 1838	Bristol, England	abt 1821
5	F A Steinmacher Esqr.	New York	15 Nov 1838	Bristol, England	abt 1808
5	James Stiff Esqr.	New York	15 Nov 1838	Bristol, England	abt 1808
5	C Tobias Esqr.	New York	15 Nov 1838	Bristol, England	abt 1810
5	Madame Vanderaghel	New York	15 Nov 1838	Bristol, England	abt 1808
5	Friend to Vanderaghel	New York	15 Nov 1838	Bristol, England	abt 1813
5	A Worthington Esqr.	New York	15 Nov 1838	Bristol, England	abt 1818

Notes

BI   Brunel Institute, ss *Great Britain* Trust
BPP   British Parliamentary Papers
TNA   The National Archives, Kew, London

1 A Bold Idea

1. Isambard Brunel, *The Life of Isambard Kingdom Brunel Civil Engineer*, 2006 edn (Stroud: Nonsuch Publishing, 1870)
2. Brunel, *The Life of Isambard Kingdom Brunel*; L. T. C. Rolt, *Isambard Kingdom Brunel*, 1st edition 1957 edn (London: Penguin, 1976), p. 249; Denis Griffiths, *Brunel's Great Western* (Wellingborough: Patrick Stephens, 1985), p. 13
3. David R. Starkey, 'The Industrial Background to the Development of the Steamship', in *The Advent of Steam: The Merchant Ship before 1900*, ed. by R Gardiner (London: Conway Maritime Press, 1993), p. 128
4. Starkey, 'Industrial Background', p. 128
5. Ronald Hope, *A New History of British Shipping* (London: John Murray, 1990), p. 267
6. David M. Williams and John Armstrong, "One of the Noblest Inventions of the Age': British Steamboat Numbers, Diffusion, Services and Public Reception, 1812 – c.1823', *Journal of Transport History*, 35 (2014), p. 19
7. John Armstrong and David M. Williams, 'Technological Advance and Innovation: The Diffusion of the Early Steamship in the United Kingdom, 1812–34', *The Mariner's Mirror*, 96 (2010), pp. 43–44
8. *Evening Post* 22 June 1815
9. Armstrong and Williams, 'Technological Advance and Innovation', p. 54
10. Armstrong and Williams, 'Technological Advance and Innovation', pp. 43–46
11. Armstrong and Williams, 'Technological Advance and Innovation', p. 48
12. *Evening Post* 22 June 1815; Williams and Armstrong, 'Technological Advance and Innovation', pp. 19–23; Starkey, 'Industrial Background', p. 217

13. Armstrong, J. and Bagwell, P. S., 'Coastal Shipping' in Aldcroft, D. and Freeman, M. (eds), *Transport in the Industrial Revolution* (Manchester: UP, 1983), p. 163

14. Armstrong and Williams, 'Technological Advance and Innovation', pp. 50–52

15. Starkey, 'Industrial Background', p. 128

16. John R. Killick, 'Bolton Ogden & Company: A Case Study in Anglo-American Trade, 1790–1850', *Business History Review*, 48 (1974), pp. 501 & 507

17. Stephen Fox, *The Ocean Railway: Isambard Kingdom Brunel, Samuel Cunard and the Revolutionary World of the Great Atlantic Steamships* (London: Harper Collins, 2004), pp. 51–55, 73; Robert G. Albion, *The Rise of New York Port 1815–1860* (New York: Charles Scribner's Sons, 1939), p. 314

18. Armstrong and Williams, 'Technological Advance and Innovation', pp. 53 & 60

19. Armstrong and Williams, 'Technological Advance and Innovation', pp. 53–54; Sarah Palmer, 'Experience, Experiment and Economics: Factors in the Construction of Early Merchant Steamers', *Proceedings of the Atlantic Canada Shipping Project* (1977), p. 234

20. John Armstrong and David M. Williams, 'The Steamboat and Popular Tourism', *Journal of Transport History*, 26 (2005), p. 63

21. Armstrong and Williams, 'Technological Advance and Innovation', pp. 55, 62

22. BPP Report on Steam Vessel Accidents 1839 appendix 120

23. John Armstrong and David Williams, *The Impact of Technological Change: The Early Steamship in Britain* (St John's, Newfoundland: International Maritime Economic Association, 2011), p. 154

24. Robert G. Albion, 'Planning the Black Ball Line, 1817', *Business History Review*, 41 (1967)

25. Denis Griffiths, *Brunel's Great Western* (Wellingborough: Patrick Stephens, 1985), p. 9

26. *Bristol Mirror* 19 December 1835

27. *Bristol Mercury* 23 January 1836

28. Armstrong and Williams, 'Technological Advance and Innovation', pp. 45 & 64

29. BPP: Report on Steam Vessel Accidents to Committee of Privy Council for Trade 1839 pp. 6–7.

30. Harold Bagust, *The Greater Genius? A Biography of Sir Marc Isambard Brunel* (Hersham: Ian Allen Publishing, 2006), p. 48

31. Bagust, *The Greater Genius?* p. 51; The National Archives (TNA): BT 107/28 Foreign Trade Shipping Registers 1815

32. Bagust, *The Greater Genius?* pp. 51 & 102

33. Andrew Lambert, 'Brunel, The Navy and the Screw Propeller' in Denis Griffiths, Andrew Lambert, and Fred Walker, *Brunel's Ships* (London: Chatham Publishing, 1999), pp. 27–30; Rolt, *Isambard Kingdom Brunel*, p. 248

34. *Kentish Weekly Post or Canterbury Journal* 8 July 1817

35. Rolt, *Isambard Kingdom Brunel*, p. 247

36. Henry Cheal, *The Ships and Mariners of Shoreham* (Shoreham: G E & P P Bysh, 1909), p. 63

37. Rolt, *Isambard Kingdom Brunel*, pp. 62 & 247

38. R. Angus Buchanan, *Brunel: The Life and Times of Isambard Kingdom Brunel* (London: Hambledon and London, 2002), pp. 43–56

39. Madge Dresser, 'Guppy, Sarah (*bap.* 1770, *d.* 1852)', *Oxford Dictionary of National Biography* (Oxford University Press, May 2016); online edn, Sept 2016 [http://0-www.oxforddnb.com.lib.exeter.ac.uk/view/article/109112, accessed 1 Feb 2017]

40. Anon, 'Obituary. Thomas Richard Guppy, 1797–1882', *Minutes of the Proceedings of the Institution of Civil Engineers*, 69 (1882), pp. 411–15; Rolt, *Isambard Kingdom Brunel*, p. 97

41. G. W. A. Bush, *Bristol and its Municipal Government, 1820 to 1851* (Bristol Record Society, 1976), p. 240

42. Buchanan, *Brunel*, pp. 200–201

43. Brunel, *Life of Isambard Kingdom Brunel*, p. 176; Griffiths, *Brunel's Great Western*, p. 13

44. Legacies of British Slave owners https://www.ucl.ac.uk/lbs/person/view/1722518733

45. Christopher Claxton, *The Naval Monitor*, 2nd edn (London, 1833), p. 4

46. Claxton, *Naval Monitor*, p. vii

47. Claxton, *Naval Monitor*, pp. viii–ix

48. Michael Lewis, *The Navy in Transition, 1814–1864* (London: Hodder & Stoughton, 1965), pp. 72–73

49. Claxton, *Naval Monitor*, p. 3

50. *Bristol Mirror* 12 August 1837

51. Claxton, *Naval Monitor*, p. 110

52. Claxton, *Naval Monitor*, p. 15

53. Buchanan, *Brunel*, p. 58

54. Christopher Claxton, *Logs of the First Voyage, Made with the Unceasing Aid of Steam, between England and America by the Great Western of Bristol* (Great Western Steamship Company 1838), p. i

2 Building the Great Western

1. Christopher Claxton, *Logs of the First Voyage, Made with the Unceasing Aid of Steam, between England and America by the Great Western of Bristol* (Great Western Steamship Company, 1838)

2. Grahame Farr, *Shipbuilding in the Port of Bristol* (Greenwich, London: National Maritime Museum, 1977), p. 3

3. Farr, *Shipbuilding in the Port of Bristol*, p. 6. Farr says Patterson was born in Arbroath 1795 in 'impoverished circumstances' and became ward of a slop seller at Wapping, London. This is a little confusing as in all census returns Patterson gives his birthplace as Aldgate, London.

4. Farr, *Shipbuilding in the Port of Bristol*, p. 8

5. Claxton, *Logs of the First Voyage*, p. ii

6. Claxton, *Logs of the First Voyage*

7. Isambard Brunel, *The Life of Isambard Kingdom Brunel Civil Engineer*, 2006 edn (Stroud: Nonsuch Publishing, 1870), p. 176–77

8. Brunel, *The Life of Isambard Kingdom Brunel*, p. 176

9. Claxton, *Logs of the First Voyage*, p. 56

10. Claxton, *Logs of the First Voyage*, p. 57
11. Claxton, *Logs of the First Voyage*, pp. 55–56
12. Brunel, *The Life of Isambard Kingdom Brunel*, p. 176
13. *Bristol Mirror* 19 December 1835
14. *Bristol Mercury* 23 January 1836
15. *Bristol Mercury* 23 January 1836
16. R. Angus Buchanan, *Brunel: The Life and Times of Isambard Kingdom Brunel* (London: Hambledon and London, 2002), p. 200
17. Paul Quinn, 'Macgregor Laird, Junius Smith and the Atlantic Ocean', *The Mariner's Mirror*, 92 (2006), p. 488
18. Quinn, 'Macgregor Laird, Junius Smith'
19. Denis Griffiths, *Brunel's Great Western* (Wellingborough: Patrick Stephens, 1985), pp 13–15
20. Grahame Farr, *Records of Bristol Ships:1800–1838* (Bristol: Bristol Record Society, 1950), p 142
21. http://www.gracesguide.co.uk/Fawcett,_Preston_and_Co
22. Andrew Lambert, 'Woolwich Dockyard and the Early Steam Navy, 1815 to 1852s', in *Shipbuilding and Ships on the Thames: Proceedings of Fourth Symposium*, ed. by Roger Owen (London Docklands Museum 2009), pp. 82–96
23. Philip Banbury, *Shipbuilders of the Thames and Medway* (Newton Abbot: David and Charles, 1971), p. 199
24. Chris Ellmers, "This Great National Object' – the Story of the Paddlesteamer Enterprize', in *Shipbuilding and Ships on the Thames: Proceedings of Fourth Symposium*, ed. by Roger Owen (London Docklands Museum 2009), pp. 59–81
25. Ellmers, 'This Great National Object', pp. 67–70
26. L.T.C. Rolt, *Isambard Kingdom Brunel*, 1st edition 1957 edn (London: Penguin, 1976), pp. 38–39
27. Brunel, *The Life of Isambard Kingdom Brunel*, p. 178
28. *Bristol Mirror* 21 January 1837
29. Denis Griffiths, Andrew Lambert, and Fred Walker, *Brunel's Ships* (London: Chatham Publishing, 1999), p. 21
30. *Bristol Mercury* 30 July 1836
31. *Bristol Mercury* 30 July 1836
32. *Bristol Mercury* 30 July 1836
33. David K. Brown, 'Seppings, Sir Robert (1767–1840)', *Oxford Dictionary of National Biography* (Oxford University Press, 2004) [http://0-www.oxforddnb.com.lib.exeter.ac.uk/view/article/25093, accessed 19 Feb 2017]
34. Griffiths, *Brunel's Great Western*, p. 8; Christopher Claxton, *The Naval Monitor*, 2nd edn (London, 1833).
35. Claxton. *Logs of the First Voyage*, First AGM Report 1838
36. Celia Brunel Noble, *The Brunels – Father and Son* (London, 1938), p. 156
37. Claxton, *Logs of the First Voyage* 1838 AGM
38. *Bristol Mirror* 15 July 1837
39. *Bristol Mirror* 6 May 1838
40. *Bristol Mercury* 22 July 1837
41. *Bristol Mirror* 6 May 1838 & Griffiths, Lambert, and Walker, *Brunel's Ships*, p 21

42. *Bristol Mirror* 6 May 1838
43. British Parliamentary Papers Report on Steam Vessel Accidents 1839 Patterson letter 14 February 1842
44. *Bristol Mirror* 6 May 1838
45. George Pattison, 'Shipping and the East India Docks, 1802–38', *The Mariner's Mirror*, 49 (1963); Griffiths, *Brunel's Great Western*, pp. 24 & 75
46. Griffiths, Denis, Andrew Lambert, and Fred Walker, *Brunel's Ships* (London: Chatham Publishing, 1999), p. 22
47. Crosbie Smith, "This Great National Undertaking'; John Scott Russell, the Master Shipwrights and the Royal Mail Steam Packet Company ', in *Re-Inventing the Ship: Science, Technology and the Maritime World, 1800–1918*, ed. by Don Leggett and Richard Dunn (Basingstoke: Ashgate, 2012), pp. 25–52
48. *Bristol Mirror* 6 May 1838
49. *Post Office Directory* 1837; *Bristol Mirror* 6 May 1838
50. *Bristol Mercury* 31 March 1838, reporting the *Sun* and *Weekly Despatch*
51. *Bristol Mercury* 31 March 1838, reporting the *Sun* and *Weekly Despatch*
52. Buchanan, *Brunel*, p. 198–7
53. Noble, *Father & Son*, p. 243
54. *Bristol Mercury* 31 March 1838
55. *Bristol Mercury* 31 March 1838
56. *Bristol Mercury* 31 March 1838
57. *Sun* 26 March 1838; *Bristol Mercury* 31 March 1838
58. Griffiths, Lambert, and Walker, *Brunel's Ships*, p. 24.
59. *Sun* 26 March 1838
60. *Bristol Mercury* 31 March 1838
61. Charles Penrose, '1838—April Fourth—1938 Centenary of Atlantic Steam Navigation', *Transactions of the Newcomen Society*, 18 (1937), p. 171
62. Quinn, 'Macgregor Laird, Junius Smith', pp. 489–90
63. Quinn, 'Macgregor Laird, Junius Smith', p. 490; Griffiths, *Brunel's Great Western*, p. 101
64. Penrose, 'Centenary of Atlantic Steam Navigation', p. 171
65. *Bristol Mercury* 31 March 1838
66. *Bristol Mercury* 31 March 1838
67. Griffiths, Lambert, and Walker, p 24.
68. Griffiths. *Brunel's Great Western* p 11; Quinn, p. 489
69. *Herald* New York 1837
70. Griffiths, *Brunel's Great Western*, p. 11; Brunel, *The Life of Isambard Kingdom Brunel*, p. 178
71. Brunel, *The Life of Isambard Kingdom Brunel*, p. 176
72. Brunel, *The Life of Isambard Kingdom Brunel*, p. 179
73. Alison Winter, 'Compasses All Awry': The Iron Ship and the Ambiguities of Cultural Authority in Victorian Britain', *Victorian Studies*, 38 (1994)
74. Quinn, 'Macgregor Laird, Junius Smith,' pp. 486 –87
75. *Herald* New York 29 February 1836
76. http://www.gracesguide.co.uk/Moses_Merryweather. This firm still exists http://www.merryweatherandsons.co.uk/company.html

77. Griffiths, Lambert, and Walker, *Brunel's Ships*, p. 26 also Brunel, *The Life of Isambard Kingdom Brunel*, p. 181–82
78. Griffiths, *Brunel's Great Western*, p. 30
79. James Hosken, *Autobiographical Sketch of the Public Career of Admiral James Hosken* (Penzance: Rodda, 1889), p 14
80. Ellmers, 'This Great National Object,' p. 68
81. Janet MacDonald, 'British Patents of Interest to Maritime Historians Filed in London between 1780 and 1820', in *Shipbuilding and Ships on the Thames: Proceedings of Fourth Symposium*, ed. by Roger Owen (Museum of London Docklands 2009), pp. 32–43, p. 33
82. Griffiths, *Brunel's Great Western*, p. 31

3 The First Record-Breaking Voyage

1. *Bristol Mercury* 7 April 1838
2. *Bath Chronicle* 29 March 1838
3. Christopher Claxton, *Logs of the First Voyage, Made with the Unceasing Aid of Steam, between England and America by the Great Western of Bristol* (Great Western Steamship Company 1838), pp. 63–64
4. Claxton, *Logs of the First Voyage*, pp. 3, 63–64
5. Claxton, *Logs of the First Voyage*
6. Roger Taylor, *Impressed by Light: Photographs from Paper Negatives, 1840–1860* (New York: Metropolitan Museum of Art, 2007), p. 50
7. Talbot, who lived near Bath, created the first photographic negative in 1835 and he presented his paper in January 1839
8. RG 10 217: 1871 Census shows him living in St Pancras, London
9. Ithiel Town, *Atlantic Steam-Ships. Some Ideas and Statements, the Result of Considerable Reflection on the Subject of Navigating the Atlantic Ocean with Steam-Ships of Large Tonnage, Etc* (New York, 1838), p. 19.; New York Passenger list; 1841 census
10. John Malcolm Brinnin, *The Sway of the Grand Saloon*, 1986 edn (London: Arlington Books, 1971), p. 61
11. Claxton, *Logs of the First Voyage*, Foster journal, p. 64
12. Claxton, *Logs of the First Voyage*, Foster journal, p. 64
13. *Inverness Courier* 16 May 1838
14. *London Dispatch* 20 May 1838
15. Claxton, *Logs of the First Voyage*, pp. 64–5
16. Claxton, *Logs of the First Voyage*
17. Claxton, *Logs of the First Voyage*
18. *Weekly Despatch* quoted in *Bristol Mercury* March 1838
19. Claxton, *Logs of the First Voyage*, pp. 12–13
20. Chris Ellmers, "This Great National Object' – the Story of the Paddlesteamer Enterprize', in *Shipbuilding and Ships on the Thames: Proceedings of Fourth Symposium*, ed. by Roger Owen (London Docklands Museum 2009), pp. 59–81
21. Claxton, *Logs of the First Voyage*, p. 27
22. Denis Griffiths, *Brunel's Great Western* (Wellingborough: Patrick Stephens, 1985), p. 35

23. Isambard Brunel, *The Life of Isambard Kingdom Brunel Civil Engineer*, 2006 edn (Stroud: Nonsuch Publishing, 1870), p. 255
24. Claxton, *Logs of the First Voyage*, Foster journal, p. 74
25. Celia Brunel Noble, *The Brunels – Father and Son* (London, 1938), p. 157
26. Charles Penrose, '1838—April Fourth—1938 Centenary of Atlantic Steam Navigation', *Transactions of the Newcomen Society*, 18 (1937), p. 175
27. Penrose, 'Centenary of Atlantic Steam Navigation', p. 174
28. *Morning Herald* 24 April 1838
29. Byard Tuckerman, *The Diary of Philip Hone, 1828 to 1851* (New York, Dodd, Mead & Co 1889)
30. *Morning Herald* 24 April 1838
31. *Courier and Enquirer* 24 April 1838
32. *Morning Herald* 24 April 1838
33. Noble, *Father and Son*, p. 157
34. Brinnin, *The Sway of the Grand Saloon*; Tuckerman, *The Diary of Philip Hone*
35. Penrose, 'Centenary of Atlantic Steam Navigation', p. 77; James Hosken, *Autobiographical Sketch of the Public Career of Admiral James Hosken* (Penzance: Rodda, 1889), p. 15. Note: The St George Society was founded in 1770 to support Englishmen and their families.
36. Penrose, 'Centenary of Atlantic Steam Navigation', p. 177
37. Griffiths, *Brunel's Great Western*, pp. 40–41
38. Claxton, *Logs of the First Voyage*, p. iv
39. Tuckerman, *The Diary of Philip Hone*
40. Penrose, 'Centenary of Atlantic Steam Navigation'
41. Tuckerman, *The Diary of Philip Hone*
42. Noble, *Father and Son*, p. 157
43. *New York Evening Post* 27 April 1838
44. Robert G. Albion, *The Rise of New York Port 1815–1860* (New York: Charles Scribner's Sons, 1939), p. 226–7
45. Edwin G. Burrows and Mike Wallace, *Gotham: A History of New York City to 1898* (Oxford: Oxford University Press, 1999), p. 601
46. Griffiths, *Brunel's Great Western*, p. 42
47. James Harrison Wilson, *The Life of Charles A. Dana* (New York: Harper Brothers, 1907) pp. 485–86
48. Griffiths, *Brunel's Great Western*, pp. 41–42; Brinnin, *The Sway of the Grand Saloon*, p.68
49. *Evening Post* 27 April 1838
50. Claxton, *Logs of the First Voyage*, Webb journal, p. 73
51. *Evening Post* 2 May 1838
52. Griffiths, *Brunel's Great Western*, p. 42
53. Tuckerman, *The Diary of Philip Hone*, p. 103
54. Claxton, *Logs of the First Voyage*
55. Claxton, *Logs of the First Voyage*, Webb journal, p. 74
56. *Evening Post* 4 May 1838
57. *Taunton Courier & Western Advertiser* 30 May 1838
58. Penrose, 'Centenary of Atlantic Steam Navigation', p. 175

59. *Evening Post* 4 May 1838
60. *Evening Post* 4 May 1838
61. Griffiths, *Brunel's Great Western*, p. 41; *Taunton Courier & Western Advertiser* 30 May 1838
62. Hosken, *Autobiographical Sketch*, p. 16
63. Griffiths, *Brunel's Great Western*, p. 43; *Gloucester Journal* 26 May 1838
64. *Bristol Mirror* quoted in the *Taunton Courier & Western Advertiser* 30 May 1838
65. *Bristol Mirror* 26 May 1838
66. *Gloucester Journal* 26 May 1838
67. Noble, *Father and Son*, p. 157
68. *Bristol Mirror* quoted in the *Taunton Courier & Western Advertiser* 30 May 1838
69. *Taunton Courier & Western Advertiser* 30 May 1838
70. *Taunton Courier & Western Advertiser* 30 May 1838
71. *Taunton Courier & Western Advertiser* 30 May 1838
72. *Bristol Mercury* 2 June 1838

4 Masters and Crew

1. Christopher Claxton, *Logs of the First Voyage, Made with the Unceasing Aid of Steam, between England and America by the Great Western of Bristol* (Great Western Steamship Company 1838). AGM 1838, p. 61
2. Hosken usually gave his place of birth as Penryn, Cornwall on the crew agreements, so saw himself as a Cornishman.
3. James Hosken, *Autobiographical Sketch of the Public Career of Admiral James Hosken* (Penzance: Rodda, 1889)
4. Hosken. *Autobiographical Sketch* p. 13. William R. O'Byrne, *A Naval Biographical Dictionary* (London: John Murray, 1849)
5. Mrs E. Dixon Diary, courtesy Caroline Welling Van Deusen
6. Hosken, *Autobiographical Sketch*, p. 21
7. Hosken, *Autobiographical Sketch*. Note Hosken refers to Broadentown but must mean Bordentown, Trenton
8. Hosken, *Autobiographical Sketch*, p. 19
9. Stephen Fox, *The Ocean Railway: Isambard Kingdom Brunel, Samuel Cunard and the Revolutionary World of the Great Atlantic Steamships* (London: Harper Collins, 2004), p. 200; *The Times* 13 April 1847, 14 April 1847; *Illustrated London News* 17 April 1847
10. *Herald* 18 June 1838
11. *Bristol Mercury* 31 September 1838
12. Claxton.AGM report March 1839; *Waterford Mail* 12 December 1838
13. *London Evening Standard* 7 September 1840
14. Hosken, *Autobiographical Sketch*, pp. 20–21
15. Philip Banbury, *Shipbuilders of the Thames and Medway* (Newton Abbot: David and Charles, 1971), p. 175
16. BI: Masters Box Item 35: testimonials from Henry Fletcher 18 February 1842
17. *Bristol Mercury* 23 January 1836
18. BI: Masters Box Letter from T R Guppy 5 February 1843

19. BPP Select Committee on Causes of Shipwrecks. Report, Minutes of Evidence 1836
20. D. Williams, 'James Silk Buckingham: Sailor, Explorer and Maritime Reformer,' in Stephen Fisher, *Studies in British Privateering, Trading and Seamen's Welfare, 1775–1900* (Exeter, University of Exeter, 1987), pp. 99–120
21. New York Passenger list October 1837 *President*
22. Williams, 'James Silk Buckingham', pp. 99–120; Certificates of Service
23. BPP Report of the Select Committee on Steamboat Accidents, 1839
24. R. G. Milburn, 'The Emergence of the Engineer in the British Merchant Shipping Industry, 1812–1863', *International Journal of Maritime History*, 28 (2016), p. 566
25. Milburn, 'Emergence of the Engineer', p. 566
26. H. Campbell McMurray, 'Ship's Engineers: Their Status and Position on Board, C. 1830–65', in *West Country Maritime and Social History* ed. by Stephen Fisher (Exeter: University of Exeter, 1980), p. 84–90
27. Milburn, 'Emergence of the Engineer', p. 571
28. McMurray, 'Ship's Engineers', p. 85–90
29. Milburn, 'Emergence of the Engineer', p. 568
30. Milburn, 'Emergence of the Engineer', p. 573
31. Milburn, 'Emergence of the Engineer', p. 563
32. *Lloyd's Register* 1834, pp. 13–27
33. Alston Kennerley, 'Stoking the Boilers: Firemen and Trimmers in British Merchant Ships, 1850–1950', *International Journal of Maritime History*, XX (2008), pp. 197–8
34. Kennerley, 'Stoking the Boilers', p. 198
35. Kennerley, 'Stoking the Boilers', p. 194
36. Kennerley, 'Stoking the Boilers', p. 210
37. Kennerley, 'Stoking the Boilers', p. 206
38. Denis Griffiths, *Brunel's Great Western* (Wellingborough: Patrick Stephens, 1985), pp. 137–38
39. Claxton, *Logs of the First Voyage*
40. Claxton, *Logs of the First Voyage*, p. 29
41. Sari Maenpaa, 'Galley News: Catering Personnel on British Passenger Liners, 1860 –1938', *International Journal of Maritime History*, XII (2000), p. 245; Griffiths, *Brunel's Great Western*, p. 64.
42. BI: *Great Western* Box AGM March 1839
43. Christopher Claxton, *The Naval Monitor*, 2nd edn (London, 1833); *Bristol Mercury* 20 January 1838
44. Valerie C. Burton, 'Apprenticeship Regulation and Maritime Labour in the Nineteenth Century British Merchant Marine', *International Journal of Maritime History*, 1 (1989), pp. 38–41, p. 33
45. Burton, 'Apprenticeship Regulation', pp. 38–41
46. Burton, 'Apprenticeship Regulation', pp. 38–41
47. Burton, 'Apprenticeship Regulation', pp. 41 & 44
48. T. C. Haliburton, *The Letter Bag of the Great Western; or Life in a Steamer* (New York: William H. Colyer, 1840), p. 87
49. Claxton, *Logs of the First Voyage*, p. 113
50. *Bristol Mercury* 20 January 1838; Haliburton, *The Letter Bag*, p. 56

51. TNA: BT 98/187 Bristol Crew Lists 28 March 1842; Griffiths, *Brunel's Great Western*, p. 137
52. Griffiths, *Brunel's Great Western*, p. 137; Certificates of Service
53. BI: *Great Western* Box AGM March 1839
54. *Morning Post* 31 December 1838
55. Sari Maenpaa, 'Galley News: Catering Personnel on British Passenger Liners, 1860 –1938', *International Journal of Maritime History*, XII (2000), pp. 243–60.
56. Maenpaa, 'Galley News', p. 247
57. George Moore, *Journal of a Voyage across the Atlantic: with Notes on Canada & the United States, and return to Great Britain in 1844* (London: s.n, 1845)
58. *Morning Post* 31 December 1838
59. Griffiths, *Brunel's Great Western*, pp. 139–40
60. Griffiths, *Brunel's Great Western*, pp. 112–13 quoting *Bristol Mirror* 8 December 1838
61. J. Jay Smith, *A Summer's Jaunt across the Water* (Philadelphia: J W Moore, 1846), p. 223
62. Haliburton, *The Letter Bag*, pp. 31 & 34
63. Burton, 'Apprenticeship Regulation', p. 47; BT xx Crew Lists
64. *The Times* 17 June 1822
65. *Bristol Mercury* 23 January 1836
66. Diary of Mrs E. L. Dixon
67. Sari Maenpaa, 'Women Below Deck: Gender and Employment on British Passenger Liners, 1860–1938', *Journal of Transport History*, 25 (2004)
68. *Evening Post* 11 August 1838
69. Claxton, *Logs of the First Voyage*
70. Griffiths, *Brunel's Great Western*, pp. 139–40; John Jay Smith, *A Summer's Jaunt across the Water* (Philadelphia: J W Moore, 1846), p. 221
71. Isambard Brunel, *The Life of Isambard Kingdom Brunel Civil Engineer*, 2006 edn (Stroud: Nonsuch Publishing, 1870), pp. 189 & 404
72. Vera Brodsky Lawrence, *Strong on Music: The New York Music Scene in the Days of George Templeton Strong, 1836–1849* (Chicago: University of Chicago Press, 1988), pp. 105–6
73. TNA: BT 98/187 Bristol Crew Lists
74. TNA: BT 98/187 Bristol Crew Lists
75. TNA: BT 98/187 Bristol Crew Lists; Griffiths, *Brunel's Great Western*, p. 138
76. Hosken. *Autobiographical Sketch*
77. L H Sigourney, *Pleasant Memories of Pleasant Lands* (Boston: James Munroe and company 1856), pp. 374–5
78. See Appendix
79. Smith, *A Summer's Jaunt*, p. 221
80. Griffiths, *Brunel's Great Western*, pp. 96–97

5 Looking after the Passengers

1. TNA: RAIL 253/111, Letter Book of the Great Western Steam Ship Company
2. TNA: RAIL 253/111, 9 April 1840, 25 July 1842
3. TNA: RAIL 253/111, 26 May 1840; 13 October 1841

4. TNA: RAIL 253/111, 25 April 1840, 31 October, 28 April 1842, 3 May
5. TNA: RAIL 253/111, 25 May 1840, 23 May
6. TNA: RAIL 253/111, 19 October 1841, 26 March 1842
7. TNA: RAIL 253/111, 30 March 1842
8. TNA: RAIL 253/111, 27 April 1842, 30 August
9. TNA: RAIL 253/111, 1 July 1843
10. Extracts from 'Diary of Mrs. E.L. Dixon of the U.S.A. On Her Honeymoon Trip to Europe', Transcript courtesy of Caroline Welling Van Deusen.
11. Diary of Mrs E. L. Dixon
12. *Bristol Mirror* 6 May 1838
13. RMSPC report in Denis Griffiths, *Brunel's Great Western* (Wellingborough: Patrick Stephens, 1985), p. 63; Douglas Hart, 'Sociability and Separate Spheres on the North Atlantic: The Interior Architecture of British Atlantic Liners, 1840–1930', *Journal of Social History*, 44 (2010), p. 190–1
14. Hart, 'Sociability and Separate Spheres', p. 194
15. Stephen Fox, *The Ocean Railway : Isambard Kingdom Brunel, Samuel Cunard and the Revoluntionary World of the Great Atlantic Steamships* (London: Harper Collins, 2004), p. 199
16. J. Jay Smith, *A Summer's Jaunt across the Water* (Philadelphia: J W Moore, 1846), p. 222–223; Note: John Tyler was US President 1841–45, a merry-andrew was a person who clowned publicly and Brother Jonathan was a term for New Englanders or Americans in general, John Bull being the epitome of an Englishman.
17. Fox, *The Ocean Railway*, p. 199
18. T. C. Haliburton, *The Letter Bag of the Great Western; or Life in a Steamer* (New York: William H. Colyer, 1840), pp. 109–10
19. Diary of Mrs E. L. Dixon
20. Diary of Mrs E. L. Dixon
21. Haliburton, *The Letter Bag*, p. 34
22. Smith, *A Summer's Jaunt*, p. 222
23. George Moore, *Journal of a Voyage across the Atlantic* (London, 1845)
24. Haliburton, *The Letter Bag*
25. Hart, 'Sociability and Separate Spheres', p. 192
26. Diary of Mrs E. L. Dixon, p. 13
27. L. H. Sigourney, *Pleasant Memories of Pleasant Lands* (Boston: James Munroe and Company, 1856), p. 371
28. Hart, 'Sociability and Separate Spheres'
29. Diary of Mrs E. L. Dixon
30. Robert G. Albion, *The Rise of New York Port 1815–1860* (New York: Charles Scribner's Sons, 1939), p. 55–6
31. Haliburton, *The Letter Bag*, p. 81 & viii
32. New York Public Library: Admiral Coffin to Philip Hone, 20 October 1836
33. Diary of Mrs E. L. Dixon
34. Moore, *Journal of a Voyage Journal of a Voyage*, p. 62
35. Moore, *Journal of a Voyage*
36. Hart, 'Sociability and Separate Spheres', p. 193
37. TNA: RAIL 253/111, 14 May 1840

38. Diary of Mrs E. L. Dixon
39. Haliburton, *The Letter Bag*, p. 28
40. Sigourney, *Pleasant Memories of Pleasant Lands*
41. Moore, *Journal of a Voyage*, p. 2
42. Moore, *Journal of a Voyage*; Haliburton, *The Letter Bag*, pp. 34–35
43. *Bristol Mirror* 6 May 1838
44. Moore, *Journal of a Voyage*
45. Diary of Mrs E. L. Dixon
46. Moore, *Journal of a Voyage*
47. Diary of Mrs L Dixon, p. 13; Stephen J Wayne, *The Road to the White House* (Boston, Cengage Learning, 2016), pp. 174–5
48. Smith, *A Summer's Jaunt*, p. 226
49. Smith, *A Summer's Jaunt*, p. 225 quoting letter from Mr Christopher Hughes, US Charge d'Affaire to the Hague
50. *Civil Engineer's and Architects Journal* March 1838
51. Diary of Mrs E. L. Dixon
52. Smith, *A Summer's Jaunt*
53. Edwin G. Burrows and Mike Wallace, *Gotham: A History of New York City to 1898* (Oxford: Oxford University Press, 1999), p. 527
54. *Herald* 18 June 1838
55. Sigourney, *Pleasant Memories of Pleasant Lands*
56. Smith, *A Summer's Jaunt*
57. BPP: Accounts of Population and Number of Houses according to Census, 1841, of each County in Great Britain, Channel Islands and Isle of Man; Comparative Statement of Population and Houses, 1801, 1811, 1821, 1831 and 1841; Account of Population of each City and Burgh in Scotland
58. Peter Malpass, 'Victorian Bristol: Chapter 3 Reshaping the City', p. 73. Unpublished. Quoting from *Chilcott's Descriptive History of Bristol*, Bristol: J Chilcott, no date, but probably 1838
59. http://physics.bu.edu/~redner/projects/population/cities/newyork.html [accessed Jan 2017]
60. Burrows and Wallace, *Gotham*, p. 450
61. Diary of Mrs E. L. Dixon
62. Smith, *A Summer's Jaunt*, p. 233; Burrows and Wallace, *Gotham*, pp. 596–599

6 A Variety of Passengers

1. *Herald* New York 18 June 1838
2. Robert G. Albion, *The Rise of New York Port 1815–1860* (New York: Charles Scribner's Sons, 1939), p. 240
3. William Patrick O'Brien, *Merchants of Independence: International Trade on the Santa Fe Trail, 1827–1860* (Missouri: Truman State University Press, 2014), pp. 160–161
4. Ancestry.com. *New York, Passenger Lists, 1820–1957* [database on-line]. Provo, UT, USA: Ancestry.com Operations, Inc., 2010
5. Edwin G. Burrows and Mike Wallace, *Gotham: A History of New York City to 1898* (Oxford: Oxford University Press, 1999), pp. 434 & 639

6. New York Passenger lists; Albion *The Rise of New York Port*, pp. 284 to 285
7. John Killick, 'Transatlantic Steerage Fares, British and Irish Migration, and Return Migration, 1815–60', *Economic History Review*, 67, 1, 2014, p. 171
8. *Sacramento Daily Union*, 26 March 1870
9. *Sacramento Daily Union*, 30 January 1875
10. Fox, *The Ocean Railway*, p. 201–2
11. Caroline Welling Van Deusen, 'Introduction to the Transcription of the Washington Diary of Elizabeth L. C. Dixon', *White House Historical Association* Issue 33, 2013. https://www.whitehousehistory.org/introduction-to-the-transcription-of-the-washington-diary-of-elizabeth-l-c-dixon
12. Smith, *A Summer's Jaunt*, pp. 229 & 231
13. Nina Baym, 'Reinventing Lydia Sigourney', *American Literature*, 62 (1990), pp. 385–6, 390
14. Sigourney, *Pleasant Memories of Pleasant Lands*, p. 3
15. Sigourney, *Pleasant Memories of Pleasant Lands*, pp. 3–31
16. http://www.accessible-archives.com/collections/godeys-ladys-book/
17. http://www.accessible-archives.com/collections/godeys-ladys-book/
18. Kathleen L. Endres (1995), *Women's Periodicals in the United States: Consumer Magazines.*(Greenwood Publishing Group, 1995), p. 115
19. Fox, *The Ocean Railway*, p. 196
20. New York Passenger Lists
21. http://www.hwlongfellow.org/ [accessed 8 Feb 2017]
22. Jacky Bratton, *The Making of the West End Stage: Marriage, Management and the Mapping of Gender in London, 1830–1870* (Cambridge: Cambridge University Press, 2011); Jacky Bratton, *New Readings in Theatre History* (Cambridge: Cambridge University Press, 2003), p. 191.; Vera Brodsky Lawrence, *Strong on Music: The New York Music Scene in the Days of George Templeton Strong, 1836–1849* (Chicago: University of Chicago Press, 1988). 60–61; BPP Theatres and Dramatic Pieces: Return of the theatres licensed by Lord Chamberlain, June 1832
23. *Morning Herald* 6 August 1838
24. Bratton, *The Making of the West End Stage*
25. Brian C. Thompson, 'Henri Drayton, English Opera and Anglo-American Relations, 1850–72', *Journal of the Royal Musical Association*, 136 (2011), p. 300
26. Lawrence, *Strong on Music*, p. 47; *Herald* New York 18 June 1838
27. Haliburton, *The Letter Bag*, p. 27
28. Diary of J W Williams
29. Lawrence, *Strong on Music*, pp. 99, 163
30. *Herald* New York 18 June 1838
31. TNA: RAIL 253/111, 29 August 1842 Ward to Gibbs, Bright
32. Moore, *Journal of a Voyage*
33. Robert Tracy, 'W C Macready in the Life and Adventures of Nicholas Nickleby', *Dickens Quarterly*, 24 (2007), pp. 161–62
34. Lawrence, *Strong on Music*, p. 189
35. *Kentish Gazette* 17 July 1838
36. *Kentish Gazette* 17 July 1838
37. *Kentish Gazette* 17 July 1838

38. Diary of Mrs E. L. Dixon
39. New York Historical Society: Louis Antoine Godey Letters. Letter to Godey 6 July 1841, author unknown
40. Moore, *Journal of a Voyage*, p. 62
41. Smith, *A Summer's Jaunt*, p. 221
42. W. H. Russell, *My Diary in India, in the Year 1858–9* (London: Routledge, 1860), p. 7
43. Claxton, *Logs of the First Voyage*, p. 72
44. Moore, *Journal of a Voyage*
45. Sigourney, *Pleasant Memories of Pleasant Lands*, p. 370
46. Diary of Mrs E. L. Dixon, p. 13
47. L. H. Sigourney, *Pleasant Memories of Pleasant Lands* (Boston: James Munroe and company 1856), p. 366
48. Diary of Mrs E. L. Dixon, p. 13
49. Diary of Mrs E. L. Dixon, p. 13

7 The Great Western Steam Ship Company

1. https://www.philadelphiabuildings.org/pab/app/ar_display.cfm/25248
2. https://founders.archives.gov/documents/Jefferson/03-06-02-0252
3. Robert G. Albion, *The Rise of New York Port 1815–1860* (New York: Charles Scribner's Sons, 1939), pp. 225–7
4. *Bristol Mercury* 31 September 1838
5. Paul Quinn, 'Macgregor Laird, Junius Smith and the Atlantic Ocean', *The Mariner's Mirror*, 92 (2006), p. 488
6. Denis Griffiths, *Brunel's Great Western* (Wellingborough: Patrick Stephens, 1985), p. 100
7. *Devizes and Wiltshire Gazette* 6 September 1838
8. *Devizes and Wiltshire Gazette* 6 September 1838
9. *Herald* New York 18 June 1838
10. My thanks to David Williams and the late John Armstrong for additional information on this aspect. For an example of this situation see details of the South Eastern Railway in Rixon Bucknall, *Boat Trains and Channel Packets* (London,1957), pp. 44–5
11. L.C.B. Gower, 'The English Private Company', *Law and Contemporary Problems*, 18 (1953), p. 535
12. *Bristol Mercury* 23 January 1836
13. John Stevens, *Bristol Politics in the Age of Peel, 1832–1847* (Bristol: Avon Local History & Archaeology, 2014), pps. 23, 20, 44; *Bristol Mercury* 30 July 1836; G W A Bush, *Bristol and Its Municipal Government, 1820–1851* (Bristol: Bristol Record Society, 1976), p. 133
14. https://www.ucl.ac.uk/lbs/person/view/41207 Legacies of British Slave-ownership
15. BPP House of Commons Return of Factories and Mills 1839
16. Denis Griffiths, Andrew Lambert, and Fred Walker, *Brunel's Ships* (London: Chatham Publishing, 1999), p. 5 see footnote 4
17. BI: *Great Western* Box AGM March 1839

18. BI: *Great Western* Box AGM March 1839
19. BI: *Great Western* Box AGM March 1839
20. *Taunton Courier and Western Advertiser* 20 March 1839
21. BI: *Great Western* Box AGM March 1839
22. *Taunton Courier and Western Advertiser* 20 March 1839
23. *Bristol Mercury* 31 September 1838
24. Extract from 'Ode to Captain Hoskin' by John Dix
25. David Large (ed.), *The Port of Bristol 1848–1884* (Bristol: Bristol Record Society, 1984), pp. 166 & 172
26. Griffiths, *Brunel's Great Western*, p. 48
27. Griffiths, *Brunel's Great Western*, p. 49; BI: *Great Western* Box AGM March 1839
28. Isambard Brunel, *The Life of Isambard Kingdom Brunel Civil Engineer*, 2006 edn (Stroud: Nonsuch Publishing, 1870), pp. 312–13
29. Brunel, *The Life of Isambard Kingdom Brunel*, p. 313
30. Francis E Hyde, *Cunard and the North Atlantic, 1840–1973* (London: MacMillan Press, 1975), p. 5; Griffiths, *Brunel's Great Western*, p. 53
31. Griffiths, *Brunel's Great Western*, p. 53
32. Quinn, 'Macgregor Laird, Junius Smith'
33. Griffiths, *Brunel's Great Western*, p. 106
34. Griffiths, *Brunel's Great Western*, p. 73
35. John G. Langley, *Steam Lion: A Biography of Samuel Cunard* (Halifax: Nimbus, 2006); Howard Robinson, *Carrying British Mail Overseas* (London: George Allen & Unwin, 1964), p. 124
36. John Malcolm Brinnin, *The Sway of the Grand Saloon*, 1986 edn (London: Arlington Books, 1971), p. 83
37. Brinnin, *The Sway of the Grand Saloon*, p. 83
38. T. C. Haliburton, *The Letter Bag of the Great Western; or Life in a Steamer* (New York: William H. Colyer, 1840), p. viii
39. Brinnin, *The Sway of the Grand Saloon*, p. 84; Ithiel Town, *Atlantic Steam-Ships. Some Ideas and Statements, the Result of Considerable Reflection on the Subject of Navigating the Atlantic Ocean with Steam-Ships of Large Tonnage, Etc* (New York, 1838)
40. Brinnin, *The Sway of the Grand Saloon*, p. 84; Langley, *Steam Lion*, p. 67
41. Stephen Fox, *The Ocean Railway: Isambard Kingdom Brunel, Samuel Cunard and the Revoluntionary World of the Great Atlantic Steamships* (London: Harper Collins, 2004), p. 54
42. Fox, *The Ocean Railway*, pp. 52–53
43. Fox, *The Ocean Railway*, p. 87
44. New York Passenger list
45. *Bristol Mercury* 31 September 1838
46. Fox, *The Ocean Railway*, pp. 85–86
47. Griffiths, *Brunel's Great Western*, pp. 53–54
48. BPP Report from the Select Committee on Halifax and Boston Mail 1846; Langley, *Steam Lion*, p. 67–72
49. Fox, *The Ocean Railway*, p. 88; New York Passenger list *Great Western* April 1839
50. Fox, *The Ocean Railway*, pp. 89–92

51. Griffiths, *Brunel's Great Western*, p. 54
52. Robinson, *Carrying British Mail Overseas*, p. 124
53. J. K. Laughton, 'Hosken, James (1798–1885)', rev. Andrew Lambert, *Oxford Dictionary of National Biography* (Oxford University Press, 2004)
54. BPP Report from the Select Committee on Halifax and Boston Mail 1846; Griffiths, p. 54
55. *The Times* 28 October 1839
56. TNA RAIL 253/111
57. Griffiths, *Brunel's Great Western*, pp. 103–104
58. Malpass, 'Victorian Bristol: Chapter 3 Reshaping the City', p. 73. Unpublished draft
59. *Bristol Mercury* 27 January1842; *Bristol Mirror* 16 July 1842
60. BI: *Great Western* Box AGM March 1842
61. *Bristol Mirror* 9 July 1842; Griffiths, *Brunel's Great Western*, p. 90
62. *Bristol Mercury* 22 October 1842
63. BI: *Great Western* Box Item 15: Article from Liverpool *Albion* quoted in the *Birmingham Journal* 27 August 1842
64. *The Times* 21 October 1842
65. *The Times* 25 October 1842
66. *Bristol Mirror* 29October 1842
67. *Bristol Mercury* 12 November 1842
68. *Bristol Mercury* 12 November 1842
69. *Bristol Mirror* 3 December 1842
70. BI: *Great Western* Box AGM 1844
71. David Hancock, *Oceans of Wine: Madeira and the Emergence of American Trade and Taste* (New Haven, Conn.: Yale University Press, 2009), p. 426
72. Hancock, *Oceans of Wine*, pp. 431, 455
73. Griffiths, *Brunel's Great Western*, p. 90
74. Griffiths, *Brunel's Great Western*, p. 91
75. *Lloyd's List* 16 April 1843
76. Griffiths, *Brunel's Great Western*, p. 91
77. BI: *Great Western* Box AGM minutes
78. Griffiths, *Brunel's Great Western*, pp. 82 & 83
79. Crosbie Smith, "This Great National Undertaking'; John Scott Russell, the Master Shipwrights and the Royal Mail Steam Packet Company ', in *Re-Inventing the Ship: Science, Technology and the Maritime World, 1800–1918*, ed. by Don Leggett and Richard Dunn (Basingstoke: Ashgate, 2012), pp. 25–52, p. 48
80. *Inverness Courier* 3 July 1844
81. Griffiths, *Brunel's Great Western*, p. 94

8 Changing Hands

1. Griffiths, *Brunel's Great Western*, p. 94
2. Moore, *Journal of a Voyage*
3. Smith, *A Summer's Jaunt*
4. Smith, *A Summer's Jaunt*, p. 221
5. TNA: RAIL 253/111

6. BI: *Great Western* Box Item 16 Letter from Grayson to Bennett Liverpool Oct 4th 1846
7. Griffiths, *Brunel's Great Western*, p. 109
8. BPP Report from Select Committee on Halifax and Boston Mail 3 August 1846
9. BPP Report from Select Committee on Halifax and Boston Mail 3 August 1846
10. *Illustrated London News* 31 October 1846
11. *Illustrated London News* 31 October 1846
12. Griffiths, *Brunel's Great Western*, p. 123
13. Griffiths, *Brunel's Great Western*
14. *Manchester Courier and Lancashire General Advertiser*, 21 April 1847
15. Robert E. Forrester, *British Mail Steamers to South America, 1851–1965: A History of the Royal Mail Steam Packet Company and Royal Mail Lines* (London: Routledge, 2016), p. 2
16. Gordon Goodwin, 'MacQueen, James (1778–1870)', rev. Elizabeth Baigent, *Oxford Dictionary of National Biography* (Oxford University Press, 2004)
17. Crosbie Smith, "This Great National Undertaking'; John Scott Russell, the Master Shipwrights and the Royal Mail Steam Packet Company ', in *Re-Inventing the Ship: Science, Technology and the Maritime World, 1800–1918*, ed. by Don Leggett and Richard Dunn (Basingstoke: Ashgate, 2012), pp. 25–52
18. Smith, 'This Great National Undertaking', p. 32; Robert G. Greenhill, 'British Shipping and Latin America 1840–1930: The Royal Mail Steam Packet Company', PhD Thesis, University of Exeter, 1971, p. 15; Anyaa Anim-Addo, 'Thence to the River Plate': Steamship Mobilities in the South Atlantic, 1842–1869', *Atlantic Studies*, 13 (2016), p. 7
19. Forrester, *British Mail Steamers to South America*, p. 1; Smith, 'This Great National Undertaking', pp. 40 & 47, 48
20. Greenhill, 'British Shipping and Latin America', p. 27
21. Forrester, *British Mail Steamers to South America*
22. Griffiths, *Brunel's Great Western*, p. 123
23. William R. O'Byrne, *A Naval Biographical Dictionary* (London: John Murray, 1849), pp. 186–87; Andrew Lambert, Denis Griffiths, Andrew Lambert, and Fred Walker, *Brunel's Ships* (London: Chatham Publishing, 1999), pp. 34–36.
24. Griffiths, *Brunel's Great Western*, p. 123
25. Griffiths, *Brunel's Great Western*, pp. 124 & 122
26. *Yorkshire Gazette* 6 May 1848
27. *Norwich Mercury* 26 January 1850
28. *Morning Post* 18 September 1850
29. Griffiths, *Brunel's Great Western*, p. 126
30. *Illustrated London News* 24 May 1851
31. *Hampshire Chronicle* 10 January 1852
32. *Durham County Advertiser* 29 April 1853
33. Griffiths, *Brunel's Great Western*, p. 145
34. Anim-Addo, 'Thence to the River Plate', pp. 10–15
35. Griffiths, *Brunel's Great Western*, p. 129

36. *Hampshire Chronicle* 15 April 1854
37. Jan Tore Klovland, 'New Evidence on the Fluctuations in Ocean Freight Rates in the 1850s', *Explorations in Economic History*, 46 (2009)
38. Griffiths, *Brunel's Great Western*, p. 129
39. Klovland, 'Ocean Freight Rates', p. 275
40. Graeme J. Milne, *Trade and Traders in Mid-Victorian Liverpool: Mercantile Business and the Making of a World Port* (Liverpool: Liverpool University Press, 2000), p. 181
41. Griffiths, *Brunel's Great Western*, p. 129
42. Milne, *Trade and Traders in Mid-Victorian Liverpool*, pp. 182–4
43. Klovland, 'Ocean Freight Rates', p. 278
44. *The Times* 6 October 1855
45. Freda Harcourt, 'British Oeanic Mail Contracts in the Age of Steam, 1838–1914', *Journal of Transport History*, IX (1988), pp. 12–13
46. Milne, *Trade and Traders in Mid-Victorian Liverpool*, p. 187
47. *Illustrated London News* 13 January 1855
48. Alston Kennerley, 'Stoking the Boilers: Firemen and Trimmers in British Merchant Ships, 1850–1950', *International Journal of Maritime History*, XX (2008), p. 209
49. *The Times* 12 March 1856; Griffiths, *Brunel's Great Western*, p. 132
50. BPP Return of Troop transports. 1856; Griffiths, *Brunel's Great Western*, p. 132
51. Ewan Corlett, *The Iron Ship: The Story of Brunel's Ss Great Britain*, 2012 edn (Bristol: ss Great Britain, 1975), pp. 207–209; R. Angus Buchanan, *Brunel: The Life and Times of Isambard Kingdom Brunel* (London: Hambledon and London, 2002)
52. Buchanan, *Brunel*, p. 180
53. *The Times* 24 June 1856

9 Influence and Legacy

1. Howard Robinson, *Carrying British Mail Overseas* (London: George Allen & Unwin, 1964), pp. 111–2
2. Robinson, *Carrying British Mail Overseas*, p. 112
3. Robinson, *Carrying British Mail Overseas*, p. 112
4. Robinson, *Carrying British Mail Overseas*, p. 113
5. Robinson, *Carrying British Mail Overseas*, p. 114
6. Robinson, *Carrying British Mail Overseas*, p. 115
7. *New York and Evening Post* 27 April 1838
8. Robinson, *Carrying British Mail Overseas*, p. 115
9. *The Patriot and Farmers Monthly*, York, Upper Canada, 13 December 1833
10. *Herald* New York 18 June 1838
11. Robinson, *Carrying British Mail Overseas*, p. 115–6
12. J. Jay Smith, *A Summer's Jaunt across the Water* (Philadelphia: J W Moore, 1846), pp. 27–28
13. Robinson, *Carrying British Mail Overseas*, pp. 115–6
14. *London Dispatch* 24 March 1839
15. BI: *Great Western* Box AGM 26 March 1840

16. BI: *Great Western* Box
17. TNA RAIL 253/111; *Bristol Mercury* 29 August 1840
18. Edwin G. Burrows and Mike Wallace, *Gotham: A History of New York City to 1898* (Oxford: Oxford University Press, 1999), p. 446
19. Jessica Lepler, "The News Flew Like Lightning", *Journal of Cultural Economy*, 5 (2012), p. 180
20. Lepler, 'The News Flew Like Lightning', p. 189
21. *Herald* New York 18 June 1838
22. Lepler, 'The News Flew Like Lightning'
23. TNA: RAIL 253/111; *New York Times* 22 October 1864
24. James Hosken, *Autobiographical Sketch of the Public Career of Admiral James Hosken* (Penzance: Rodda, 1889), pp. 19–20
25. *Inverness Courier* 12 December 1838
26. *The Times* 5 October 1839
27. *Bristol Times & Mirror* 6 May 1843; *Illustrated London News* 6 May 1843
28. *Dublin Evening Packet and Correspondent*, 4 May 1843
29. *Dublin Monitor* 9 June 1843
30. *Herald* New York 18 June 1838
31. Hosken, *Autobiographical Sketch*, p. 15
32. *Gloucester Chronicle* 2 February 1838
33. *Herald* New York 18 June 1838
34. BI: *Great Western* Box AGM 7 March 1839
35. *Herald* New York 18 June 1838
36. *London Dispatch* Sunday 30 December 1838
37. BI: *Great Western* Box AGM 26 March 1840
38. TNA: RAIL 253/111;
    http://www.hairraisingstories.com/Proprietors/PHALON.html
39. Burrows and Wallace, *Gotham*, p. 437
40. L. H. Sigourney, *Pleasant Memories of Pleasant Lands* (Boston: James Munroe and company 1856).
41. *Herald* 18 June 1838
42. *Morning Herald* 14 September 1838
43. *Worcester Journal* 20 May 1847
44. Winterthur Library, Downs Collection. Item no 1328 Toast of the Atlantic
45. *Norfolk News* 16 January 1847
46. Bodleian Library, Oxford: Harding B 16 (107d) Broadside Ballad printed in London 1838
47. *The Era* 2 December 1838
48. BI: *Great Western* Box letter to Hosken
49. *Herald* New York 31 May 1838
50. Crosbie Smith, "This Great National Undertaking'; John Scott Russell, the Master Shipwrights and the Royal Mail Steam Packet Company ', in *Re-Inventing the Ship: Science, Technology and the Maritime World, 1800–1918*, ed. by Don Leggett and Richard Dunn (Basingstoke: Ashgate, 2012), pp. 42 & 48;
51. BI: University of Bristol Collection DM 1758/9/4 letter from Christopher Claxton to IKB 30 March 1853
52. *London Evening Standard* 9 February 1852

53. Edward W. Sloan. 'The First and (Very Secret) International Steamship Cartel, 1850–1856', in Starkey, D J and Harlaftis, H (eds) *Global Markets : The Internationalization of the Sea Transport Industries since 1850* (St John's, Newfoundland) 1998, 29–52.

54. Denis Griffiths, *Brunel's Great Western* (Wellingborough: Patrick Stephens, 1985), p. 107; Paul Quinn, 'Macgregor Laird, Junius Smith and the Atlantic Ocean', *The Mariner's Mirror*, 92 (2006), p. 494

55. J. K. Laughton, 'Hosken, James (1798–1885)', rev. Andrew Lambert, *Oxford Dictionary of National Biography* (Oxford University Press, 2004); 1871 Census

56. Ewan Corlett, *The Iron Ship: The Story of Brunel's Ss Great Britain*, 2012 edn (Bristol: ss Great Britain, 1975), pp. 195–199; BI: Captains Box Funeral notice in *The Age* 27 April 1869

57. BPP: Report of the Commissioners appointed to Inquire as to the Proposal for an Irish Packet Station 1851.

58. http://www.ucl.ac.uk/bloomsbury-project/articles/individuals/lardner_dionysius.htm

59. J. N. Hays, 'Lardner, Dionysius (1793–1859)', *Oxford Dictionary of National Biography* (Oxford University Press, 2004)

60. Grahame Farr, *Shipbuilding in the Port of Bristol* (Greenwich, London: National Maritime Museum 1977), pp. 9–10

61. R. Angus Buchanan, *Brunel: The Life and Times of Isambard Kingdom Brunel* (London: Hambledon and London, 2002), pp. 200–201; Anon, 'Obituary. Thomas Richard Guppy, 1797–1882', *Minutes of the Proceedings of the Institution of Civil Engineers*, 69 (1882), pp. 411–15

62. Anon, 'Obituary. Joshua Field (Ex-President and Vice-President), 1786–1863(?)', *Minutes of the Proceedings of the Institution of Civil Engineers*, 23 (1864), pp. 488–92

63. *Monmouthshire Merlin* 9 Oct 1847 quoting *Railway Gazette*

64. East Sussex Record Office: dhbg/DH/B/157/262 List of names of speakers on plans for floating harbour

65. *Staffordshire Advertiser* 12 November 1864; *Bristol Times and Mirror* 1 February 1864; *Bristol Times and Mirror* 4 April 1868

66. Denis Griffiths, Andrew Lambert, and Fred Walker, *Brunel's Ships* (London: Chatham Publishing, 1999), p. 27

67. Griffiths, *Brunel's Great Western*, p. 133

68. Robert and Linda Tait, 'Castle's Shipbuilders & Shipbuilders on the Thames' in Rankin, Stuart (ed.) *Proceedings of Symposium on Shipbuilding on the Thames*, Rotherhithe September 2000, pp. 29–31

69. Isambard Brunel, *The Life of Isambard Kingdom Brunel Civil Engineer*, 2006 edn (Stroud: Nonsuch Publishing, 1870), p. 182

Sources and Bibliography

Primary Sources
National Archives, London
BT 98/187 Bristol Crew Lists 1837–1844
BT 98/597 Bristol Crew Lists 1845
BT 98/873 Bristol Crew Lists 1846
BT 98/1173 Bristol Crew Lists 1847
BT 98/1315 London Crew Lists 1847
BT 98/1669 London Crew Lists 1848
BT 98/1959 London Crew Lists 1849
BT 98/2237 London Crew Lists 1850
BT 98/2607 London Crew Lists 1851
BT 98/3031 London Crew Lists 1852
BT 98/3452 London Crew Lists 1853
BT 98/3863 London Crew Lists 1854
BT 98/4227 London Crew Lists 1855
BT 98/4585 London Crew Lists 1856

BT 107/7 London Coasting Register 1814–1820
BT 107/29 Foreign Trade Shipping Registers 1815
BT 107/28 Foreign Trade Shipping Registers 1816

C 114/128: Chancery Exhibits Re Fricour, a bankrupt: Hotel inventory and account books, London 1839

CUST 130/40 London Registers of shipping 1846 to 1847

PROB 11/1580 Will of Thomas Hall 1816

RAIL 1014/8 Early Steamships in which the Company were indirectly interested through I.K. Brunel and D. Gooch. Misc collection of material
RAIL 253/111 Letter Book of the Great Western Steam Ship company

Bodleian Library, Oxford
Harding B 16 (107d) Broadside Ballad printed in London 1838

East Sussex Record Office
dhbg/DH/B/157/262 List of names of speakers on plans for floating harbor

Brunel Institute, ss Great Britain Trust
University of Bristol Collection
DM 162/10 Brunel Letter Books no 1 and no 2
DM 407 *Great Western* fire insurance document 2 December 1843
DM 1758/9/4 letter from Christopher Claxton to IKB 30 March 1853
Transcript of diary of Mrs E. L. Dixon, courtesy Mr and Mrs Welling

Library of Congress
MSS45849 1839–1895 John Warren Williams
Family Diary of John W Williams 1839–1842

M1 A15 vol 8 Great Western March
composed and respectfully dedicated to Capt. James Hosken R.N. commander of the Great Western by Charles Jarvis. Published by Osbourn's Music Saloon (between 1820 and 1860), Philadelphia

Connecticut Historical Society
Lydia Sigourney material

New-York Historical Society
Louis Antoine Godey Letters. Letter to Godey 6 July 1841, author unknown
Astor House invitation

New York Public Library
Letter Admiral Coffin to Philip Hone, 20 October 1836

Winterthur Library
Downs Collection. Item no 1328 Toast of the Atlantic

Online Collections
Ancestry.com
Passenger Lists of Vessels Arriving at New York, New York, 1820–1897. Microfilm Publication M237, 675 rolls. NAI: 6256867. Records of the U.S. Customs Service, Record Group 36. National Archives at Washington, D.C.

HO 3: Returns of alien passengers, July 1836-December 1869 returns made of alien passengers on ships arriving at British ports as required by the Aliens Act, beginning in 1836; formerly known as Lists of Immigrants

UK and Ireland, Masters and Mates Certificates, 1850–1927 [database on-line]. Provo, UT, USA: Ancestry.com Operations, Inc., 2012.
Original data: *Master's Certificates*. Greenwich, London, UK: National Maritime Museum

UK Census 1841–1861

Newspapers

Bristol Mirror
Bristol Mercury
Courier and Enquirer
Devizes and Wiltshire Gazette
Dublin Evening Packet
Dublin Monitor
Durham County Advertiser
Evening Post
Gloucester Journal
Hampshire Chronicle
Herald
Illustrated London News
Inverness Courier
Kentish Weekly Post
Liverpool Albion
Lloyds List
London Dispatch
London Evening Standard
Morning Post
New York Evening Post
Norwich Mercury
Patriot and Farmers Monthly
Staffordshire Advertiser
Sun
Taunton Courier & Western Advertiser
The Times
Worcester Journal
Yorkshire Gazette

Websites

Longfellow Society (http://www.hwlongfellow.org/)
US Population data (http://physics.bu.edu/~redner/projects/population/cities/newyork.html)
Godey's Lady's Book (http://www.accessible-archives.com/collections/godeys-ladys-book)
Philadelphia Architecture (https://www.philadelphiabuildings.org/pab/app/ar_display.cfm/25248)

USA National Archives online (https://founders.archives.gov/documents/Jefferson/03-06-02-0252)

University College London (https://www.ucl.ac.uk/lbs/person/view/41207Legacies of British Slave-ownership)

Edward Phalon & Sons (http://www.hairraisingstories.com/Proprietors/PHALON.html)

British Parliamentary Reports

BPP Theatres and Dramatic Pieces: Return of the title licensed by Lord Chamberlain, June 1832

BPP Select Committee on Causes of Shipwrecks. Report, Minutes of Evidence 1836

BPP Return of British Shipping and Consuls in United States 1836

BPP Report on Steam Vessel Accidents to Committee of Privy Council for Trade, 1839

BPP House of Commons Paper, Return of Factories and Mills 1839

BPP Accounts of Population and Number of Houses according to Census, 1841, of each County in Great Britain, Channel Islands and Isle of Man; Comparative Statement of Population and Houses, 1801, 1811, 1821, 1831 and 1841; Account of Population of each City and Burgh in Scotland

BPP Report from the Select Committee on Halifax and Boston Mail 1846

BPP Report of the Commissioners appointed to Inquire as to the Proposal for an Irish Packet Station 1851.

BPP Return of Troop Transports 1856

Nineteenth-Century Publications

Post Office Directory 1837

Lloyd's Register 1834

Anon, 'Obituary. Joshua Field (Ex-President and Vice-President), 1786–1863(?)', *Minutes of the Proceedings of the Institution of Civil Engineers*, 23 (1864), pp. 488–92.

Anon, 'Obituary. Thomas Richard Guppy, 1797–1882', *Minutes of the Proceedings of the Institution of Civil Engineers*, 69 (1882), pp. 411–15.

Claxton, Christopher, *Logs of the First Voyage, Made with the Unceasing Aid of Steam, between England and America by the Great Western of Bristol* (Great Western Steamship Company, 1838).

Claxton, Christopher, *The Naval Monitor*. 2nd edn (London: 1833).

Haliburton, T.C., *The Letter Bag of the Great Western or Life in a Steamer*. (New York: William Colyer, 1840).

Hosken, James, *Autobiographical Sketch of the Public Career of Admiral James Hosken* (Penzance: Rodda, 1889).

Mackay, Alexander, *The Western World; or, Travels in the United States in 1846–47: exhibiting them in their latest development, social, political and industrial, including a chapter on California* (Philadelphia: Lea & Blanchard, 1849).

Moore, George. *Journal of a voyage across the Atlantic: with notes on Canada & the United States, and return to Great Britain in 1844* (London: s.n., 1845).

Russell, W. H., *My Diary in India, in the Year 1858–9* (London: Routledge, 1860).

Sigourney, L.H., *Pleasant Memories of Pleasant Lands* (Boston: James Munroe and company 1856).

Smith, John Jay, *A Summer's Jaunt across the Water* (Philadelphia: J W Moore, 1846).

Town, Ithiel, *Atlantic Steam-Ships. Some Ideas and Statements, the Result of Considerable Reflection on the Subject of Navigating the Atlantic Ocean with Steam-Ships of Large Tonnage, Etc.* (New York: 1838).

Trollope, Frances, *Domestic Manners of the Americans* (London: Whittaker, Treacher & Co, 1832).

Tuckerman, Byard (ed.), *The Diary of Philip Hone, 1828 to 1851* (New York, Dodd, Mead & Co 1889).

Bibliography

Adams, Sean Patrick, 'The Perils of Personal Capital in Antebellum America: John Spotswood Wellford and Virginia's Catharine Furnace', *Business History*, 55 (2013), pp. 1339–60.

Albion, Robert G., 'Planning the Black Ball Line, 1817', *The Business History Review*, 41 (1967), pp. 104–07.

Albion, Robert G., *The Rise of New York Port 1815–1860* (New York: Charles Scribner's Sons, 1939).

Anim-Addo, Anyaa, 'Thence to the River Plate': Steamship Mobilities in the South Atlantic, 1842–1869', *Atlantic Studies*, 13 (2016), pp. 6–24.

Armstrong, J. and Bagwell, P. S., 'Coastal Shipping' in Aldcroft, D. and Freeman, M. (eds), *Transport in the Industrial Revolution* (Manchester: UP, 1983).

Armstrong, John, and Williams, David, *The Impact of Technological Change: The Early Steamship in Britain*. Vol. 47, *Research in Maritime History* (St John's, Newfoundland: International Maritime Economic Association, 2011).

Armstrong, John and Williams, David M., 'The Beginnings of a New Technology: The Constructors of Early Steamboats 1812–22', *The International Journal for the History of Engineering & Technology*, 81 (2011), pp. 1–21.

Armstrong, John and Williams, David M., 'The Steamboat and Popular Tourism', *Journal of Transport History*, 26 (2005), pp. 61–77.

Armstrong, John and Williams, David M., 'Technological Advance and Innovation: The Diffusion of the Early Steamship in the United Kingdom, 1812–34', *The Mariner's Mirror*, 96 (2010), pp. 42–61.

Bagust, Harold, *The Greater Genius? A Biography of Sir Marc Isambard Brunel* (Hersham: Ian Allen Publishing, 2006).

Banbury, Philip, *Shipbuilders of the Thames and Medway* (Newton Abbot: David and Charles, 1971).

Baym, Nina, 'Reinventing Lydia Sigourney', *American Literature*, 62 (1990), pp. 385–404.

Bratton, Jacky, *The Making of the West End Stage: Marriage, Management and the Mapping of Gender in London, 1830–1870* (Cambridge: Cambridge University Press, 2011).

Bratton, Jacky, *New Readings in Theatre History* (Cambridge: Cambridge University Press, 2003).

Brinnin, John Malcolm, *The Sway of the Gand Saloon*. 1986 edn (London: Arlington Books, 1971).

Brodie, Marc, 'Free Trade and Cheap Theatre: Sources of Politics for the Nineteenth-Century London Poor', *Social History*, 28 (2003), pp. 346–61.

Brown, David K.,'Seppings, Sir Robert (1767–1840)', *Oxford Dictionary of National Biography* (Oxford University Press, 2004).

Brunel, Isambard, *The Life of Isambard Kingdom Brunel Civil Engineer*. 2006 edn (Stroud: Nonsuch Publishing, 1870).

Buchanan, R. A. and Doughty, M. W., 'The Choice of Steam Engine Manufacturers by the British Admiralty, 1822–1852', *The Mariner's Mirror*, 64 (1978), pp. 327–47.

Buchanan, R. Angus, *Brunel: The Life and Times of Isambard Kingdom Brunel* (London: Hambledon and London, 2002).

Bucknall, Rixon, *Boat Trains and Channel Packets* (London, 1957).

Burrows, Edwin G. and Wallace, Mike, *Gotham: A History of New York City to 1898* (Oxford: Oxford University Press, 1999).

Burton, Valerie C., 'Apprenticeship Regulation and Maritime Labour in the Nineteenth Century British Merchant Marine', *International Journal of Maritime History*, 1 (1989), pp. 29–49.

Bush, G. W. A. Bush, *Bristol and Its Municipal Government, 1820–1851* (Bristol: Bristol Record Society, 1976).

Chaloner, W. H. and Henderson, W. O., 'Aaron Manby, Builder of the First Iron Steamship', *Transactions of the Newcomen Society*, 29 (1953), pp. 77–91.

Cheal, Henry, *The Ships and Mariners of Shoreham* (Shoreham: G E & P P Bysh, 1909).

Claybaugh, Amanda, 'Toward a New Transatlanticism: Dickens in the United States', *Victorian Studies*, 48 (2006), pp. 439–60.

Clydesdale, Greg, 'Thresholds, Niches and Inertia: Entrepreneurial Opportunities in the Steamship Industry', *Journal of Enterprising Culture*, 20 (2012), pp. 379–404.

Cohen, Daniel A., 'The Murder of Maria Bickford: Fashion, Passion, and the Birth of a Consumer Culture', *American Studies*, 31 (1990), pp. 5–30.

Cohn, Raymond L., *Mass Migration under Sail: European Immigration to the Antebellum United States* (Cambridge: Cambridge University Press, 2008).

Cohn, Raymond, 'The Transition from Sail to Steam in Immigration to the United States', *The Journal of Economic History*, 65 (2005), pp. 469–95.

Cookson, Gillian, 'Submarine Cables: Novelty and Innovation, 1850–1870', *Transactions of the Newcomen Society*, 76 (2006), pp. 207–19.

Corlett, Ewan, *The Iron Ship: The Story of Brunel's Ss Great Britain*. 2012 edn (Bristol: ss Great Britain, 1975).

Cottrell, P.L., 'The Steamship on the Mersey, 1815–80', in *Shipping, Trade and Commerce: Essays in Memory of Ralph Davis* ed. by P.L. Cottrell and D.H. Aldcroft (Leicester: Leicester University Press, 1981), pp. 137–64.

Daunton, M. J., 'Rowland Hill and the Penny Post ', *History Today*, 35 (1985), pp. 31–37.

de Oliveira Torres, Rodrigo, 'Handling the Ship: Rights and Duties of Masters, Mates, Seamen and Owners of Ships in 19th Century Merchant Marine', *International Journal of Maritime History*, 26 (2014), pp. 587–99.

Dresser, Madge, 'Guppy, Sarah (*bap.* 1770, *d.* 1852)', *Oxford Dictionary of National Biography* (Oxford University Press, May 2016).

Duckham, Baron F., 'Railway Steamship Enterprise : The Lancashire and Yorkshire Railway's East Coast Fleet', *Business History*, 10 (1968), p. 44.

Ellmers, Chris, "This Great National Object' – the Story of the Paddlesteamer Enterprize', in *Shipbuilding and Ships on the Thames: Proceedings of Fourth Symposium*, ed. by Roger Owen (London Docklands Museum 2009), pp. 59–81.

Endres, Kathleen L., *Women's Periodicals in the United States: Consumer Magazines.*(Greenwood Publishing Group, 1995)

Farr, Grahame, *Records of Bristol Ships:1800–1838* (Bristol: Bristol Record Society, 1950).

Farr, Grahame, *Shipbuilding in the Port of Bristol, Maritime Monographs and Reports* (Greenwich, London: National Maritime Museum 1977).

Forrester, Robert E., *British Mail Steamers to South America, 1851–1965: A History of the Royal Mail Steam Packet Company and Royal Mail Lines* (London: Routledge, 2016).

Fox, Stephen, *The Ocean Railway : Isambard Kingdom Brunel, Samuel Cunard and the Revoluntionary World of the Great Atlantic Steamships* (London: Harper Collins, 2004).

Freema, Mark, Pearson, Robin, and Taylor, James, 'Law, Politics and the Governance of English and Scottish Joint-Stock Companies, 1600–1850', *Business History*, 55 (2013), pp. 633–49.

Gassan, Richard, 'Tourists and the City: New York's First Tourist Era, 1820 – 1840', *Winterthur Portfolio*, 44 (2010), pp. 221–46.

Gillin, Edward John, "Diligent in Business, Serving the Lord': John Burns, Evangelicalism and Cunard's Culture of Speed, 1878–1901', *Journal for Maritime Research*, 14 (2012), pp. 15–30.

Goodwin, Gordon, 'MacQueen, James (1778–1870)', Rev. Elizabeth Baigent, *Oxford Dictionary of National Biography* (Oxford University Press, 2004).

Gower, L. C. B., 'The English Private Company', *Law and Contemporary Problems*, 18 (1953), pp. 535–45.

Greenhill. Robert G., 'British Shipping and Latin America 1840–1930 : The Royal Mail Steam Packet Company' (University of Exeter, 1971).

Griffiths, Denis, *Brunel's Great Western* (Wellingborough: Patrick Stephens, 1985).

Griffiths, Denis, Andrew Lambert, and Fred Walker, *Brunel's Ships* (London: Chatham Publishing, 1999).

Hamilton, C. I. Hamilton, 'Three Cultures at the Admiralty, c.1800–1945: Naval Staff, the Secretariat and the Arrival of Scientists', *Journal for Maritime Research*, 16 (2014), pp. 89–102.

Hancock, David, *Oceans of Wine: Madeira and the Emergence of American Trade and Taste* (New Haven, Conn.: Yale University Press, 2009).

Harcourt, Freda, 'British Oceanic Mail Contracts in the Age of Steam, 1838–1914', *Journal of Transport History*, IX (1988), pp. 1–18.

Harcourt, Freda, 'The High Road to India: The P&O Company and the Suez Canal, 1840–1874', *International Journal of Maritime History*, XXII (2010), pp. 19–72.

Hart, Douglas, 'Sociability and "Separate Spheres" on the North Atlantic: The Interior Architecture of British Atlantic Liners, 1840–1930', *Journal of Social History*, 44 (2010), pp. 189–212.

Hays, J. N. Hays, 'Lardner, Dionysius (1793–1859)', *Oxford Dictionary of National Biography* (Oxford University Press, 2004); online edn, Oct 2007 [http://0-www.oxforddnb.com.lib.exeter.ac.uk/view/article/16068].

Herzl-Betz, Rachel, 'Reading England's Mail: Mid-Century Appropriation and Charles Dickens's Traveling Texts', *Dickens Quarterly*, 30 (2013), pp. 131–40.

Hope, Ronald, *A New History of British Shipping* (London: John Murray, 1990).

Hyde, Francis E., *Cunard and the North Atlantic, 1840–1973* (London: MacMillan Press, 1975).

Jaher, Frederic Cople, 'Nineteenth-Century Elites in Boston and New York', *Journal of Social History*, 6 (1972), pp. 32–77.

Jordan, H. Donaldson, 'Richard Cobden and Penny Postage: A Note on the Processes of Reform', *Victorian Studies*, 8 (1965), pp. 355–60.

Kaukiainen, Yrjo 'Shrinking the World: Improvements in the Speed of Information Transmission, C. 1820–1870', *European Review of Economic History*, 5 (2001), pp. 1–28.

Kelly, Andrew and Kelly, Melanie, *Brunel, in Love with the Impossible : A Celebration of the Life, Work, and Legacy of Isambard Kingdom Brunel* (Bristol: Bristol Cultural Development Partnership, 2006).

Kennedy, Greg, 'Maritime Strength and the British Economy, 1840–1850', *The Northern Mariner/Le Marin du nord*, VII (1997), pp. 51–69.

Kennerley, Alston, 'Early State Support of Vocational Education: The Department of Science and Art Navigation Schools, 1853–63', *Journal of Vocational Education and Training*, 52 (2000), pp. 211–24.

Kennerley, Alston, 'Nationally Recognised Qualifications for British Merchant Navy Officers, 1865–1966', *International Journal of Maritime History*, XIII (2001), pp. 115–35.

Kennerley, Alston, 'Stoking the Boilers: Firemen and Trimmers in British Merchant Ships, 1850–1950', *International Journal of Maritime History*, XX (2008), pp. 191–220.

Killick, John, 'Transatlantic Steerage Fares, British and Irish Migration, and Return Migration, 1815–60', *Economic History Review*, 67 (2014), pp. 170–91.

Killick, John R., 'Bolton Ogden & Company: A Case Study in Anglo-American Trade, 1790–1850', *Business History Review*, 48 (1974), pp. 501–19.

Kippola, Karl M., *Acts of Manhood: The Performance of Masculinity on the American Stage, 1828–1865* (Palgrave Macmillan, 2012).

Klovland, Jan Tore, 'New Evidence on the Fluctuations in Ocean Freight Rates in the 1850s', *Explorations in Economic History*, 46 (2009), pp. 266–84.

Laakso, Seija-Riitta, *Across the Oceans: Development of Overseas Business Information Transmission 1815–1875* (Helsinki: Studia Fennica, 2007).

Lambert, Andrew, 'Captain Sir William Symonds and the Ship of the Line: 1832–1847', *The Mariner's Mirror*, 73 (1987), pp. 167–79.

Lambert, Andrew, 'John Scott Russell: Ships, Science and Scandal in the Age of Transition', *The International Journal for the History of Engineering & Technology*, 81 (2011), pp. 60–78.

Lambert, Andrew, 'Woolwich Dockyard and the Early Steam Navy, 1815 to 1852s', in *Shipbuilding and Ships on the Thames: Proceedings of Fourth Symposium*, ed. by Roger Owen (London Docklands Museum 2009), pp. 82–96.

Lambert, Andrew, 'Brunel, the Navy and the Screw Propeller' in Griffiths, Denis, Andrew Lambert, and Fred Walker, *Brunel's Ships* (London: Chatham Publishing, 1999).

Lambert, Andrew D., 'Preparing for the Long Peace: The Reconstruction of the Royal Navy 1815–1830', *The Mariner's Mirror*, 82 (1996), pp. 41–54.

Langley, John G., *Steam Lion: A Biography of Samuel Cunard* (Halifax, Nimbus, 2006)

Large, David (ed.), *The Port of Bristol 1848–1884* (Bristol: Bristol Record Society, 1984)

Laughton, J.K., 'Hosken, James (1798–1885)', Rev. Andrew Lambert, *Oxford Dictionary of National Biography* (Oxford University Press, 2004).

Lawrence, Vera Brodsky, *Strong on Music: The New York Music Scene in the Days of George Templeton Strong, 1836–1849* (Chicago: University of Chicago Press, 1988).

Leggett, Don, and Davey, James, 'Introduction: Expertise and Authority in the Royal Navy, 1800–1945', *Journal for Maritime Research*, 16 (2014), pp. 1–13.

Lepler, Jessica, "The News Flew Like Lightning", *Journal of Cultural Economy*, 5 (2012), pp. 179–95.

Lewis, Michael, *The Navy in Transition, 1814–1864* (London: Hodder & Stoughton, 1965).

Lin, Chih-lung, 'The British Dynamic Mail Contract on the North Atlantic: 1860–1900', *Business History*, 54 (2012), pp. 783–97.

Luskey, Brian P., '"What Is My Prospects?": The Contours of Mercantile Apprenticeship, Ambition, and Advancement in the Early American Economy', *The Business History Review*, 78 (2004), pp. 665–702.

MacDonagh, Oliver, 'The Regulation of the Emigrant Traffic from the United Kingdom 1842–55', *Irish Historical Studies*, 9 (1954), pp. 162–89.

MacDonald, Janet, 'British Patents of Interest to Maritime Historians Filed in Londmn between 1780 and 1820', in *Shipbuilding and Ships on the Thames: Proceedings of Fourth Symposium*, ed. by Roger Owen (Museum of London Docklands 2009), pp. 32–43.

Macleod, Christine, 'Negotiating the Rewards of Invention: The Shop-Floor Inventor in Victorian Britain', *Business History*, 41 (1999), pp. 17–36.

Macleod, Christine, Stein, Jeremy, Tann, Jennifer, and Andrew, James, 'Making Waves: The Royal Navy's Management of Invention and Innovation in Steam Shipping, 1815–1832', *History and Technology*, 16 (2000), pp. 307–33.

Maenpaa, Sari, 'Galley News: Catering Personnel on British Passenger Liners, 1860–1938', *International Journal of Maritime History*, XII (2000), pp. 243–60.

Maenpaa, Sari, 'Women Below Deck: Gender and Employment on British Passenger Liners, 1860–1938', *Journal of Transport History*, 25 (2004), pp. 57–74.

Malpass, Peter, 'Victorian Bristol: Chapter 3 Reshaping the City', unpublished.

Tyrrell, Margot and Alex, 'The Hosken Family Papers: A Naval Genealogy', *The Mariner's Mirror*, 74 (1988), pp. 273–82.

Markovits, Stefanie, 'Rushing into Print: "Participatory Journalism" During the Crimean War', *Victorian Studies*, 50 (2008), pp. 559–86.

Marsden, Ben, and Smith, Crosbie, *Engineering Empires: A Cultural History of Technology in Nineteenth-Century Britain* (London: Palgrave, 2005).

Matson, Cathy, 'Introduction: The Ambiguities of Risk in the Early Republic', *The Business History Review*, 78 (2004), pp. 595–606.

McGoverin, Ken, 'William Pitcher and the Northfleet Dockyard, 1830–60 ', in *Shipbuilding and Ships on the Thames: Proceedings of Third Symposium*, ed. by Roger Owen (Greenwich Maritime Institute: 2006), pp. 22–38.

McMurray, H. Campbell, 'Ship's Engineers: Their Status and Position on Board, C. 1830–65', in *West Country Maritime and Social History* ed. by Stephen Fisher (Exeter: University of Exeter, 1980).

McOwat, Peter, 'Henry Bell's Comet: The Account Book for 1820', *The Mariner's Mirror*, 99 (2013), pp. 455–63.

Milburn, R. G., 'The Emergence of the Engineer in the British Merchant Shipping Industry, 1812–1863', *International Journal of Maritime History*, 28 (2016), pp. 559–75.

Milne, Graeme J., *Trade and Traders in Mid-Victorian Liverpool: Mercantile Business and the Making of a World Port* (Liverpool: Liverpool University Press, 2000).

Moody, Jane, 'The State of the Abyss: Nineteenth Century Performance and Theatre Historiography in 1999', *Journal of Victorian Culture*, 5 (2000), pp. 112–28.

Morgan, Kenneth, 'The Bristol Chamber of Commerce and the Port of Bristol, 1823–1848.', *International Journal of Maritime History*, 18 (2006), pp. 55–77.

Neill, Elizabeth, *Fragile Fortunes; The Origins of a Great British Merchant Family* (Wellington: Halsgrove, 2008)

Noble, Celia Brunel, *The Brunels – Father Anc Son* (London: 1938).

O'Brien, William Patrick, *Merchants of Independence: International Trade on the Santa Fe Trail, 1827–1860* (Missouri: Truman State University Press, 2014).

O'Byrne, William R., *A Naval Biographical Dictionary* (London: John Murray, 1849).

Owen, J. R., 'The Post Office Packet Service, 1821–37: Development of a Steam-Powered Fleet', *The Mariner's Mirror*, 88 (2002), pp. 155–75.

Palmer, Sarah, 'Experience, Experiment and Economics: Factors in the Construction of Early Merchant Steamers', *Proceedings of the Atlantic Canada Shipping Project* (1977), pp. 233–49.

Palmer, Sarah, 'The Most Indefatigable Activity: The General Steam Navigation Company, 1824–50 ', *Journal of Transport History*, 3 (1982), pp. 1–22.

Pattison, George, 'Shipping and the East India Docks, 1802–38', *The Mariner's Mirror*, 49 (1963), pp. 208–12.

Penner, Barbara, 'Colleges for the Teaching of Extravagance: New York Palace Hotels', *Winterthur Portfolio*, 44 (2010), pp. 159–92.

Penrose, Charles, '1838—April Fourth—1938 Centenary of Atlantic Steam Navigation', *Transactions of the Newcomen Society*, 18 (1937), pp. 169–79.

Sources and Bibliography

Quinn, Paul, 'I K Brunel's Ships — First among Equals?', *The International Journal for the History of Engineering & Technology*, 80 (2010), pp. 80–99.

Quinn, Paul, 'Macgregor Laird, Junius Smith and the Atlantic Ocean', *The Mariner's Mirror*, 92 (2006), pp. 486–97.

Rankin, Stuart, 'William Evans, Shipbuilder of Rotherhithe and His Steamships', *Shibuilding on the Thames and Thames-built ships; Proceedings of a second symposium* (2004), pp. 47–76.

Robinson, Howard, *Carrying British Mail Overseas* (London: George Allen & Unwin, 1964).

Rolt, L. T. C., *Isambard Kingdom Brunel*. 1st edition 1957 edn (London: Penguin, 1976).

Scholl, Lars U., 'The Loss of the Steamship *President*: A Painting by German Artist Andreas Achenbach', *The Northern Mariner/Le Marin du nord*, 15 (2005), pp. 53–71.

Sheppard, T., 'The Sirius: The First Steamer to Cross the Atlantic', *The Mariner's Mirror*, 23 (1937), pp. 84–94.

Sloan, Edward W., 'The Baltic Goes to Washington: Lobbying for a Congressional Steamship Subsidy, 1852', *The Northern Mariner/Le Marin du nord*, 5 (1995), pp. 19–32.

Sloan, Edward W., 'The First and Very Secret International Steamship Cartel, 1850–1856', in *Global Markets: The Internationalization of Sea Transport Indutried Snce 1850* ed. by David R. Starkey and Gelina Harlaftis (St John's, Newfoundland: International Maritime Economic Association 1998), pp. 29–52.

Smigel, Libby, 'Minds Mad for Dancing: Polkamania on the London Stage', *Journal of Popular Culture*, 30 (1996), pp. 197–207.

Smith, Crosbie, "This Great National Undertaking'; John Scott Russell, the Master Shipwrights and the Royal Mail Steam Packet Company ', in *Re-Inventing the Ship: Science, Technology and the Maritime World, 1800–1918*, ed. by Don Leggett and Richard Dunn (Basingstoke: Ashgate, 2012), pp. 25–52.

Smith, Crosbie, Higginson, Ian, and Wolstenholme, Phillip, '"Avoiding Equally Extravagance and Parsimony": The Moral Economy of the Ocean Steamship', *Technology and Culture*, 44 (2003), pp. 443–69.

Smith, Crosbie, '"Imitations of God's Own Works": Making Trustworthy the Ocean Steamship', *History of Science*, 41 (2003), pp. 379–426.

Smith, Crosbie and Scott, Anne, '"Trust in Providence": Building Confidence into the Cunard Line of Steamers', *Technology and Culture*, 48 (2007), pp. 471–96.

Starkey, David R., 'The Industrial Background to the Development of the Steamship', in *The Advent of Steam: The Merchant Ship before 1900*, ed. by R Gardiner (London: Conway Maritime Press, 1993).

Stevens, John, *Bristol Politics in the Age of Peel, 1832–1847* (Bristol: Avon Local History & Archaeology, 2014).

Sylla, Richard, Wilson, Jack W. and Wright, Robert E., 'Integration of Trans-Atlantic Capital Markets, 1790–1845', *Review of Finance*, 10 (2006), pp. 613–44.

Taylor, Roger, *Impressed by Light: Photographs from Paper Negatives, 1840–1860* (New York: Metropolitan Museum of Art, 2007) p. 50.

Thompson, Brian C., 'Henri Drayton, English Opera and Anglo-American Relations, 1850–72', *Journal of the Royal Musical Association*, 136 (2011), pp. 247–303.

Tracy, Robert, 'W C Macready in the Life and Adventures of Nicholas Nickleby', *Dickens Quarterly*, 24 (2007).

Tyrrell, Margot & Alex, 'The Hosken Family Papers: A Naval Genealogy', *The Mariner's Mirror*, 74 (1988), pp. 273–82.

Van Deusen, Caroline Welling, 'Introduction to the Transcription of the Washington Diary of Elizabeth L. C. Dixon', *White House Historical Association* Issue 33, 2013 [https://www.whitehousehistory.org/introduction-to-the-transcription-of-the-washington-diary-of-elizabeth-l-c-dixon].

Wayne, Stephen J., *The Road to the White House* (Boston, Cengage Learning, 2016).

Weber, William, 'Redefining the Status of Opera: London and Leipzig, 1800–1848', *Journal of Interdisciplinary History* 36 (2006), pp. 507–32.

Wilson, James Harrison, *The Life of Charles A. Dana* (New York; Harper Brothers, 1907).

Williams, D., 'James Silk Buckingham: Sailor, Explorer and Maritime Reformer,' in Stephen Fisher, *Studies in British Privateering, Trading and Seamen's Welfare, 1775–1900* (Exeter, University of Exeter, 1987), pp. 99–120

Williams, David M., and Armstrong, John, "One of the Noblest Inventions of the Age': British Steamboat Numbers, Diffusion, Services and Public Reception, 1812 – C.1823', *Journal of Transport History*, 35 (2014), pp. 18–34.

Winch, Julie, '"A Person of Good Character and Considerable Property": James Forten and the Issue of Race in Philadelphia's Antebellum Business Community', *The Business History Review*, 75, pp. 261–96.

Zboray, Ronald J. and Zboray, Mary Saracino, 'Books, Reading, and the World of Goods in Antebellum New England', *American Quarterly*, 48 (1996), pp. 587–622.

List of Illustrations

1. Bristol Harbour showing site of Patterson's yard. (Denis Griffiths)
2. Launch of the *Great Western*. (Denis Griffiths)
3. Saloon of the *Great Western*. (Brunel Institute, ss Great Britain Trust)
4. *Great Western* longitude, 1836. (Denis Griffiths)
5. *Great Western* layout, 1836. (Denis Griffiths)
6. *Great Western* arriving in New York, April 1838. (New York Public Library)
7. Crowds greeting arrival of *Great Western* in New York. (New York Public Library)
8. *Sirius*. (New York Public Library)
9. Drawing of New York showing Pike Street where *Great Western* had mooring and coal yard. (Denis Griffiths)
10. Astor House invitation.
11. Voyage no. 1. (Denis Griffiths)
12. Engraving celebrating *Great Western*, 1840. (New York Public Library)
13. A portrait of Captain Hosken as a naval officer. (Michael Hosken)
14. George Macready, surgeon on *Great Western*. (Brunel Institute, ss Great Britain Trust)
15. *Great Western* sailing from River Avon. (Denis Griffiths)
16. Guppy. (*A Short History of Great Western*, published 1938)
17. Patterson. (*A Short History of Great Western*, published 1938)
18. *Great Western* in gale, 1846. (*Illustrated London News*)
19. *Great Western* longitude, 1846. (Denis Griffiths)
20. *Great Western* layout, 1846. (Denis Griffiths)
21. *Great Western* ship's bell. (Brunel Institute, ss Great Britain Trust)
22. *Great Western* butter dish. (Brunel Institute, ss Great Britain Trust)
23. Barnard Mathews and his officers and cadets on ss *Great Britain*. (Brunel Institute, ss Great Britain Trust)
24. Cabin plans of 1839, used by booking office. (Denis Griffiths)
25. *Great Western* at her moorings. (*A Short History of Great Western*, published 1938)
26. Poster for voyage to Madeira, 1843. (Brunel Institute, ss Great Britain Trust)

27. Drawing of the Ice Field Incident, 1840, by Lydia Sigourney. (Connecticut Library)
28. Astor House. (New York Public Library)
29. Madame Celeste. (New York Public Library)
30. Fanny Elssler in Park Theatre dressing room, 1845. (New York Public Library New York Public Library)
31. Cartoon of Aroostook War; Queen Victoria, Melbourne and President Van Buren. (New York Public Library)
32. Letter carried on board *Great Western* to Miss Anne Hemmings, 1845. (Brunel Institute, ss Great Britain Trust)
33. Britannia Bridge engineers, 1850. (Institution of Civil Engineers)
34. The Royal Mail Steam Packet Company's West Indies routes, 1850. (Denis Griffiths)
35. *Great Western* in drydock and *Orinoco* ready for launching at Northfleet on 17 May 1851. (*Illustrated London News*)
36. The Royal Mail Steam Packet Company's Brazil and Crimea routes. (Denis Griffiths)
37. Balaclava Harbour. (*Illustrated London News*)

Index

Acraman, William Edward   38, 43, 45, 140, 141, 156, 171
Admiralty   18, 23, 24, 54, 146, 148–154, 161, 163, 171–174, 179, · 182
Aroostook   186
Aspinwall, W. H.   121
Astor, John Jacob   71
Astor House   71, 134

Bagster, Cornelius Birch   61
Balaclava   178–180
Barings Bank   103, 104, 171, 186
Baring, Thomas   171
Bates, Mr Joshua (banker)   104, 109, 121, 186, 188
Bayley, George (surveyor)   147
Bell, Henry   15
Bennett, James Gordon   66, 71, 83, 117, 119, 139, 183, 185
Blandy, John, & sons   161
Bolton, Ogden and Company   18
Boston   21, 77, 81, 82, 122, 127, 133, 153, 158, 162, 167
Bright, Robert   26, 141, 160, 162, 188
Bristol, visitor arrivals at   134–135
Bristol Dock Company   28, 143, 145, 146
Britannia Bridge   196

British Association for the Advancement of Science   40, 53, 55
British and American Steam Navigation Company   34, 51, 54, 138, 148, 155, 194
Brocklebank   92
Brown and Shipley   103, 121
Brunel, Isambard Kingdom   13, 19, 24–26, 29, 41, 44, 48, 53–56, 65, 87, 96, 142, 147, 162, 196–198
Boulton and Watt   15, 35, 36
Brunel, Sir Marc Isambard   23, 24, 36, 37, 41, 55
Buckingham, James Silk   86–87
Bucklins Patent Stove   190
Burns, George   153
Bush, Henry   140
Byerley, Samuel   121

cadets   90–92
Canadian border dispute   154, 186
Carmichael-Smythe, Captain Robert   150
Castles (shipbreakers)   197
Celeste, Madame   127–128
Chappell, Edward   169, 172, 173
Claxton, Berkeley   96
Claxton, Christopher   26–29, 31–32, 38–40, 41, 43, 55–56, 90, 102, 142, 144–148, 155, 158, 162, 167, 181, 196

Claxton, William   26, 40
coffee houses   77, 104, 112, 182, 183
Cookson, Joseph   140
Copley, Sir Joseph   108, 114
cotton   141, 188–189
Courthope and Sons   23
Crane, Judge William   151, 152
Crawford, William (steward)   93,
  107, 133, 134
Crimean War   177–180
Crooks, (stoker)   65
Cross, Eliza   61, 76, 96
Cunard, Samuel   82, 151–154, 156,
  162, 167, 168
Cunard company   82, 95, 162
Curling and Young   51

Delano, Frederick   82
Dickens, Charles   95
Dixon, Elizabeth   80, 105, 107, 111,
  114, 123, 130–131, 134
Dodworth band of musicians   75, 97
Douglass, Frederick   82

earthenware trade   190, 191
East India Dock   45
Elssler, Fanny   127
Ely, Richard   111
engineers   87–89

Fairbanks, Charles   150
Fawcett & Co   35
Field, Joshua   44, 56, 89
firemen and trimmers   89–90
Fletcher, Henry   84
Flinn, James (City of Dublin treasurer)
  187, 188
Foster, W   59–62, 133

Ghega, Carl   104
Gibbs, Bright & Co   141, 166, 179,
  194
Girdwood, Claude & Co   51
Glenelg, Lord   151–153
Godey's Lady's Book   124, 189
Godey, Louis   124
Gordon, John   61

Government mail contract   148, 167,
  168
Graham, Colonel Vernon   61, 73
Great Western Railway   19, 102, 139,
  141, 187
Great Western, steamship
  arrival New York   66
  attempted sale   157, 163, 164
  booking agents   59
  Bristol Dock problems   143, 146,
    146
  Brunel accident   55, 56
  coal   64, 89, 143
  construction description   44, 45
  crew desertions   98
  death of Chief Engineer   69
  design influence   193
  engine room   63, 64, 100, 101
  engine trials   49, 50
  female passengers   109
  fire on board   55, 56
  grounding   161
  ice encounter   98–100
  interior design   46–48
  launch   42, 43
  life preservers   105
  move to Liverpool   156
  New York welcome   69–70
  passenger complaints   130–132,
    165, 166
  passenger food   93, 94, 115, 116
  sale to RMSPC   169, 170
  saloon description   46–48
  ship motion   112, 119
  shipboard routine   113
  stern frame raising   38–48
  terrible storm   100, 101, 168, 169
  trip to London   46–48
  troopship   178–180
Great Western Steam Ship Company
  29, 30, 33, 34
  Building Committee   29, 31, 35, 38,
    44, 46, 48, 130, 143, 163, 195
  cadets   90–92
  directors   140, 141
  establishment   139, 140
  financial woes   167

mail contract   149–154
shareholder disputes   159, 160
trustees   140, 141
Guppy, Sarah   25–26, 32, 40

Hall, Thomas   23
Haliburton, Judge Thomas (aka Sam Slick)   94, 107, 108, 112, 127, 149–153
Hardy, Sir Thomas Masterman   41
Harford, John   140, 141
Harrison, William, President of United States   114, 115
Harmony, Peter   120
Hilhouse, shipbuilders   30, 31
Hone, Philip   67, 68, 70, 110, 126
Hosken, James   41, 60, 65, 79–84
Howe, Joseph   149–151

ice field   98–100
Irving, John   140

Jackson and Sons   47
Jacques, John   144
James, Henry   122
Jellicoe, John Henry   175
Jones, George   159

Kington, Thomas   140, 141

Laird, Macgregor   34, 54
Lang, Oliver   41, 172
Lardner, Dr Dionysius   52–54, 195
Lawrence, Amos A   122
Lee & Perrins Worcestershire Sauce   190
Letrosne, Felix   92
Guppy, Thomas   13, 19, 25–26, 29, 85, 140, 144, 152, 162, 195, 196
London
   theatres   126
   visitor impressions of   116, 118
Longfellow, Henry   124–125

MacQueen, James   170, 173
Madeira   42, 161, 173
mail contracts   148–154

Marine Act 1850 & Certificates of Service   86–87
Marks, Israel   196
masters   86–87
Mathews, Barnard   84–85, 100–101, 132, 133, 164–166, 168, 169, 194
Matthews, Charles, actor   126–127
Maudslay, Sons & Field   36–38, 45, 172
Maze, Peter   43 140, 142
McIver, David and Charles   153
Mercer, John   31
Merryweather fire engine   55
Miles, Mrs   42
Miles, William, MP   43, 58
Moore, George, merchant   108, 111, 113, 133, 165, 195
Morell Dr, school at Hove   25
Murat, Joachim, Prince of Pontecorvo   81, 122–123
music   191, 192

Napier, Robert   35.51
naval lieutenants, half pay   27, 28, 41, 172
New York
   sailing lines   21, 22, 151, 182
   theatre   127–129
   passenger arrival at   118, 133–134
North and South American Coffee House   77, 104, 112, 182, 183

Osborn and Ward solicitors   140, 157

Parris, Edward Thomas   47
Paton & Stewart   189
Patterson, William   30–31, 43, 45, 46, 169, 171, 195
Peach, William Henry   92
Pearne, George   56, 57, 63, 69, 75
Peninsular Steam Navigation Company (P&O)   132, 155, 163, 164, 179
Pitcher, Thomas of Northfleet   36, 171, 177, 175
Portishead Pier   147, 148
Power, Tyrone   126
Pycroft, Thomas   140

quay warden (harbourmaster) 28, 160

Roberts, Richard 68, 69, 70, 73, 150, 156
Roberts, William (engineer) 97
Rooseveldt, James 122
Royal Mail Steam Packet Company (RMSPC) 169–180, 193
  extension of mail contract to South America 176
  founding of 170, 171
  purchase of *Great Western* 169
  ship losses 173, 175
Russell, John Scott 171, 196
Russell, William Howard (journalist) 132, 178

Scott, Robert 140, 142, 156
Seppings, Sir Robert 40
ship letters 181–185
ships *see* separate index
Sigourney, Lydia 98–100, 109, 112, 117, 123–124, 133, 134, 189, 190
Slick, Sam see Haliburton
Smith, John Jay 100, 101, 106, 116, 123, 131, 132, 165
Smith, John Junius 34–51, 138, 194
Society of Merchant Venturers 39, 40, 140
St George Steam Packet Company 51, 148
Stafford of Bath 58
Stafford, Cedrick 92
steam vessel accidents 22, 23
Stephenson, Robert 34
steward 93, 94, 113, 114
stewardess 70, 95
Strickland, William architect and engineer 137
surgeons 96

Swartwout, Samuel Collector of Customs New York 137
Symons, William 41

Talbot, Fox 61
Tappan, Lewis 120
Tate (Tait), Charles 61
theatres
  London 126
  New York 127–129
Tidcombe, Thomas 92
Tontine Coffee House, New York 182
Transatlantic Steamship Company 149, 155
transport ship 178–180
Trollope, Fanny 118, 123
Tyler, John President of United States 114, 115

Valentia Island, Ireland 53, 54
Van Buren, Martin, President of United States 114, 115, 186
Vestris, Madame, actress 126, 127
Victoria, Queen 48, 52, 110, 117, 124

Wallack family (actors) 126
Wapping dock, Bristol 31
Ward, Thomas, London Office 102–105, 111, 141, 155
Webb, Colonel James Watson, editor 68, 71, 72, 74, 126
Welman, James 61
Were, Thomas Bonville 140
Whitehead, G M 92
Wigram and Green 92
Winwood & Co 35, 37, 44

yellow fever 175

Index of ships

Aaron Manby 17
Aetna 80
Amazon 175
Archimedes 172
Banshee, HMS 194
Belle-Isle 194
Benledi 42, 45, 85
Britannia 95
British Queen 51, 119, 138, 149, 151, 155, 156, 187
Bulwark, HMS 80
Cambrian 76, 157
Charlotte 95
Charlotte Dundas 15
City of Glasgow 88
Clermont 14
Clifton 42
Columbia 154
Comet (1812) 15, 16
Comet (1838) 50
County of Pembroke 85
Enterprize 36, 56, 64
Garrick 42
George IV 30
Great Britain 13, 88, 97, 142, 159, 160, 163–170, 176, 179, 193–195, 197
Great Eastern 13, 42, 48, 193, 196, 197, 198
Harriet 84
Henry Brougham 62
Highlander 74
Hope 16
Lady Charlotte 31

Liverpool 149, 155
Maria Louisa 85
Medina 173
Medway 177
Moselle 73, 74
Mountaineer 31
Nassau 30
Orinoco 175, 177
Palmerston 30
President 35, 155, 194
President (packet ship) 87
Princess Elizabeth 80
Rattler, HMS 13
Redwing 172
Regent 23, 24, 36
Richard Watson 80
Richmond 36
Royal William (1831) 19, 151
Royal William (1838) 149
Saint George 42
Savannah 19, 61
Severn 196
Sirius 51, 52, 60, 62, 66–76, 138, 139, 148–150, 170, 182, 192
Talbot 95
Thames 15, 17,
Torridge 42
Trent 177
Tweed, 173
Tyrian 80, 150, 151
Valiant 84
Wellington 75

Also available from Amberley Publishing